Faith and Politics in the Public Sphere

Religion and Politics
Michael Barkun, *Series Editor*

SELECT TITLES IN RELIGION AND POLITICS

Blood and Faith: Christianity in American White Nationalism
Damon T. Berry

Cultural Conversions: Unexpected Consequences of Christian Missionary Encounters in the Middle East, Africa, and South Asia
Heather J. Sharkey, ed.

Ecumenism, Memory, and German Nationalism, 1817–1917
Stan M. Landry

Islamist Opposition in Authoritarian Regimes: The Party of Justice and Development in Morocco
Eva Wegner

Localizing Islam in Europe: Turkish Islamic Communities in Germany and the Netherlands
Ahmet Yükleyen

Missionary Politics in Contemporary Europe
José Pedro Zúquete

Religion and the Rise of Nationalism: A Profile of an East-Central European City
Robert E. Alvis

Women of Faith and Religious Identity in Fin-de-Siècle France
Emily Machen

For a full list of titles in this series, visit https://press.syr.edu/supressbook-series/religion-and-politics/.

Faith and Politics in the Public Sphere

The Gülen Movement and the Mormon Church

ETGA UGUR

Syracuse University Press

Syracuse, New York 13244-5290

First Edition 2019
19 20 21 22 23 24 6 5 4 3 2 1

∞ The paper used in this publication meets the minimum requirements of the American National Standard for Information Sciences—Permanence of Paper for Printed Library Materials, ANSI Z39.48-1992.

For a listing of books published and distributed by Syracuse University Press, visit https://press.syr.edu.

ISBN: 978-0-8156-3629-8 (hardcover) 978-0-8156-3647-2 (paperback)
978-0-8156-5475-9 (e-book)

Library of Congress Cataloging-in-Publication Data

Names: Ugur, Etga, 1979– author.

Title: Faith and politics in the public sphere : the Gülen movement and the Mormon church / Etga Ugur.

Description: First edition. | Syracuse, New York : Syracuse University Press, 2019. | Series: Religion and politics | Includes bibliographical references and index. | Description based on print version record and CIP data provided by publisher; resource not viewed.

Identifiers: LCCN 2019005830 (print) | LCCN 2019006140 (ebook) | ISBN 9780815654759 (E-book) | ISBN 9780815636298 (hardcover : alk. paper) | ISBN 9780815636472 (pbk. : alk. paper)

Subjects: LCSH: Religion and politics. | Church of Jesus Christ of Latter-day Saints. | Gülen Hizmet Movement.

Classification: LCC BL65.P7 (ebook) | LCC BL65.P7 U38 2019 (print) | DDC 322/.109561–dc23

LC record available at https://lccn.loc.gov/2019005830

Manufactured in the United States of America

To my grandfather, Ali Nadir Uğur (1925–2004),
the kind and humble intellectual giant who introduced
me to religion and politics

Contents

Illustrations and Tables

Illustrations

Tables

Preface

My interest in religion and politics goes back to the confusion of my childhood and the ensuing curiosity of my adolescence regarding Turkey's highly charged political environment. The first time I felt the elusive boundary between the public and the private domains was when I was a first grader. Unlike most of my fellow classmates, my biggest struggle was neither with math nor grammar, but with a common core requirement called *Hayat Bilgisi* ("Life Knowledge"). Despite its broad and vague name, in hindsight the earliest lesson plans in this subject were in fact very specific and systematic: the life of modern Turkey's founding father, Mustafa Kemal Atatürk, as a model for young citizens. As a student who excelled in learning by listening, the life story of Atatürk that I heard from my teachers was full of the heroism, altruism, wisdom, and overall greatness of the founding father, whose last name literally means "father of Turks." Of course, my parents, like most others, would ask me what I was learning in school. Our family environment was a good example of the modernizing Turkish society, where the nucleus family was on its way to replace the more traditional extended families, but gradually. We had a separate apartment with my parents and my two sisters, yet we also lived in the same building with my grandparents, and we ate our meals and spent most evenings together. As I tried to impress my family with how much I was learning, my grandfather always listened to me with what I later figured was his critical thinking smile.

The stories my grandfather told me about the Ottoman sultans and Atatürk would directly contradict what I was hearing from my teachers. Amid the concerned and disapproving gazes of my parents, my grandfather would not refrain from telling the complete opposite story of Turkey's foundation. According to my grandfather's version, Atatürk was not the great hero who took it upon himself to organize the resistance in Anatolia and who led the war of independence; he was, rather, an opportunist and a disloyal Ottoman general who turned his back against the last Ottoman sultan, Vahdettin, who almost couldn't convince him to leave Istanbul under the watchful presence of the British navy. While I was hearing about the incompetency, fanaticism, weakness, and backwardness of the Ottoman Empire at school, I was hearing about the wisdom, power, glory, and tolerance of the Ottomans at home. As a child, while I enjoyed the hours of my most memorable conversations with my grandfather, I was feeling distressed, caught in between the Turkish nationalist narrative and the Islamist counternarrative. Perhaps most discomforting of all, I was not allowed to discuss our private skepticism and the counternarrative with any of my friends in public, which was dominated by the official state ideology, known as Kemalism.

My grandfather was born two years after the founding of the Republic (1923) and his life story exemplified the complicated story of Turkish modernization. On the one hand, the public education system was almost solely responsible for his upward mobility. Born to a large family who lost everything during the economic hardships of interwar years in a small provincial town in central Turkey, he would end up going to the only high school in Konya and later to Istanbul, where one of the only two medical schools in the country was located. After some initial struggles and, of course, hard work, he would join the ranks of Turkey's new professional middle class. On the other hand, he would spend his summers in his hometown, learning how to read and write in the defunct Ottoman script, as a form of passive resistance to the republican Westernization reforms. Despite its endurance and elimination of its rivals, after three decades the Kemalist model that combined Turkish nationalism with Western secular modernization was nowhere near winning the hearts and minds of most people, and Atatürk's party would lose to the populist Democrat

Party in its first free multiparty elections in 1950. The sort of passive resistance and the counterpublics that my grandfather participated in and supported was for sure a big factor in the emerging rift between the republican state and the populist and conservative governments that came to power after 1950.

Turkish politics was for decades deeply shaped by what preeminent Turkish sociologist Şerif Mardin called center-periphery relations. As the Kemalist bureaucracy controlled the state apparatus, the Kemalist intelligentsia and the media manufactured consent among the less politicized public, and the Istanbul-based Kemalist bourgeoisie shared the economic power with the state. It wasn't so far-fetched to think of the byproduct of this Kemalist hegemony as creating a small minority of privileged "white" Turks and large majority of oppressed "black" Turks. Despite my grandfather's achievements and the relatively comfortable living standards he offered to his family, I felt more like a black Turk for not sharing the Kemalist ideology and not being able to publicly criticize it. Religion was a key battleground and fault line in the Turkish public sphere between the Kemalist establishment and the conservative Islamic actors. Adopting a stricter form of French secularism, *laïcité*, Kemalism subjugated religion to state control while pragmatically using it as a tool for its nation-building project. While we were receiving a secular education, often in a secularist form hostile to religion, we also had a class called *Din Kültürü ve Ahlak Bilgisi* (religious culture and ethical knowledge) from the fourth grade to the end of high school. This course was introduced into the curriculum by the Turkish military after the 1980 coup, as a response to its Cold War fears of leftist ideologies "poisoning" the Turkish youth. The textbooks for this course were written from a very basic introductory comparative religion perspective, yet they clearly favored the Turkish interpretation of Sunni Islam. While there was an evident shift in the balance between coercive and cooptation measures it adopted to control religion, the Turkish-Islamic synthesis was criticized from the Left and the Right. Some secular and non-Sunni, especially Alevi, families strived to exempt their children from the religion course in public schools as some conservatives and religious studies teachers strived to turn it into a course on Islam. Often finding the course contents insufficient, conservative families sought additional informal summer camps and courses for their children.

In the context of Turkey's secularist republican public sphere, piety would become an identity marker, often stigmatized and politicized. The implication for me as a child was the realization of an uncomfortable dichotomy between the modern and the traditional lifestyles. While my modern friends went on summer vacations, usually somewhere by the sea, I would feel that my only choice was to go to the mosque and learn how to read the Quran and memorize the prayers. In addition to going to the beach, alcohol and women's clothing would become other symbolic boundaries between the secular and the conservative lifestyles.

While my early childhood was shaped by my grandfather's Islamist outlook toward modernity and the Kemalist state, during my adolescent years I was exposed to a different form of Islamism that seemed to underplay the tensions between tradition and modernity, and Islam and secularism. I heard about a group of college students mentoring some of my classmates in middle school. They seemed to be doing additional tutoring for the high school placement exams, as well as a host of social and recreational activities. They seemed to be pious yet more private about their piety. They seemed to be less confrontational with the Kemalist ideology in the public sphere. They also seemed to have strong fraternal solidarity. These elders (*abiler*) were influenced by an enigmatic *hocaefendi*. For many of my teenaged peers struggling with the dichotomy between our pious and traditional upbringing and the secular republican ethos and the modernity, hocaefendi's approach was appealing, perhaps to demonstrate that Islam and modernity can be compatible. I would later learn the enigmatic leader that his followers called *hocaefendi* was Fethullah Gülen.

When I asked my grandfather, as my primary intellectual guide, about Gülen, he was ambivalent. On the one hand, he would commend Gülen's piety and his movement's educational accomplishments; on the other hand, he was critical of Gülen's accommodationist approach to the Kemalist state. Islamists like my grandfather were particularly disappointed with Gülen's appeasement when the military forced the resignation of the Islamist Welfare Party–led coalition government in 1997. The 1980s had ushered Turkey into a relatively liberal era in its economy, civil rights, and politics. Both the Islamists and the Gülen movement had benefited from the liberal openings, albeit in different forms. Encouraged by their growing popularity and electoral success in local and national elections, Islamists had become more vocal in their critique of Kemalist secularism in the public sphere. Being aware of the power of the Kemalist bureaucratic establishment over the elected politicians, the Gülen movement was much more concerned about expanding its presence in the state and civil society. During my high school and college years, the movement would become much more visible in the public sphere through organizing interfaith gatherings, fund raising activities, and public platforms, claiming the moderate Islamic center.

Unfortunately for the Kemalists, the 1997 intervention in politics was short-lived and an economic crisis in 2000 resulted in a fundamental restructuring of Turkish politics. For my part, the economic crisis would mean limited job prospects in Turkey's private sector. Despite earning a bachelor's degree in international relations at a top private university in Turkey, my chances of getting into foreign service was also slim, due to my black Turk background. I had some college friends who seemed to follow Gülen's advice to underplay or hide their piety (*tedbir*) to get into the civil service, and perhaps received help with their exam and interview preps. The Gülen movement was organized in a series of concentric circles, with the most loyal members in the core functioning more like a hierarchic organization and outer circles more like a loose civil society network. To me and many other less ideologically inclined Turks with contacts in the outer circles, Gülen was offering a middle way between the ideological poles of the secularists and the Islamists, and perhaps a way forward to ease the political tensions in the country. Despite this promise, the movement continued to keep its inner circles out of reach and mysterious for the public. In addition to the limited job opportunities in the private sector, I knew *tedbir* wasn't something I would do just to get in the public sector, either. My only realistic option seemed to be academia.

I decided to apply to graduate school and was admitted to the University of Utah. When I first arrived in Salt Lake City, I was struck by the similarity of the landscape and the climate with my home town Konya, which also had its own salt lake (Tuz Gölü). There were also cultural similarities; like Utah's reputation in the US, Konya was known as one of the most conservative provinces in Turkey. Konya was also one of the hubs of Islamic capitalism and a conservative form of modernity, much like Mormon Church's success in capitalism and modernization in Utah in the twentieth century. The University of Utah and Salt Lake City were relatively more diverse and liberal compared to Utah in general, yet I was struck by the generally negative attitude of non-Mormons toward Mormons. It appeared to be more than the typical secular-religious or liberal-conservative tensions. I was somewhat puzzled by this, as my initial experience with Mormons in general was quite pleasant and friendly. However, much like my experience with the Gülen movement folks in Turkey, I realized there was a more closed inner culture that outsiders could not easily permeate.

I had started hearing about the grievances of non-Mormons regarding what they called "the dominant religion" as soon as I arrived in Utah. Moving in the more diverse university community and owing to the fact that the Mormon population made up less than 50 percent of the population of Salt Lake City population, I first thought most of these grievances were more perceived than real. The civil society initiatives that emphasized diversity, pluralism, and the religious divide were very vocal and impressive, given the stereotypical perception of Utah. I was able to understand the sources of resentment only when I participated in some of these initiatives, such as "Bridging the Religious Divide" between 2004 and 2006, and, briefly, "The Culture of Connection" in 2007. Most of the grievances were based on the lack of a meaningful dialogue and the absence of mutual trust between Mormons and non-Mormons. Many of these grievances were also historically based. There was an awareness of diversity but not the necessary social institutions and the bridging social capital. The problems minority families faced, especially in raising their children, were some of the most important observations I made during my attendance at the civil society initiatives.

As I pondered the role of religion in Utah and Turkey, I became interested in an intellectual puzzle. The Gülen movement and the Mormon Church were both conservative religious groups who emphasized traditional family and moral values. They were also quite modern in their emphasis on secular as well as religious education, quite aware of the importance of mass media, and quite keen on managing their public image. These modernist conservative movements differed in one key area: their public relations strategy. Mormons were more direct and assertive about their positions on public issues, whereas Gülen movement remained quite indirect and ambivalent on similar public questions. This book is my humble attempt to address this puzzle. I am thankful for my advisors, colleagues, and friends at the University of Utah, Michigan State University, and University of Washington for discussing many of the earlier versions of my work. I'd like to extend my special thanks to the anonymous readers and the publication team at Syracuse University Press, especially the editor-in-chief, Suzanne E. Guiod, and the series editor, Dr. Michael Barkun, for their amazing support. I am indebted to my family in Turkey for always prioritizing my education and their seemingly infinite confidence in me. I'm thankful for colleagues, friends, and interviewees from both communities for sharing their experiences and ideas with me. Last, but not least, I'm thankful for my son Ekrem, whose early cries, smiles, and later critical questions on when I will get this book published have been major sources of inspiration and motivation for me.

The ideas and analysis I offer in this book are neither validation nor refutation of either movement's beliefs or practices; they are rather a humble attempt at understanding and explaining how political context shapes public strategies of religious groups. I hope the readers will find the comparison useful and forgive the book's shortcomings. I appreciate the skepticism readers may have about comparing two theologically very different religious groups. I will use a Turkish saying that I heard from my grandfather countless times as the opening statement in my defense: *teşbihte hata yoktur* (there is no mistake in comparison). There is much to be learned from comparative inquiry. What follows is a longer justification.

Faith and Politics in the Public Sphere

Introduction

Religion unites and divides. The faithful find solace in religious teachings, find meaning in behaving certain ways, and feel a sense of belonging to a greater cause. Religious organizations unify individuals by providing resources to promote piety and fellowship, and by instilling a common social identity in their members. As churches, synagogues, mosques, and temples advance bonding among their congregants, they also get involved in representing them in the public sphere. Most modern religions are involved in their community, albeit to varying degrees and forms. The majority of Americans believe that religion contributes to solving important social problems.[1] Religion acting as a civil society agent by providing social services and engaging advocacy for social issues receives high marks in general even

1. In 2009, Pew Research Center found that 75 percent of Americans surveyed believed religion contributes a great deal or somewhat to solving important social problems, compared to 39 percent who believed religion contributed not much or nothing. These percentages had shifted by 2016 (58 percent and 39 percent, respectively). Despite the increasing skepticism, the majority of the public continued to see religion's social contribution positively ("Are Churches Key to Solving Social Problems? Fewer Americans Now Think So," Pew Research Center, July 18, 2016, http://www.pewresearch.org/fact-tank/2016/07/18/are-churches-key-to-solving-social-problems-fewer-americans-now-think-so/).A Gallup survey also found that 55 percent of Americans believed "religion can answer all or most of today's problems," compared to 34 percent who believed "religion is largely old-fashioned and out of date." ("Majority in US Still Say Religion Can Answer Most Problems," Gallup News, June 2, 2017, http://news.gallup.com/poll/211679/majority-say-religion-answer-problems.aspx?g_source=position7&g_medium=related&g_campaign=tiles.

from the more skeptical nonreligious sectors. Religion becomes a more divisive force, however, when it comes to its involvement in politics, through taking positions and endorsing candidates.[2] Disagreements on the limits to religious freedoms, scope of the separation of church and state, and the danger of the entanglement of religion and politics place religion as one of the most controversial forces in a polity.

Between those who believe religion should be confined to the private sphere and those who believe religion cannot be forced or wished away from the public arena emerges a tension and a debate concerning the legitimate role of religion in the public sphere across the world. Whether the concern is the relations between majority and minority religious groups, the legitimacy of religious symbols in public, or the expression of reasoning informed by religious doctrine in debates regarding moral and public policy issues, the public sphere of both the advanced developed and developing countries is fraught with an increasingly "deprivatized religion" (Casanova 1994; Haynes 1998). Religion going public, however, takes many forms, ranging from formal political participation to issue-based lobbying and community projects. What explains these varying forms and degrees of involvement in the public sphere? Is it religious doctrine or political opportunities that ultimately motivate the public activism of religious groups?

The impact of motives, means, and opportunities is key to understanding particular evolution stories and political strategies of religious groups in the public sphere. The Gülen movement and the Church of Jesus Christ of Latter-day Saints (the LDS Church, whose members are commonly known as Mormons) are two influential contemporary modernist-conservative movements. They carry elements of social conservatism, such as a belief in the importance of traditional family values. They both emphasize religion as an indispensable part of public culture and as a crucial source of social mores, and they believe in

2. Gregory Smith, "Most Americans Oppose Churches Choosing Sides in Elections," Pew Research Center Fact Tank, February 3, 2017, http://www.pewresearch.org/fact-tank/2017/02/03/most-americans-oppose-churches-choosing-sides-in-elections/.

religion's legitimate and positive contribution to public debate in their respective societies. These two movements are also similar in their attitude toward politics. They are natural allies of politically active conservative platforms, yet they often make a considerable effort to distance themselves from groups that they perceive to be more politicized than themselves: in the American context, the Christian Right, and in the Turkish context, the Islamists. The Gülen movement and the LDS Church are both very conscious of the importance of public relations and image in an age of mass communications. Indeed, both groups have invested heavily in the media and public relations.

Despite these striking similarities, the Gülen movement and the LDS Church employ very different strategies to achieve their goals in the public sphere. The LDS Church is a formally established church with a unified institutional structure, and it regularly takes positions on public moral issues, such as same-sex marriage, liquor laws, pornography, and gambling. In contrast, the Gülen movement remains less formally structured and is more like an amalgam of fraternal organizations, social service institutions, project groups, social solidarity platforms, and business networks. As its structure remains opaque, the movement is marked by its strategic ambiguity and emphasis on coalition building in addressing social and political issues in Turkey, rather than by taking clear policy stances on controversial issues.

Named after its founding leader (Fethullah Gülen), the Gülen movement emerged in the 1960s from the Turkish-Islamic periphery with the goal of moving to the center. By the mid-1990s it adopted an increasingly universal-humanist language, and it achieved a considerable global reach during the next decade. Despite its growth and publicity, the movement is still informally organized around a core of dedicated full-time *abiler-ablalar* (elders) who are supported by volunteers and supporters with varying degrees of commitment and skill sets. The movement's public face remained within the civil society and featured civic and social-service projects. The main areas of activity include education, business associations, community organizations, interfaith/intercultural diversity platforms, humanitarian aid, health care, and the media. Despite its clear stakes in policy outcomes, the movement largely refrained from direct involvement in party politics yet strongly and systematically encouraged its participants to pursue influential professions in society and strategic positions in the state bureaucracy. The movement's success in attracting and recruiting bright and talented students, offering them mentorship and support in advancing their careers, and creating business opportunities enabled its rapid growth. This combination of upwardly mobile human capital, trust-based social capital, and a community-oriented business model translated into political influence and access to power. While some in Turkey rushed to join its ranks for the perceived network benefits, others were alarmed by its organizational secrecy, recruitment methods, and growing influence. Ironically, the movement that aimed to bridge societal divisions itself became a major source of polarization between those who loved the movement and those who reviled it, with very few in between.

The origins of the Gülen movement's publicity reaches back to the mid-1990s, which marked its coming of age. During this period, Fethullah Gülen initiated an outreach effort with a purported vision of a pluralist and dynamic public sphere that would be founded on understanding, tolerance, and dialogue. The movement found itself a mission in the much-fragmented and polarized Turkish public sphere marked by ethnic, religious, sectarian, and ideological fault lines.

To implement such an ideal, the movement organized meetings under its Abant Platform, which brought together intellectuals and politicians with diverse beliefs and affiliations to address divisive political issues. In practice, this meant that the movement adopted a strategy of building a civil society shield vis-à-vis the powerful and penetrating state in Turkey without necessarily taking clear positions on controversial issues, and, hence, without drawing the ire of the secular establishment. This strategy was informed by both its principled efforts to create a society with a meaningful dialogue among its constituents in the core and in the periphery of politics, and its more strategic calculations of legitimizing an Islamic movement's position in the public sphere under a restrictive form of republican secularism.

However, this self-defined arbiter role and civil society-building mission paradoxically made the members of the Gülen community rather cautious and uncomfortable when expressing their own positions on controversial issues. The movement traditionally preferred finding third parties with more standing and legitimacy to convey their messages and opinions. The leadership eschewed opposing the state openly on controversial issues, such as the ban on wearing headscarves, restrictions on religious education, and limits to political liberties. Thanks to this strategy of cautious activism, the movement initially survived the state crackdown on Islamic movements between 1997 and 2002 and was well positioned to maximize its growth and access to power during the next decade of the Islamist Justice and Development Party (AKP) government. However, its success created resentment among its rivals and its strategy of caution and secrecy also left the movement under constant suspicion by Islamists and secularists alike. The movement's gains were dramatically reversed after its fallout with the AKP government starting in 2013: closing down or losing control of all its formal organizations, leaving many of its leaders and supporters in jail or in exile, and endangering its international activities due to pressure from the Turkish government on other governments abroad.

Mormons, in comparison, have a well-structured and hierarchical formal church government with a lay ministry. The church as an institution has openly taken positions on certain moral issues. In contrast to the Gülen movement's indirect approach to public issues, the LDS Church takes a direct approach: its representatives deliver speeches and declarations on a regular basis through official channels.[3] The church has sought to influence public opinion on social and political issues primarily at the local level (liquor laws, gaming ordinances, pornography regulations, and laws concerning education

3. The church maintains an official newsroom to provide its own statements on public issues: http://www.mormonnewsroom.org/news-releases.

and immigration in Utah), but it has also been involved in some key national issues (the Equal Rights Amendment, same-sex marriage, and religious liberties).

In contrast to the loosely affiliated organizations of the Gülen movement, such as the Istanbul-based Journalists and Writers Foundation (JWF), the LDS Church created an official public affairs office to deal with these types of issues concerning the relationship of the Mormons with the society at large. Like the Gülen movement, the LDS Church also claims to refrain from direct involvement in party politics and maintains a distance from the various iterations of the Christian Right. One can argue that the LDS Church often acts as an independent interest group within the pluralistic American political system by participating in public debates if and when it deems it necessary for the interest of the church and its members. Indeed, the welfare of the church and its members is an oft-cited justification for the church's positions on social and political matters. This contrasts with the Gülen movement's emphasis on the public good, the national interest, and social harmony as a discursive strategy and source of legitimacy.

This brief overview of the two cases exposes an interesting puzzle on how religious movements operate under conditions of adversity. *Given the similarities in terms of fellowship ties, the emphasis on conservative social values, and religious doctrine concerning political neutrality, why do the LDS Church and the Gülen movement act differently in the public sphere?* To put it another way, *why is Mormonism more self-assertive in the American public sphere and the Gülen movement less direct in its participation in the Turkish public sphere?* This book argues that the solution to this puzzle lies in the primary political context in which these two religious groups operate. More specifically, the *liberal public sphere* in the US and the *republican public sphere* in Turkey explain the divergent public behavior of the LDS Church and the Gülen movement. These different types of public spheres have direct and indirect implications on the actors' strategies and behaviors in three important domains of the polity: *the state, political society,* and *civil society.*

A liberal public sphere is a context in which citizens engage in multiple communications and produce shared but plural identifications in these three domains. Liberal public spheres are marked by their emphasis on negative liberty: individual freedoms, political liberties, and legal protections vis-à-vis a limited government. A republican public sphere, in contrast, prioritizes the values of the republic and a positive liberty that is promoted by the state: national unity, civic virtues, and an often-abstract notion of the public good. The type of a public sphere is closely related to a specific relationship between the state and political and civil society. In the liberal public sphere, political and civil society are strong entities with degrees of autonomy from the state; in the republican public sphere, the state plays a much more dominant role and concedes more limited autonomy to the other domains.

One plausible explanation for the difference in strategy between the Gülen movement and the LDS Church might be found in organizational factors: the LDS Church is a hierarchical religion and the Gülen movement is an amalgam of service-oriented institutions and loose networks of social relations. Acknowledging the merits of this explanation, this book argues that the relationship between the organizational structure and the public strategies of these two groups is spurious: a third factor can explain both the organizational structure and the political strategies of both groups. This factor is the political context in which these two groups have emerged, evolved, and flourished.

The choice to formally or informally organize is closely related to the nature of state-society relations in each country. Turkey is a polity in which the state has clearly been the dominant actor in the public sphere. The Gülen movement, or, indeed, any other Islamic group, could not garner official status as a religious group because the state recognizes only one form of Islam and controls religious services, education, and places of worship. The US offers a sharp contrast to the regulated religious market of Turkey. The strong tradition of decentralization and institutional separation—together with a robust religious freedoms regime—offers more autonomy to religious groups in public life in the US.

This book covers the time period between 1994 and 2018 to develop a public profile of the two groups; this time period also permits a comparative examination of the historical context in which each group moved from the periphery of its respective society toward the center.

The changing structure and substance of the public sphere offers a strong explanation not only for each group's historical trajectory in the last two and a half decades but also alludes to subsequent developments and provides useful insights regarding future developments in each society. For example, parallel to a liberalizing trend in Turkish politics between 2003 and 2011, the tone and substance of the Gülen movement's public message changed: it began to offer more vocal critiques of the exclusionary form of Turkish secularism, the role of the military in politics, and the discriminatory policies and civil rights violations of the state toward its citizens, and, consequently, the movement moved toward more direct forms of involvement in politics. Evidently, as the public sphere had temporarily shifted away from its strongly republican character to a more liberal one, the movement had become relatively more self-confident and assertive than it had been in the past. However, this access to power was short-lived and exposed the movement. After its alliance with the ruling AKP collapsed, the movement attempted to return to its politics of coalition building with other civil society organizations and political parties, but had limited success due to the erosion of its credibility during its almost blind support of the AKP's political hegemony. When the movement encountered the wrath of the Turkish state after its daring opposition to the AKP government in 2013, there were very few Turks outside of the movement to offer sympathy. Between 2013 and 2016, the movement tried to adopt methods of civil disobedience and transform its nonconfrontational activism into contentious activism. A failed coup attempt in July 2016 implicated civil and military persons with links to the movement, and the ensuing crackdown under emergency rule sent many of its members to prison or exile, and the remnants underground in Turkey. Even during its relatively assertive period, the movement's approach remained quite general and allusive compared to the LDS Church's official positions and declarations on substantive policy matters. The Gülen movement continued to emphasize liberal democratic values and European Union (EU) membership protocols as the legitimacy for its public discourse and opposition to the government. The findings in this study suggest that religious movements adapt their political strategies, public discourse, and organization in response to the changing political contexts in which they operate, and the continuum of liberal-republican public spheres explains the forces at work in each context.

The existence of either a liberal or republican public sphere is linked to several factors, such as the prevalent political culture, the state ideology, and the history of nation-state building. In the US, the earlier phase of Protestant immigration, the First and Second Great Awakenings, the American Revolution, the constitutional process, and the increasingly clashing notions of liberal rationalism and conservative populism have been crucial in the formation of a liberal public sphere. With respect to the shape of the contemporary public sphere, there have been two key developments since the American Revolution. One is the gradual increase in the powers of the national government and the extension of the Bill of Rights freedoms to the state. The second is the rise of a pluralistic minority rights regime alongside an increasing amount of diversity within the society. Significant legal and political developments in the US, such as constitutional amendments and court rulings, can be better understood with reference to the pressures arising from these two parallel developments.

In the case of Turkey, the Ottoman state tradition and bureaucracy, center-periphery relations, multilegalism under the *millet* system, and the ideological basis of the Turkish modernization project are key for an understanding of the origins of Turkey's republican public sphere. The founder of modern Turkey, Mustafa Kemal Atatürk, believed in the necessity of a strong centralized authority to accomplish his reform project. He was influenced by the positivist values and enlightenment ideals of the French republican model. In particular, the secularism of the Turkish republican model is similar to its French counterpart (*laïcité*) in both its understanding and practice of secularism. Under Atatürk, the republican public sphere was introduced to replace the old Ottoman confessional public sphere. This confessional public sphere was arguably more inclusive of multiple ethnic and religious identities, but it had a lower degree of integration among them. The amalgamation of social forces in the public sphere was part of a nation-building project controlled by a strong ideological state. This started off as a form of one-party authoritarianism in the 1920s and evolved into an illiberal "guided democracy" in the latter part of the twentieth century. The strong centralized state tradition in the Ottoman Empire played a decisive role in the formative years of the Turkish Republic. Although Atatürk tried to distance the new republic from its Islamic and imperial past, modern Turkey was built upon the remaining core of the multiethnic Ottoman Empire. The dismemberment of the Ottoman state as a result of ethnonationalist movements left an indelible mark on the new republican elite's relations with social or ethnic forces at the periphery.

While the Turkish Republic remained wary of the separatist potential of ethnic and religious identities, the US was formed as a result of separation from the British Empire. Consequently, the US political system was based on restrictions over the powers of the federal government and more autonomy was granted to the states and the civil society in general. This is in stark contrast to the paranoia of the Turkish state regarding diverse societal identities after the collapse of the Ottoman Empire, which decisively shaped the republican elite's attempts to create a homogenous nation. This exclusionary and top-down Turkish modernization and nation-building project is quite different from the American experience with the semi-independent colonies with their own legislative bodies, albeit under the final authority of the British Crown. This early colonial structure gave rise to the development of political autonomy, self-determination aspirations, and the eventual contractual nature of state-society relations during the formative years following the Revolutionary War. As opposed to the strongly centralized unitary Turkish state reacting to the trauma of ethnic separatism, the US was created as a confederation of thirteen colonies and later evolved into a federal political system with strong checks and balances on the powers of the central government.

Its relatively pluralist and liberal history notwithstanding, the American public sphere also witnessed its own share of exclusionary policies and discrimination toward various social groups, such as African Americans, Catholic and Jewish immigrants, Mormons, Japanese Americans, and, more recently, Muslims. Despite these examples of exclusion from the American public sphere, there is one key difference in the historical trajectories of the two countries. While the fault lines in Turkey were between the modernizing state and the ethnic and religious identity groups in society, the struggle in America was between different ideological forces and religious traditions *within* society. This struggle internal to society originally translated into political cleavages in a more organic process. In the American case, the social majority and their political representatives discriminated against different minorities in different periods. In the Turkish case, a privileged minority and the ruling class led the nation-building process. This state-centric modernization process enacted a host of discriminatory policies against various ethnic and religious groups, effectively pitting the state against the society. These dynamics of top-down and bottom-up forces are closely related to the types of public spheres in a country and significantly shape the public behavior and strategies of religious groups in a polity.

Methodology and Case Selection

The practices and attitudes of religiously oriented groups that engage with society as a whole regarding social and political issues are the basic indicators of public activism. In particular, civic associations; public platforms of debate and deliberation; declarations on public policy, moral, and political issues; and publications of this nature are ways of assessing the public participation of a religious community or a movement. In the case of the LDS Church, this book focuses on the practices of the Church Public Affairs department and official documents, memos, letters, and exchanges between different local groups in Utah on what the church terms "moral issues." For the Gülen movement, the focus is on the practices of the Gülen-affiliated organizations; the opinions of Fethullah Gülen; and the editorials in the affiliated traditional print and visual media organizations and social media platforms.

In order to interpret the objectives of these public activities and the impact of the political context on them, this book employs content analysis to examine speeches, pamphlets, and media appearances by each group. Additional data is drawn from an archival study of the authoritative LDS Church First Presidency letters, internal memos, and official statements in the Church History Library in Salt Lake City, Utah. Elite interviews with the leadership of the Gülen-inspired Journalists and Writers Foundation in Istanbul and the LDS Church Public Affairs officials in Salt Lake City offer a second layer of evidence regarding how elites within these two religious communities view their positions in their respective public spheres. I also participated in Salt Lake City Mayor Rocky Anderson's "Bridging the Religious Divide" initiative in 2004 and 2005, shortly before initiating this project. The honest and heartfelt grievances, opinions, and exchanges between various members of the community were quite revealing of the perceived position of the LDS Church as a sociopolitical actor in Utah. Similarly, taking part in interfaith activities coordinated by the Salt Lake Interfaith Roundtable between 2004 and 2008 gave me an additional chance to observe and better understand the dynamics of religious representation in a local setting.

It is challenging to offer a balanced view of religious groups in general, but this challenge is heightened when the religious groups in question are those whose current affairs or history have generated significant controversy and division in the societies they are part of. Both the LDS Church and the Gülen movement have had their detractors and even enemies during much of their existence. The opponents of these religious groups portray a darker side and raise suspicions about the ulterior motives for their public activities. There is always a journalistic reflex to address these issues by offering a thorough investigation of such claims, accusations, and critiques. Although it is important to understand the sources of these grievances, legitimate or illegitimate, the scope of this study was shaped by its research question and the available data. Much of the data used here is publicly accessible for anyone interested in the subject. While this project does not directly address the more polemical and controversial aspects of the two movements, the value of this kind of a study comes explicitly from its engagement with the observed behavior of such religious movements. Moreover, understanding public profiles and movement dynamics is not easier or less important than uncovering the "hidden" aspects.[4] Indeed, the very question of what kind of strategies these movements develop in order to present and position themselves in face of skeptical and inquisitive publics is at the core of this book.

This study conducts two forms of comparison: longitudinal and cross-national. Through the historical comparative method, the longitudinal part identifies the changes and continuities in the public role of religion in Turkey in general and in the Gülen movement in particular. Similarly, the evolution of the public image and the doctrine of the LDS Church after its formation and the admission of Utah to the Union, and the different forms of publicity in these periods, are taken as points of historical comparison. In terms of cross-national comparison, the Gülen movement and the LDS Church offer a useful juxtaposition to underscore the influence of the two different types of public spheres over the identity, interests, and practices of these religious groups in the public sphere. The cross-national comparison between the two movements looks at the different public attitudes of the Gülen movement and the LDS Church despite their key similarities.

Although here I primarily focus on two cases, these cases yield a number of observations because I examine the transformation of the two movements over time (King, Keohane, and Verba 1994). Even though studies with a narrow focus such as this one may not be ideal

4. I owe this point to Elisabeth Özdalga, who explains it eloquently in her work, which aptly examined public manifestations of modern Islamic movements from a Weberian outlook of ascetic piety (2003b).

for demonstrating causality, they are useful in understanding causal mechanisms or other crucial factors that may be overlooked in studies with a larger number of cases, and, thus, help in theory building (Eckstein 1975).

The Gülen movement and the LDS Church provide variation on both the independent variable (different religious groups in the republican and liberal public spheres) and on the dependent variable (the modes of operation vis-à-vis the state, political society, and civil society). Among the various historical points the book zeroes in on, survey data from 2008 sharply illustrates this variation. At this point, the Gülen movement was one of the largest—and, arguably, the most influential to date—Islamic movement in modern Turkey. Despite its popularity and strong social support across the country, the movement continued to display insecurity, behaving guardedly in the Turkish public sphere.[5] Almost the opposite was true for the LDS Church: Mormons made up only 1.7 percent of the American population, yet the church was quite assertive and self-confident in the American public sphere.[6] The two cases were at critical political junctures in their respective polities, which offer an instructive contrast: a highly popular group acting far less assertively and a highly unpopular group acting far more assertively.[7] Being similar in terms of their *relevant* group

5. In a 2008 GENAR Poll, 65.4 percent of the respondents said they endorsed the Gülen movement functions in general ("Operasyona Turk Halkindan Destek" [The Turkish Public Supports the Operation] *Yeni Safak*, July 18, 2008). In a more detailed survey-based study of Islamic communities in Turkey, the Gülen movement was identified as the most well-known group in Turkey with the greatest number of adherents (Çaha et al. 2011).

6. "Religious Affiliation: Diverse and Dynamic," US Religious Landscape Survey, Pew Forum on Religion and Public Life, February 2008. Accessed August 12, 2018. http://www.pewforum.org/files/2013/05/report-religious-landscape-study-full.pdf.

7. For example, Mormons fared third (only after atheists and Muslims) in terms of being least likely to be voted as president in a Pew survey ("Religion in Campaign '08: Clinton and Giuliani Seen as Not Highly Religious; Romney's Religion Raises Concerns," Pew Research Center, September 6, 2007. Accessed August 12,

characteristics, such as commitment to the promotion of a positive public image and the pursuit of public influence, this study points to the influence of outside factors, such as the political context in which these groups operate. The US and Turkey are also two interesting cases for comparison. In particular, these states are characterized by electoral politics, albeit with different institutions and practices; a vivid public religion; and different, but comparable, forms of the public sphere.

The role of religion in the public sphere is a contested issue in both Turkey and the US. The US Constitution outlaws religious tests for office and the First Amendment prohibits establishment of religion by the government (Establishment Clause) and protects religious liberty (Free Exercise Clause). Despite their brevity, these two clauses have been anything but straightforward in their implementation and have been the basis of many cases to come before the US Supreme Court. In the twentieth century, separationists, who tended to prioritize the Establishment Clause and argue that the First Amendment erects a wall of separation between religion and the state, won legal victories in landmark cases related to school prayer, tax exemptions, and parochial school funding. In combination with increasing ethnic and religious diversity, such rulings mobilized social conservatives and led to the rise of the Christian Right and politics of moral values. Mormons, as one of the most active religious groups—and one increasing in both numbers and influence—have been a natural ally of the new Republican coalition, albeit a less vocal one. The LDS Church's selective accommodation of modernity and its conservative-but-mainstream profile in the liberal American public sphere is comparable to the Gülen movement's efforts to distance itself from more partisan and ideological Islamist parties and forging alliances with more center-right political parties.[8]

2018. http://people-press.org/report/353/clinton-and-giuliani-seen-as-not-highly-religious-romneys-religion-raises-concerns.

8. The use of the term liberal can be especially confusing for American readers, given how its meaning evolved over time as a political ideology and political attitude.

As the Gülen movement constantly tried to assure the Turkish state of its loyalty to the secular order and the benign nature of its activities, the LDS Church acted assertively with minimal fears of government persecution but with consciousness about its public image and public opinion in general. Both movements demonstrate awareness of public image and legitimation, yet their primary targets in their public relations management are different: the state in the Turkish republican public sphere and the society in the liberal American public sphere. Mormons learned after bitter lessons that the protections provided by the government are often incomplete and subject to the interests of other societal groups and the dominant understandings of morality and religious liberties. The Gülen movement, on the other hand, must have realized the limits of popular support in a republican public sphere where the state remains to be a dominant, if not hegemonic, actor.

In regard to theoretical implications, the comparison of the LDS Church and the Gülen movement sheds light on the discussions regarding constitutions and the functioning of the public sphere as well as how the public sphere is utilized by religiously-based social actors. Thus, this study develops a model to explain the political participation of religious groups in the public sphere. The republican-liberal typology developed in this study combines elements of structural and contextual political analysis. As these structural and contextual factors shape the environment in which religious groups go public and develop their political strategies, their preferences are shaped by their group interests and social identities. Identities and interests mutually constitute the set of preferences, priorities, and repertoires of action available to the religious organizations. In other words, all social groups are motivated by their desire to promote their own well-being in the public arena. However, their preferences are not exogenous.

I use the term liberal in this study to refer to open, unregulated, and free public space that lacks a dominant organizing force, rather than to indicate a particular political position in the continuum between those who might characterize themselves and others as liberals or conservatives.

Rather, these preferences are constructed within the context of their interactions with the entirety of the political system in which they function (Wildavsky 1987).

The typologies of the republican and liberal public spheres developed by this study are not confined to issues related to religion or religious groups. This understanding of political participation and group behavior is broadly applicable to any social movement or group that attempts to enter into the public sphere. Ultimately, social groups formulate their preferences and strategies by interacting with political institutions, culture, and other actors.

Organization and Outline

The book comprises seven chapters. The next chapter details the theoretical framework of the study and makes a case for situating public activism within the three analytical domains of the polity: the state, political society, and civil society. Religious groups, including the Mormons and the Gülen movement, target a combination of these domains for their activism. The type of public sphere shapes the preferences of the religious groups, through the restrictions, opportunities, incentives, and disincentives present in each type of public sphere.

The concept of social capital is also important in understanding the broader impacts of collective action originating in the civil society. Social capital refers to organizations, networks, norms, and mutual trust that enable cooperation and collective action in a society. Different types of social capital form when social actors create ties among like-minded individuals (*bonding*), reach out to groups with different identities and beliefs (*bridging*), and cultivate relationships with political leaders and state institutions (*linking*). Generation and utilization of different forms of social capital illustrate how religious organizations engage with the society at large. The Mormons are known for their strong fellowship ties and in-group solidarity, which translates into *bonding* social capital. Such solidarity was a key factor in the success of the Mormons as they faced outside pressures to the point of existential threats in their faith's early years, both before and immediately after the migration to Utah. The institutional and spiritual capital of the LDS Church is very effective in organizing community programs, such as helping the poor, disaster preparedness, and disaster relief efforts. The Gülen movement has also demonstrated in-group cohesion both in response to the restrictive policies of the state and to mobilize a grassroots movement in support of their educational goals. Since the mid-1990s, the Gülen movement has also actively sought to rebuild relations across ethnic, religious, and ideological boundaries. This translates into *bridging* social capital. Since 2000, the success of movement-affiliated business associations, humanitarian aid organizations, and cultural projects has also helped to develop strong ties among the civil society, socioeconomic interest groups, politicians, and the state bureaucracy. These ties suggest the development of a more vertically connected *linking* social capital.

Such social outcomes and implications are critical factors for the performance and legitimacy of political institutions in a democracy (Putnam 1994). Variation in the types of social capital generated by religious groups points to the incentives generated by the particular form of public sphere. The preferences and strategies of the religious groups are shaped by the political structure and are the products of a mutually constitutive relationship between group identity and group self-interest. Chapter 1 delineates the republican and liberal types of public spheres; the public sphere shapes interactions and facilitates reciprocal relations among social groups. These two types are not rigid models; rather, they are ideal types. Most political contexts are located somewhere on a continuum between the liberal and republican public sphere ideal types. Political contexts can change, meaning that a given public sphere may move closer to one type over time. Such a dynamic approach makes it possible to trace the changing political behavior of religious groups in tandem with the changing contours of the public sphere in their respective societies.

After laying out its conceptual foundations and theoretical arguments, the book provides an empirical analysis of the two movements in three sections following its analytical model: religion and the state, religion and politics, and religion and civil society. To develop a comparative perspective, each part consists of a designated chapter for the two cases.

In the first part, chapter 2 traces the evolution of the public sphere in its republican form in Turkey and examines public debates on religious representation, especially the conflict over wearing the headscarf in the universities. The paternalistic Ottoman state, which reigned over a multiethnic and multireligious society, was replaced by a republican state that undertook an ambitious nation-building project to promote a homogenous secular-Sunni-Turkish citizenry. This nation-building project was truly revolutionary under a one-party political system; the republican zeal was tempered only after World War II, when Turkey transitioned to a multiparty political system. From 1950 to 2000, Turkey witnessed two direct and two indirect military interventions, as well as numerous other examples of military's meddling in politics. The Gülen movement emerged in this period as another informal Islamic movement in the tightly controlled Turkish religious market. The movement was successful in transforming what started as a community-building project in the sociopolitical periphery into one of the best organized, most influential and, yet, most controversial social movements at the center of Turkish politics. In order to survive the external pressure of a hostile state, the movement employed a strategy of adopting a lower profile in public and forming broad coalitions as a counterweight to the power of the state in the public sphere. The chapter contextualizes the movement's puzzling behavior to underplay the symbolic importance of the headscarf controversy in the 1990s and 2000s and its attempts to appease the secularist establishment.

Chapter 3 offers a historical perspective on the politics of minority religious identity in nineteenth-century America. The Mormon struggle for self-preservation and self-rule can be better understood with reference to the gradual increase in the power of the federal government and the judicial and legislative policies promoting a common American public identity. Diversity and pluralism have always been factors in the American nation-state building project, yet their definition and boundaries have been conditioned by time and space. Diversity through much of the nineteenth century was primarily understood as diversity within Protestantism; non-Protestants, including Mormons, were forced to conform to a system of Protestant semiestablishment. For example, the public school system was designed to assimilate the Catholic minority as well as to provide a free education to the Protestant majority. The Victorian moral values of the Protestant majority shaped their attitudes toward the Mormons and their distinctive beliefs and practices. Hierarchical church structure, new sacred revelations, and the practice of polygamy put the Mormons at odds with the rest of the public. In the absence of a robust minority rights regime at the state level, Mormons often faced discrimination and persecution in Missouri and Illinois. The chapter also discusses the roots of American patriotism and exceptionalism in the Mormon doctrines and situates them in their political context.

In the second part, "Religion and Politics," chapters 4 and 5 use process tracing to illustrate the relationship between political context and group behavior. Chapter 4 uncovers the impact of republicanism evident in the Gülen movement's discursive and organizational strategies. An empirical analysis of Fethullah Gülen's initial ideas concerning politics and social issues underscores the influence of republicanism on questions of an ideal political system, state authority, religion, and state-society relations. In comparison, his post-1999 interviews and statements reflect a more liberal turn, with a greater emphasis on freedom, democracy, and limited government. Gülen's immigration to the US and the short-lived liberal openings in the Turkish political system are the primary reasons for this discursive change. The chapter demonstrates that, on the one hand, the movement itself benefited from the liberalization in Turkey between 2000 and 2012 and became relatively more assertive in the public sphere. On the other hand, by the end of 2013, the movement became a victim of its success by alienating other social groups with its Machiavellian tactics and Byzantine politics inside the state bureaucracy, and by entering into an all-out power struggle in 2013 against its former ally, the Islamist AKP government.

Chapter 5 looks at the struggles of the Mormons in more historical detail and explains a Mormon logic of resistance through an examination of the economic, political, and legal strategies the Mormons pursued in their relations with the federal government. In the late nineteenth century, the "Mormon question" occupied a central place in the Supreme Court's interpretation of the First Amendment. The court's differentiation between religious belief and religious practice in terms of the protection accorded to each under the First Amendment of the Constitution made *Reynolds v. United States* (1879) a landmark case. The court would uphold the antibigamy laws applied by the federal government in the Utah Territory. These laws constituted a central part of what can be considered a crusade against polygamy. After decades of living on the periphery of American society and under the federal government's economic and political sanctions, the LDS Church in Utah went through a tremendous transformation to secure a place for their faith in the mainstream of the American polity. As church policies and practices moved away from polygamy, economic communalism, and bloc voting, the "Americanization" of Utah, the disestablishment of the LDS Church, and the mainstreaming of the Mormons accelerated.

In the third section, "Religion and Civil Society," chapter 6 analyzes the public relations of the Gülen movement by looking at the Abant Platform of the Journalists and Writers Foundation as the Gülen movement's most prominent—yet still unofficial—public affairs organ. The platform's approach to social issues differs from the LDS Church's public relations, as the latter offers a more direct and autonomous voice. The Gülen movement undertook the role of a facilitator, offering moral and logistical support for bringing together prominent intellectuals, media representatives, civil society organizations, politicians, and members of the state bureaucracy. Such a diverse group of participants were invited to discuss politically polarizing issues with a "collective intellect and spirit." The platform was successful in promoting a much-needed dialogue among different social groups and in parsing complex problems into manageable pieces and achieving agreement on some key principles and procedures.

The Abant Platform demonstrates the Gülen movement's investment in an ambitious project that aims to organize civil society and empower it by increasing cohesion among diverse constituents of the society. This appeared to be an effective strategy, given the predominance of the Turkish state over Turkish civil society, whose influence was further limited owing to the Turkish civil society's fragmentation along ethnic, ideological, and religious lines. However, the chapter also argues that, despite the Gülen movement's primary role as a facilitator and organizer, the movement relied almost exclusively on others to debate issues and thus failed to develop its own independent voice. This lack of assertiveness and its increasing bureaucratic presence came at the expense of its soft power, undermining the public trust in the movement and causing many to question its intentions. In light of the movement's public engagement, the chapter also discusses the broader implications of the Abant Platform on issues related to Islam, secularism, and democracy; questions of pluralism, diversity, and freedoms; and the rule of law.

As a result of their struggle for statehood in Utah and their efforts to respond to critics of polygamy, the LDS Church has long understood the importance of public image and has developed strategies to influence public opinion. Chapter 7 examines the efforts of the church to carefully manage its public relations with the rest of society. The transformation of an archetypal Mormon from a bearded, polygamous outsider to a clean-cut, industrious, middle-class American patriot is a great achievement not only for the Mormons, but also for the American body politic. In this process, Mormons felt increased pressure to be seen as good representatives of their community, demonstrate their patriotism, and promote a mainstream-but-unique American profile. The efforts of the LDS Church to provide a clear position on questions of official doctrine and to publicly articulate these positions differentiates it from the Gülen movement's preference for a more decentralized system of representation through multiple channels in the media and civil society. The chapter demonstrates that the church excelled in public affairs, especially starting in the latter part of the twentieth century. However, beneath these organized and professional publicity efforts problems with diversity, credibility, and transparency remain. The church continues to face the challenge of balancing its support for conservative measures in moral issues while upholding its political neutrality principle amid demographic and attitudinal changes among its members.

The concluding chapter summarizes the main argument and findings of the study in order to provide a discussion of the future prospects of each religious group in its respective public sphere. The political developments since 2013 suggests that the LDS Church is acting even more assertively in the post-Romney American body politic. On the other hand, the Gülen movement has lost even its restrained public identity in the face of the Turkish government's insistence that the movement was the mastermind behind a failed coup attempt in July 2016, resulting in a crackdown on suspected Gülen movement supporters in the bureaucracy, business, education, and civil society organizations. These more recent developments suggest the fragility of gains made by societal actors in a republican public sphere, especially when actors usher in a power struggle and the regime slides into authoritarian nationalism. Having lost even very basic protections for property rights, due process, and freedom of assembly in Turkey, the Gülen movement is likely to go through a process of soul-searching and to turn back to its grassroots community organization. As for the liberal American public sphere, the primacy of the societal actors and public opinion continue to shape American politics. Antiestablishment sentiments and populism have become more consequential in American politics since the rise of the Tea Party movement in 2008 and the election of Donald Trump as president in 2016. Likely due to its own history of persecution and discrimination, the LDS Church so far remained skeptical of the anti-immigration and Islamophobic wing of the Republican Party. Despite its conservative preferences, its minority status is likely to shape the Mormon politics in the coming years.

1

Religion in the Public Sphere

The Liberal-Republican Axis

As social movements across the world have increasingly challenged the existing political institutions and intensified citizen activism beyond conventional party politics, the public sphere has become a focal point for contemporary political analysis. The public sphere itself is a fuzzy concept with institutional, discursive, and normative dimensions. The concept is generally used by political theorists, but it has been largely ignored by scholars of comparative politics. This book brings this understudied concept into the comparative politics literature by synthesizing insights from structural-functional political analysis and sociology of religion. Alfred Stepan's conceptualization of modern polities and José Casanova's study of religion in the public sphere have been two seminal works that are uniquely suited for such a synthetic approach on politics of religious representation. From his extensive study of democratization and civil-military relations, Stepan calls for a more analytical study of politics at different levels. According to him, modern polities can be conceptually divided into three distinct domains for conceptual purposes: the state, political society, and civil society (Stepan 1988; 2001). In his path-breaking sociological study of public religions, Casanova (1994) traces the "deprivatization" of religion in modern societies to these three domains of the polity.

If we think of the public sphere as the juncture between state and society, we can argue that this ideally autonomous space is often negotiated between the state, the political society, and the civil society.

As scholars of the state-in-society approach maintain, the terms of interaction between the state and the society are not fixed, nor are they monolithic. Rather, the terms are highly dependent on the issue-area, which draws particular societal groups and compartments of state bureaucracy (Migdal, Kohli, and Shue 1994). From this point of view, the boundaries between the state and the society are fluid and the relative influence each has in the public sphere—and its function therein—can shift back and forth.

The *state* refers to a continuous administrative, legal, bureaucratic, and coercive system with its own institutions, regulations, and enforcement mechanisms. The state level includes symbolic and legal functions. The constitution, civil service, law enforcement, public education, and the judiciary are some examples of venues in which religion can manifest itself in the state apparatus. The *political society* is an arena in which societal groups struggle to gain control over the state apparatus and influence policy. This competition usually takes place through political parties, interest groups, lobbies, and other more informal channels. The *civil society* is made up of a body of associations, platforms, and organizations beyond the immediate reach and control of the state. The civil society also requires a certain reference to the public good, as opposed to the pure market rationality and self-interest that are the vehicles of the economic society. Voluntary organizations and members of the associational life in civil society offer social services in education, health care, gender equality, and minority rights; they also promote different issue-based platforms. Just like any other social actor, religious groups may choose to utilize a combination of these three domains. The political context limits and expands the options available to social groups through incentives and disincentives.

This book seeks to explain the public profile of religious groups, which includes their social activities, their channels and modes of representation, and their positions on specific issues. The public profiles of select religious groups emerge along the aforementioned three domains of the polity. Social groups act within or across the boundaries of these domains when they enter into the public sphere.

Civil Society, Social Movements, and Religion

This book utilizes key insights from the civil society literature and social movement theory. Civil society is the primary domain in which religiously based social movements originate and interact with the public. The norms and networks of civic engagement significantly influence the quality of public life, including the performance of political institutions. Robert Putnam attaches great importance to civic culture and defines social capital as "features of social organization such as networks, norms and social trust that facilitate coordination and cooperation for mutual benefit." (Putnam 1995, 66). Civic engagement facilitates communication and creates social bonds and social trust, which, in turn, make collective action easier and opportunism and cheating less likely (Coleman 1990, 302). Participation in voluntary civic associations advances the socialization of individuals and cultivates values and mores regarding communal life, such as reciprocity, trustworthiness, and friendship. Engagement in civic life exposes the citizens to politically relevant information and enhances their social skills (Putnam 2000).

Networks of civic engagement are crucial for a vibrant society with a meaningful dialogue among its constituents. Social capital can be understood at two separate but interrelated levels. One is the individual level, pertaining to the degree to which individuals are community minded and have a sense of the common good. The other level is more intersubjective and structural, related to the absence or existence of trust between individuals in a society. James Coleman argues that social capital is embedded in social relations and is evident in three main forms: obligations and expectations, information channels, and social norms (Coleman 1988, 98; 101–5). In essence, voluntary organizations in civil society play an important role in transforming the anonymous masses into communities; it is trust that "lubricates" this cooperation for mutual benefit (Smidt 2003; Putnam 1993).

Religion continues to be an important source of social capital in many modern societies. Religion as a body of beliefs, values, and norms motivates believers to volunteer in community affairs, to provide social services such as health care and education, and to help the poor. Moreover, religion offers a common identity to its followers and creates bonds between them. Obviously, religion is only one such source of social capital or civic engagement. But how does religion influence civil society? Is there anything unique about religion when it comes to generating social capital?

In comparison to "secular" sources, religion may have an advantage in promoting a strong sense of reciprocity. First, the centrality of an afterlife and an all-seeing omnipotent higher authority in many religious traditions provides a strong foundation for engagement. In that sense, the nonmaterial basis of volunteering and self-sacrifice are key aspects of religious social capital. Second, most religions claim universal appeal, which, in turn, fosters a sense of common identity and purpose across ethnic, racial, and economic lines. Third, because most religions are motivated by salvation rather than by strict definitions of worldly success, they may be willing to take on bold initiatives and politically risky ventures. Last, religion also provides a symbolic language enmeshed in the grammar of the society by speaking the language of the masses and utilizing the "cultural capital" (Williams 2003).

The particular role of religion in civil society is initially shaped by the organizational structure of the religious groups and their religious doctrine. Religious groups whose organizations are congregational tend to promote a more active and engaged laity than hierarchically structured groups (Harris 2003, 127). Particular religious teachings may also play a role in either enhancing or hindering social capital. Religions that emphasize the distinctiveness of their beliefs, especially religions with exclusive evangelism, are more likely to be inward looking, whereas religions that emphasize social justice and interfaith dialogue are more likely to work across faiths and socioeconomic classes.

While the literature on social capital studies various sites and networks that host civic engagement, the social movement literature explains how societal groups utilize those sites and networks to create movements and become actors of social change. A broad understanding of contentious politics first provides the foundation for an eventual definition of politically relevant collective action by religious groups. Contentious politics includes "all situations in which actors make collective claims on other actors, claims which, if realized would affect the actors' interests, when some government is somehow party to the claims" (McAdam, Tarrow, and Tilly 1998, 143). Thus, religious groups that take positions on moral-political-national questions, build coalitions, mobilize support on policy issues, and publicly express their positions through direct and indirect ways are engaging in politically relevant collective action. Politically relevant collective action, therefore, includes both what religious groups say and what they do. Accordingly, this study treats both the Gülen community and the Mormons as part of the broader world of contentious politics, making collective claims, on the state and other societal actors, with their specific agendas and strategies, rather than as simple ascetic spiritual actors.

In their pivotal work on social movement theory, McAdam, Tarrow, and Tilly (1998) advocated for an integrated perspective to bridging the otherwise divided literature of contentious politics by emphasizing the centrality of *cultural frames*, *resources*, and *structure*. Wald, Silverman, and Fridy (2005) advocate utilizing this "unified" social movement theory approach to explain the translation of religious grievances into political action on the basis of *motive*, *means*, and *opportunity*. In looking at the life cycle of the two movements in this study, one can see the utility of such a synthesis. Both movements started with a lofty idealism and strong ambitions for transforming the larger world; in the early years, then, motives and ideas provide explanations for their emergence, perseverance, and survival under external pressure and very unfavorable political conditions. These formative years also influenced the development of a defensive group posture, group cohesion, and group solidarity. Each group's ability to build community in the face of opposition as well as their growing economic and organizational resources tell the story of their respective maturation phases. The limits of utopian visions are tested by challenges related to leadership, financial resources, and human capital. One can argue that both the LDS Church and the Gülen movement became victims of their own success by alarming more powerful and established social, economic, and political interest groups. In explaining why the Gülen movement and the LDS Church chose to engage with the outside world and the types of activities that they have promoted in the public sphere, this study will look at the motives and means of each group. To clarify why the two groups have adopted different public profiles in spite of comparable resources and cultural frames, the subsequent chapters will illustrate the significance of the opportunity factor in determining the particular form of each religious group's public engagement.

A more recent line of research in social movement theory stresses collective or shared beliefs. Social movement theorists have long been preoccupied with the process of meaning creation. Movements help to create and recreate meanings through *framing*: by turning new or alternative ideas into messages that delineate the issues at stake and the appropriate strategies for action (Klandermans 1997). Framing occurs not only through what movements say, but also through what they do—through their choices of tactics and the connections between their actions and their rhetoric (McAdam, McCarthy, and Zald 1996). Social movements use framing for tactical and strategic purposes, such as to build consensus and to appease opponents. Transnational social movements and their strategies of issue framing and advocacy networking have also garnered attention in social movement theory (Tarrow 2001; Smith, Chatfield, and Pagnucco 1997). Indeed, social movement theory offers a set of functional tools for the analysis of religious groups in the public sphere. Different framing efforts regarding "moral issues" or in public debates can hint at the conditioning effects of the dominant political culture and political socialization.

A mere cultural frame explanation would overemphasize the role of the theological differences in religions. While Islam and Mormonism represent different theological approaches, it would be erroneous to conceptualize these two cases exclusively as accounts of religious actors. An exclusive resource-based approach would fail to explain why the Gülen movement had long maintained a relatively lower public profile despite its vast financial and organizational resources. The argument developed in this book is based on the analysis of the distinct impacts of two different types of public spheres; it thus affirms the structural/opportunity explanation.

Religious communities emerge from civil society and use religious teachings to create frames of meaning and social identity for their members. To strengthen solidarity among their believers, they rely on the bonding type of social capital. As they aim to expand their membership and geographic scope, religious communities encounter other societal groups and the larger body politic. This outreach and expansion necessitates the building of horizontal relationships with other communities through bridging social capital and vertical relationships with the state institutions and political elite through linking social capital.

However, despite comparable generic goals of survival, expansion, and access, religious communities use quite different strategies to promote the well-being of their organizations and members. The literature on social movements suggests that grievances, resources, and opportunities are potential explanations for religiously based societal group behavior. This study argues that the Gülen movement and the LDS Church have similar aims of survival, expansion, and access to power, and both command significant economic and organizational resources. However, the opportunity structure in which they operate differs with respect to the prevalent model of the public sphere.

Public Spheres: Liberal and Republican

The dynamics of subordination, coexistence, and domination between the state and society constitute the structure of the public sphere. This structure can be understood by looking at two ideal types: republican and liberal public spheres. A good starting point for understanding variations in the structure of the public sphere is the private/public demarcation and the implications this has for the polity. Political scientist Guillermo O'Donnell succinctly compares liberal and republican political traditions on this aspect:

> Both the liberal and republican traditions distinguish between a public and a private sphere, but to different ends. For liberalism,

> the private sphere is the proper arena in which to pursue the fullness of human development. Hence liberalism's inherent ambivalence toward the public sphere and more particularly the state: the latter must be strong enough to guarantee the freedoms enjoyed in private life, yet limited enough to prevent it from encroaching on those same freedoms. Republicanism, by contrast, holds that wholehearted dedication to the public good—not the lesser undertakings of the private sphere—is what demands and nurtures the highest virtues. (O'Donnell 1998, 113)

The republican and the liberal models constitute two public sphere ideal types on the basis of core political values, priorities, and the private/public demarcation. These models interact with the existing political institutions and cultural norms of a society and significantly mold the substance of public debates and the boundaries of the acceptable forms of public activism, and, hence, the public behavior and strategies of social groups. The formation of a particular type of public sphere is related to factors such as the historical-institutional background of a given polity, which shapes state-religion relations, and the founding ideology of a given state, which encompasses the dominant political traditions and collective assumptions about politics.

The Republican Public Sphere

Republicanism[1] sees the public sphere as the domain of public virtue. The republican public sphere is not a place for the articulation of individual or group interests nor is participation therein a quest for the

1. The term republicanism may be used in different ways. One would be the founding principle of republican governments, which rely on popular sovereignty as opposed to the personal or hereditary rule under monarchies. Republicanism can be used to describe indirect democracy, where citizens control politics through their elected representatives. Republicanism can also be used to describe separation of powers and checks and balances between branches of government (executive, legislative, and judiciary). Republicanism in this study is treated as a political tradition with a particular view of the private-public demarcation as summarized above in the O'Donnell quote.

representation of particularistic values or identities. Individuals ought to set aside their private attributes and act as virtuous citizens seeking the realization of the common good. The state and the public, as conceptualized by republican ideals, have a common goal: achieving the collective good. In that sense, the state needs to guide public discussions to prevent private agendas from dominating public discussions. There is a distinction between the public and the private sphere, but the public sphere is inherently superior to the private, and thus should be kept autonomous from encroaching private agendas.

Hannah Arendt is most commonly associated with a republican line of argument. According to her, as a result of modernity, the economy became a public matter and the public sphere diminished as formerly excluded groups were gradually included in politics. The state and society also became intertwined; the boundaries between public and private became murky. These two processes of the intrusion of the pursuit of private socioeconomic interests into the public and the shifting boundaries of the public and the private led to the loss of the ideal public space. Arendt has two ways of understanding the public sphere. The first is the "agonistic" notion, which sees the public sphere as "the space of appearances in which moral and political greatness, heroism, and prominence are revealed, displayed, and shared with others. This is a competitive space in which one competes for recognition, precedence and acclaim" (Benhabib 1992, 78).

One can see how this definition carries the republican understanding of public sphere as a place of political and public moral virtues. Arendt's second approach is an associational way of looking at the public sphere, where the public sphere is defined as the space that emerges whenever and wherever "men act in concert" (Benhabib 1992, 79). From this associational point of view, the inclusion of certain issues in the public agenda is an expression of a struggle for justice and freedom, which makes any quest for inclusion and representation a public issue. According to Arendt, the associational understanding of the public sphere—or the "rise of the social"—leads to the loss of the public space. Arendt's concern is that this affects the distinction between public and private, and, thus, divides the line between the realms of "necessity" and "freedom" reducing political life to a form of "household administration" (Arendt 1958, 33–49; Charney 1998, 97). Consequently, the agonistic version is implied as being more desirable for an autonomous and productive public sphere, as public virtue plays a key role in the agonistic understanding of the public sphere.

In the republican tradition, the state can easily dominate the public sphere, because the public sphere is a state-supervised site of citizen socialization. In a republican public sphere, the state tries to promote public virtues by assuming a regulatory role in order to enlighten the masses with republican ideals. The republican public sphere, therefore, tends to be more homogeneous and under the state's close scrutiny. In this context, the public sphere often becomes a zone of conflict for the private identities that seek recognition and the state that sets the boundaries of public and private through law, regulatory procedure, and public policy.

Republicanism offers a normative model of the public sphere. In this model, the public interest (not private needs), justice (not the good life), and norms (not values) should prevail (Benhabib 1992, 88). However, the definition of the acceptable values and ideas in the public sphere is problematic from a liberal view of diversity and pluralism.

The Liberal Public Sphere

Liberal theory puts the individual—rather than the public—at the center of its analysis. The liberal model of the public sphere is rights centered. Legitimation takes place through dialogue without necessarily convincing or denouncing the other (Benhabib 1992, 84). The public sphere is not inherently superior to the private in liberal theory. Therefore, calls for the public good or public order do not easily trump individual rights. Public virtues are acceptable as long as they do not restrict individualism, diversity, and pluralism. Individuals can play the role of both public citizens and private persons at the same time and can carry both of these roles into the public sphere. In the liberal public sphere, individuals do not have to leave aside their human values in order to participate fully. This is not to deny the necessity of social norms and order, but is an effort to make those norms acceptable and practical and to make the public order viable by way of creating space for the individual. Public reasoning should not lead to a strict separation of public and private, but should mediate between the shared values of the public and particular individual value systems (Macedo 1991). Public discussion is not a means to solve philosophical, moral, and religious problems; the liberal public sphere draws sharp boundaries between the realm of the state's and the civil society.

The goal of public discussion in the liberal model is not the creation of a fixed set of public values, but a culture of coexistence based on mutual respect and recognition. Otherwise, some sectors of the society would be alienated from the common good and morality, rather than being integrated (Erdoğan 1999). The liberal public sphere generally reflects minimal state control over social issues. Therefore, it is most likely to be civil and pluralistic; a full-fledged state ideology is not common.

Republican and Liberal Public Spheres in Turkey and the United States

In most republican models of public sphere, one can find an ideology attached to the state. In those settings, the visibility and participation of societal groups in the public sphere is determined by a group's compatibility with the state ideology. The public sphere in modern Turkey has been dominated by the state since the founding of the republic in 1923. The founding elite established one-party rule and undertook an ambitious top-down modernization project, known as Kemalist modernization. The public sphere functioned as an arena for promoting a homogenous Western-oriented Turkish-secular national identity. After three decades of one-party political control over the polity, the transition to multiparty politics in 1950 marked the beginning of a differentiation between the bureaucratic state and the political society. However, this was not a firm separation and the state constantly watched and maneuvered to keep tabs on the political society. As religious and traditional identities became more visible and politicized, the republican state elite clashed with populist politicians in government, culminating in the 1960 military coup. This coup resulted in the overthrow of the popularly elected Democrat Party and execution of its leadership. Even though the Turkish military opted to return to civilian rule, it did so after writing a new constitution. This new constitution named the military as the guardian of republican order and further identified other unelected bureaucratic institutions to serve as a check on elected politicians. The years 1971, 1980, and 1997 witnessed other ruptures in civilian rule in Turkey through direct or indirect military interventions. These interventions point to the assertive role of the state over the ineffective political society and the polarization in the civil society.

The military justified its 1980 coup as an effort to restore law and order in the face of an increasingly violent left-right political polarization. The military rulers aimed to depoliticize the society in response. Coupled with the privatization and deregulation taking place under the neoliberal reform model, politically oriented left-right ideological groups were replaced by religious, professional, and ethnic identity groups in the public sphere. The ensuing rise of Kurdish and Islamic identity movements alarmed the Kemalist state establishment, however. The state, in turn, reasserted the Kemalist notion of a homogenous Turkish secular citizenship and republican identity.

Turkey made significant progress toward liberalizing its politics between 2003 and 2011: elected governments were gradually empowered vis-à-vis the appointed state officials. The liberalization and privatization reforms initiated by Prime Minister Özal in the 1980s, the initiation of the EU membership accession talks in 2005, and the rise of a more autonomous civil society and private media are some key structural factors to account for the change in this process (Yavuz 2003a, 75–81). After 2010, just as the Turkish public sphere was seemingly moving toward a more liberal direction, the power struggle between the Islamist AKP government and the Gülen movement once again reinforced the primacy of the state in the polity. In sum, one can argue that the gradual and nonlinear process of democratization in Turkey since 1950 is the story of the state and society negotiating the boundaries of the three domains of the polity. Civil society groups, like the Gülen movement, have operated with the same state-centered political culture as the Republican Kemalist elite and have strived for penetration into bureaucracy and even control of state institutions.

In contrast to Turkey's strong tradition of a state-dominant political culture, American political culture has been deeply influenced by a widely held skepticism toward government in general. Ideologically, the founding political principles of the United States were influenced by the Scottish Enlightenment and liberal philosophers like John Locke. This stands in contrast to the experience in Turkey, where the founding principles were influenced more by the French Enlightenment and Republican thinkers like Jean-Jacques Rousseau as well as a Hobbesian understanding of state authority. Consequently, key concepts of general will, citizenship virtues, and positive freedoms characterize the Turkish political culture; in comparison, the American political culture is characterized more by ideals of limited government, freedom of conscience, and negative freedoms. Aside from ideology, the American public sphere has historically been diverse and open to pluralism, albeit with limitations. Federalism and decentralization have been other factors resulting in a less dominant national government vis-à-vis the civil society.

The skepticism of the American public toward government has oscillated between a healthy check on politicians and political institutions and a populist cynicism toward Washington, DC. A 1998 Gallup survey, for example, identified an unsurprising correlation between the national mood and public (dis)trust in government, explaining the oscillation.[2] These findings have been supported by more recent studies looking at rising populism in the United States in general, and, especially, the rise of the Tea Party movement[3] and

2. "How Americans View Government: Deconstructing Trust," Pew Research Center, March 10, 1998, http://people-press.org/report/95/how-americans-view-government.

3. "Distrust, Discontent, Anger, and Partisan Rancor: The People and Their Government," Pew Research Center, April 18, 2010, http://people-press.org/report/606/trust-in-government.

Table 1. A structural and an institutional comparison of the liberal and republican public spheres in Turkey and the United States

	Governance Structure	State Ideology	Promotion of Homogenous National Identity	State Autonomy	State Capacity
Turkey	Unitary	Yes	Yes	Medium to High	Low to Medium
US	Federal	No	No	Low to Medium	Medium to High

election of President Donald Trump.[4] Therefore, as table 1 demonstrates, the terms of the relationship between the state and society in Turkey and the United States are almost exactly opposite. In Turkey, one can identify the state as the main political actor; the state has enjoyed high levels of autonomy and medium to low levels of capacity. In the United States, the state has been significantly less autonomous and has also demonstrated more capacity than in Turkey. As the chief vulnerability of the American system has been populism from the right and the left, the Turkish polity has suffered from an authoritarian state and a weak society.

Other Conceptual Approaches to the Public Sphere

There are other analyses of the public sphere that do not neatly fit with the republican-liberal distinction. The most prominent scholar on the theory behind the public sphere is Jürgen Habermas. In *The Structural Transformation of the Public Sphere*, Habermas (1989a) analyzes the emergence and evolution of the public sphere in western Europe. He argues that the public sphere as a distinctive arena appeared for the first time in eighteenth-century Europe, within bourgeois civil society. Habermas developed his model of the public sphere with reference

4. "Political Typology Reveals Deep Fissures on the Right and Left," Pew Research Center, October 24, 2017, http://www.people-press.org/2017/10/24/political-typology-reveals-deep-fissures-on-the-right-and-left/.

to the specific historical and social factors of that time. Accordingly, the public sphere is a literary and discursive space in which public opinion is formed. The public sphere is not a physical place—it is a discursive space that emerges whenever private individuals exchange ideas on matters of public interest; these discussions might take place in salons, cafes, or even through letters. Television, radio, newspapers, and magazines can be seen as the media of the public sphere, facilitating discussions of public issues. In its earlier form, the public sphere was not "public": it was located in the private realm of civil society. In other words, the public sphere became an autonomous space that mediated between the state and the society. The public discussion that takes place in the public sphere was guided by rationality, and individuals in the public sphere shared a common public culture grounded in their socioeconomic experience and interests vis-a-vis the state.

Habermas argues that a specific set of historical conditions produced the particular form of the autonomous public sphere that emerged in eighteenth-century Europe. The most distinguishing feature of this public sphere was its reliance on critical rational discourse by private citizens (Calhoun 1992). Before then, there was hardly any distinction between the realm of the ruler and the realm of the public, as the French king Louis XIV's famous equivalence of state and self, "*L'état, c'est moi*," indicates.

Capitalism and modernization brought important changes that made an autonomous public sphere possible in England, France, and the German territories. Industrialization and trade gradually made the economy a public matter, taking it out of the private-necessity realm of the household. The need for information for the efficient functioning of the new economy made newspaper and print capitalism critical components of these modernizing societies. Newspapers not only shared information about the economy, but also about political matters, thereby becoming a literary space for the critical rational discussion of politics. In addition to this discursive space, a new sociability emerged in salons, cafes, and similar public places that hosted the male heads of bourgeois households. As the society created this public space, modernization made the state more bureaucratized and impersonal. The secularization process also helped the rise of the bourgeois public sphere, by limiting the role of the church in state administration, education, and social services. Secularization theorists have described this reduced role of the church as privatization and differentiation (Casanova 1994). Modernization—particularly, capitalism and secularism—positioned the state against the society and created the critical rational public sphere as an autonomous space (Habermas 1989b).

Unlike its early stages, the subsequent stages of modernization undermined the bourgeois public sphere. As the public sphere gradually expanded to incorporate the working class and other formerly excluded sectors of society, competing identity and ideology claims called into question the universality claims of the rational-critical discourse. The rise of the social welfare state further undermined the autonomy of the public sphere and created the conditions for the state's penetration into society. Habermas's historical analysis of the rise and fall of the bourgeois public sphere implies that the rise of social identities and interests undermined the coherence and autonomy of the political public sphere. With the greater social inclusion, private economic interests started to dominate public discussions, replacing the notion of a rationally articulated public good.

Habermas's analysis is in line with Arendt's above-mentioned critique of modernization regarding the loss of public space in its ideal agonistic sense.[5] This ideally functioning public sphere approaches the republican civic virtue tradition of the public sphere that restricts public discussion to matters of the common good and excludes private individual concerns (Fraser 1992). However, in his later work Habermas has developed "communicative rationality" as the guiding principle of contemporary public sphere, moving away from his seeming idealization of the "universal" critical rationality of the bourgeois public sphere. This more recent work appreciates institutional,

5. For a comparison of Arendt and Habermas on the public sphere, see Benhabib 1996, especially 203–10.

cultural, and personal practices of modernity and integrates them into a model that, arguably, can be understood as a third model located between the liberal and republican models (Seyla Benhabib 1992).

Critical theory, especially feminism, offers another theoretical understanding of the public sphere, challenging the mainstream dichotomies and functional explanations regarding the public/private distinction. Feminist critical theorists argue that mainstream theories do not pay enough attention to the power struggles and power relations that characterize the public/private debate. Accordingly, the separation of public and private has normative implications and power implications. As a result of this separation, the private domain becomes impervious to public pursuits of justice and the channels by which private issues make their way to the public domain in search of solutions are restricted. Feminists argue that the democrats of the public domain are autocrats in private and this behavior is legitimized by the suggestion that there are different normative standards for each sphere. Operating with the understanding that "the personal is political," feminists favor bringing so-called private issues to public sphere to seek justice.

In this approach, the public sphere is not, cannot be, and should not be neutral, contrary to the suggestions of liberals. The public sphere is not simply a place of deliberation and rationalization of the public good but—inescapably—a site of power relations expressed in terms of representation, recognition, and identity. Rather, the idea of neutrality based on rationality and deliberative communication is, in fact, a mechanism of control: the state or the hegemonic class uses the recourse to neutrality and rationality to suppress dissent and silence those who promote alternative notions of society and the good life. In short, critical theory provides useful insights by drawing attention to underlying power relations and unpacking the assumptions in standard explanations. Critical theory's understanding of the public sphere can be used as a proxy to understand the broader context in which the rivalry between the liberal and republican models of the public sphere takes place.

The Gülen Movement and the LDS Church in the Public Sphere

The Gülen movement is an Islamic social movement, which bases its philosophy on empowering individuals with piety, discipline, and education, and seeks to mobilize community resources for social engagement and presence in the public sphere. Since the movement's start in the 1970s, participants have used educational and business networks to promote a Muslim model of modernity in Turkey. From the 1990s onward, the movement exported and adapted its model of human and social capital-building to a transnational context. It emerged from Turkish civil society, but its growing appeal and access to power eventually led to conflict with other political actors and the Turkish state. The movement has refrained from direct involvement in formal party politics. Yet the leadership often made their preferences for centrist parties known through cues in the affiliated public platforms and the media. The movement demonstrates elements of a congregational organizational structure; there is a core cadre of devotees around Fethullah Gülen who provide inspiration and technical skill to others for movement activities such as building schools, opening cultural centers, running dialogue platforms, and forming business associations. The bulk of the movement's activism remains at the local level, though. The idea of volunteering and committing one's time and money plays a key role in the activities of the group. Islam is at the center of the movement's operational codes of piety, service, and activism. However, consonant with its increased public visibility, the movement has strategically evolved to incorporate a more inclusive humanist language vis-à-vis other religions, ethnicities, and ideological groups, making claims to promote the public good and the national interest in whichever host country it finds itself.

Turkey's ethos of civic republicanism, national unity, and general will has strongly shaped the movement's outlook. Rather than emphasizing the welfare of its members, the interest of the movement, or Islam itself, movement participants have sought public legitimacy by referring to the national interest and the public good in their public discourse. One of the ways the Gülen movement has tried to influence public debate and policy has been by building institutions and hosting events that would bring different sectors of the society together to discuss public issues, including philosophical and moral questions. In addition to a large web of informal ties, the movement participants established many business associations, education foundations, and dialogue platforms. The Abant Platform is the most well-known dialogue platform the movement initiated; this project has brought intellectuals and politicians of diverse beliefs and affiliations together to discuss controversial issues in Turkey. The movement's self-declared goal of organizing civil society became a key source of its legitimacy and a major public strategy in navigating state-society relations in the state-dominated Turkish public sphere.

The LDS Church, whose followers are known as Mormons, emerged in nineteenth-century American civil society, and its religious missions quickly became entangled with politics. The church was both an agency and a source of contention, and a topic of public debate. The series of communal conflicts Mormons encountered were not primarily rooted in religious beliefs, but more related to competition over land, economic resources, and political power. During the formative years of Mormonism, the US was deeply influenced by a Protestant revivalist movement known as the Second Great Awakening (1790–1850). Mormons' missionary zeal, restorationist theology, and millennialism were shared by various other new contemporaneous denominations and movements. Moreover, utopian-communalist ideals and the emerging Temperance movement against hard liquor provided a context for some of the Mormon practices that are often seen as peculiar (Howe 2015). Mormons, however, had a record of communitarian resource management and bloc voting that could quickly shift as a result of church instructions. These economic and political reasons turned other frontier communities against Mormons. The liberal public sphere with its limited federal protections and the prevalent majoritarianism of Jacksonian America was of very little help. Mormons had a strong belief in American exceptionalism and the divinely inspired nature of the Constitution; however, they were disappointed in how institutions and politics at the time were so far from fully implementing the country's founding principles. Despite the gap between the ideal and the reality, the liberal model of public sphere shaped Mormon attitude toward politics.

The first Prophet and President of the church, Joseph Smith, was initially indifferent to politics. However, this gradually gave way to involvement in local and national political processes (Bushman 2016). As the growing numbers of Mormons and their strong communalism alarmed other communities, Mormons found themselves in a struggle for survival that had them moving ever-westward in search of hospitable neighboring communities. First, Mormons discovered the power of bloc voting and the group's leadership negotiated with politicians and institutions at the state and county levels. However, anti-Mormon sentiments increased as Mormon communities in Missouri and Illinois grew, which led to violent conflicts. Joseph Smith tried to use his brief candidacy for the president of the US in 1844 as a platform to promote minority rights, religious freedoms, and federalism under the American Constitution, which Mormons believe to be divinely inspired.

Ultimately, the Mormons were unable to cultivate political allies to protect their lives or property; nor were they able to prevent the death of Joseph Smith at the hands of a mob while incarcerated in an Illinois jail in 1844. These failures resulted in disillusionment among the believers, leading to quests for self-determination outside of what were US territories at the time. A smaller number of Mormons chose to remain in the Midwest while many Mormons migrated westward en masse to the Great Plains and the Mountain West.

The Mormon Pioneers first sought to claim a vast state they called Deseret; after conflict with the US government, they retained control over a much smaller territory, Utah. In almost a complete reversal of Joseph Smith's pleas for the federal government to be more active in matters of religious freedoms and minority rights in Missouri and Illinois, the LDS Church under Brigham Young's leadership sought maximum autonomy on governing their own affairs in Utah. However, being a territory under federal administration, Utah lacked the autonomy enjoyed by other states in the Union and the federal government refused to grant statehood until after the church abrogated polygamy and loosened control over local politics. When Utah was admitted to the Union in 1896, the LDS Church also initiated its transformation into a more mainstream American religion. During much of the nineteenth century, Mormons remained outcasts in American society, appealing to the basic organizing principles of the liberal American public sphere, such as freedom of religion, minority rights, and states' rights, either to counter the excesses of populist Jacksonian democracy or advocate for local autonomy against the growing influence of the federal government.

The twentieth century brought a fundamental shift in Mormon behavior in the public sphere. After decades of struggle for communal autonomy and for the protection of its particular religious beliefs and practices, such as polygamy, economic stewardship, and conformist politics, the church shifted gears and sought to downplay its uniqueness. The aim was integration to the mainstream American society. The church strove to establish a conventional, wholesome American patriotic image through its Tabernacle Choir, tourist sites, and strong showing in civil service and the United States' wars. In less than two centuries since the church began in upstate New York, the level of Mormon integration in the American public sphere is striking. In a symbolic illustration of how far Mormonism has come, the World's Parliament of Religions—an organization that denied participation to the LDS Church at its 1893 Chicago meeting—convened in Salt Lake City, Utah, in 2015, mere blocks away from the flagship Salt Lake Temple, and with a prominent participation of the LDS Church.

Mormons are organized around a well-structured and hierarchical formal church system, which is the lynchpin of the Mormon public voice and identity. As Mormonism sought to locate itself firmly within the mainstream American culture, its public affairs since the end of World War II have revolved around managing its public image, promoting Mormon values, and securing the interests of the church and the welfare of its members. The church regularly releases statements on various social and political platforms regarding a wide range of public issues, such as liquor laws in Utah, same-sex marriage, immigration, and public education.[6] The Public Affairs Office of the LDS Church provides professionalized control over the relations of the church with the public at large. Similar to the Gülen movement, the LDS Church claims to refrain from overt party politics and purports to abide by its principle of political neutrality. The church does take positions on what it terms "moral issues," following its principles. In general, church beliefs align closely with those held by the conservative bloc in American politics led by Evangelical Christians. This overlap can be seen clearly on issues of same-sex marriage and the institutional, moral, and financial support provided by Mormons to the conservative causes on various ballot initiatives. This support for the common conservative cause has been the strongest in Utah, California, Hawaii, and Alaska, all states with relatively large Mormon communities. On other issues, such as abortion, immigration, and war, the LDS Church is less closely aligned with the beliefs of the evangelical bloc due to the church's more nuanced doctrine on these issues as well as the church's concern for its international missionary work and public image abroad. Within the liberal American public sphere of the twenty first century, the LDS Church now acts as an interest group and participates in public debates if it deems this necessary for the interest of the church and its members.[7]

Both the Gülen movement and the LDS Church have well-supported organizations with different features; the Gülen movement has a largely informal structure, while the LDS Church has a very formal one. Both groups are very outreach oriented and seek to increase their appeal worldwide. However, the nature of outreach activities is

6. See, for example, "Statement before the Alcoholic Beverage Control Commission," *Mormon Newsroom*, February 10, 2003, http://www.mormonnewsroom.org/article/alcohol-legislation-in-utah.

7. For an analysis of how and when the LDS Church involves itself in public and political issues, see Bruce L. Olsen, "LDS Church: No Thumbs Up or Down Are Given to the Legislature," *Salt Lake Tribune*, March 16, 2003.

understood and practiced in different fashions. The LDS approach is more direct and includes conveying the teachings of the church through visible missionary work. The Gülen movement's method, on the other hand, is focused on recruiting volunteers by employing the language of everyday service, social transformation, and community-focused actions through networks of schools, businesses, and fellowships. The method is to teach by example rather than to proselytize. This difference in terms of teaching strategy and outreach style also influences the public discourse of each group. LDS Church declarations do not shy away from referring to religious doctrine as the basis of their position, whereas followers of the Gülen movement try to articulate their thoughts with frequent references to broader moral values, global human rights discourses, pluralism, public welfare, and tolerance for others.[8]

In comparing the two cases, this study exposes a puzzle. Despite their core goals of producing conservative modernity, the two religious communities approach public representation and public engagement quite differently. Mormonism takes a more self-assertive approach in the public sphere whereas the Gülen movement is quite indirect in public. The answer to the puzzle of this different group behavior lies in the differences between liberal public sphere in the US and the republican public sphere in Turkey. In each case, the public sphere is a formative force that has conditioned and shaped the public strategies of the LDS Church and the Gülen movement.

A brief historical survey of the role of religion in the Turkish and American polities provides insight regarding the formation of these two types of public spheres. In Turkey, Ottoman history stands as the most influential period for the relationship between the public and the religious. The dissolution of the traditional patrimonial Ottoman state and the ensuing formation of the modern-secular-republican

8. For an analysis of secularization trends in the Gülen movement, see Özdalga 2003a. Yavuz 2003a has argued these trends were in line with "internal secularization" of the movement.

Turkish state was the turning point in the Turkish political culture and public sphere. The changes and continuities between the two periods in terms of state-society relations and secularism shed light on the parameters of Turkish political culture and the way in which religious groups function within the public sphere. When the founding fathers of the Republic declared the Ottoman era as an ancien régime, they paved the way for the struggle between the modern republican political core and the traditional conservative periphery, molding the modern history of state-society relations. In the US, the history of the colonies, Puritanism, and the American Revolution shaped the contractual nature of state-society relations, limited government, and the Bill of Rights that comprise the core characteristics of the liberal American public sphere. Subsequent legal and political developments, such as Supreme Court rulings, the assimilation of non-Protestant immigrants, the struggle between liberals and conservatives, and the rise of the Christian Right have all taken place within the basic framework of a liberal public sphere. Although the American public sphere today is more pluralist than it was two centuries ago, the boundaries of inclusion and the limits of tolerance are still being negotiated for minority religious groups, such as Muslims, and, to a lesser extent, Mormons.

The public profiles of the two religious movements differ despite their key similarities in modernist conservatism and centrist political doctrine. The first step in explaining the reasons behind the variation is to specify and measure proxies for religious group behavior in the public domain. The practices and attitudes of religiously oriented groups that target society as a whole regarding social and political issues are basic indicators of public behavior. In particular, civic associations; public platforms of debate and deliberation; and public declarations and publication on public policy, moral conflicts, and political issues are ways of assessing the public participation of a religious community or movement. To explain the variation in the public strategies of the two religious groups, this study investigates each group's political context and delineates the changes and continuities in the structure of the public sphere along the continuum of liberal and republican models of the public sphere. In the republican model, the state actively takes part in regulating religious representation and organization of religious groups and the state expects individuals to act as citizens in the public arena and thus sets limits on the display of particular social, political, or economic identities. Many republican countries have constitutional provisions to defend the state against forces of "darkness," "obscurantism," or "backwardism," terms for perceived threats from certain sectors of the society that may not have internalized the republican civic principles and, thus, whose behavior as virtuous citizens may be suspect. The state needs to be protected against infiltration, capture, or domination from those forces. The politicization of a religious or subnational ethnic identity can be criminalized, and such political groups or group members can then be accused of seeking control of the state, be seen as regime threats, and could ultimately be tried in state security courts. The social and political struggle of the Islamists and Kurdish nationalists in Turkey throughout much of the republican period have been characterized by such resistance from the regime.

In the liberal public sphere, the state does not enjoy higher levels of autonomy and cannot wield power independently from the public. This dynamic means that the society approaches the state with skepticism, rather than the other way around, as is the case in the republican public sphere. The aim of the society in the liberal public sphere is to keep state power checked and limited: the state should have just enough power to maintain order, security, and provide a limited number of public goods. Thus, political debates in the liberal public sphere often revolve around the idea of containing the state rather than trying to capture or control it. In the case of the US, the de facto Protestant establishment in the nineteenth century was a function of the predominant Protestant social identity, which was reflected in policy regarding the public school system, the ban on government funding for private schools, and the absence of some government services on Sundays, including mail delivery. The de facto Protestant establishment was also at work in how the federal government treated the Mormon practices of hierarchical church organization, theocratic government, economic communalism, and polygamy. The theocratic state of Utah (or the earlier State of Deseret attempt) was an anomaly in the US, but its treatment by the government was not: the federal government's pressures coming from all three branches of the executive, the legislative, and the judiciary on Mormons to conform to the larger Protestant norms of the society were largely supported by the American public. This is quite different from Turkey, where the state-imposed restrictions on manifestations of Islam in politics and civil society against the will of the majority.[9] Obviously, the Turkish state's actions were a combined function of authoritarianism and republicanism. Yet, even after the beginning of multi-party politics in 1950, the bureaucratic establishment, with the help of the intelligentsia and the media, maintained much of its influence in the public sphere. In fact, the state establishment only shared its power with the elected politicians, adopting a watchful, praetorian stance toward government policies and intervening in politics on a regular basis. The EU-inspired Turkish reforms of the 1990s and 2000s helped the Islamist AKP weaken and eliminate the Kemalist state establishment. However, the AKP's consolidation of power created the conditions for a new hegemonic order rather than hearkening the arrival of liberal democracy in the country.

How Political Context Matters

Interest groups find it easier to act—and are thus more likely to do so—within the political society in the liberal public sphere than in the republican public sphere. Notably, the LDS Church has been more likely to engage public issues through formal spokespeople and lobbyists in the US, whereas the Gülen movement has been more

9. The Republican People's Party (CHP), the party of the Kemalist state bureaucracy and top-down modernization, has lost nearly every election since the first democratic elections took place in Turkey in 1950. Only Bülent Ecevit was able to lead the CHP to victory in the 1973 parliamentary elections, thanks to his realignment of the party's ideology toward social democracy and left-of-center politics (Yavuz 2003a; Özbudun 1976; Kasaba 1993).

likely to use informal networks and loosely affiliated media to address public issues.

The state in the republican tradition tends to be skeptical of both the forms and sources of public identity other than national citizenship. Therefore, any group acting in the public arena in the republican public sphere is expected to bracket its particular religious identity and act as a group of citizens, making their arguments on the basis of "the public good" without primarily referencing their particularistic beliefs. This mindset has informed the ban on religious symbols in France and Turkey, albeit with a different scope in each case. The idea of the public good can also be found in the liberal public sphere, yet religious groups in the liberal public sphere can still act as interest groups and represent their particularistic agendas, almost like any other interest group in society. Lobbying and interest groups carry negative connotations in Turkey; the Gülen movement has stayed away from such language even in the US. For example, when various local nonprofits formed an umbrella organization in Washington, DC, they called this group the Turkic-American Alliance, rather than using the name of the movement itself. Such local and national organizations have sponsored trips to Turkey and have visited congressmen and senators to offer alternate historical perspectives in response to the activities of the Armenian lobby on proposed congressional resolutions regarding the Armenian genocide. Gülen associates understand well the importance of money in American politics and make campaign contributions accordingly. Yet these contributions are usually made as private individuals and thus lack movement affiliation.[10]

As the comparison above illustrates, religious groups may adopt a variety of strategies. This study's analytical framework suggests that the same religious groups should be acting differently in different

10. The donations through individuals led to reports in the American media about the movement's connections and lack of transparency: "US Lawmakers Got Suspect Turkish Campaign Cash," *USA Today*, November 23, 2015, http://www.usatoday.com/story/news/nation/2015/11/20/lawmakers-got-suspect-turkish-campaign-cash/75982732/.

contexts. The inverse design of this study—the Gülen movement in the US and the LDS Church in Turkey—is limited by the brief history of each group in each alternate context as well as by the questionable reliability of available information. However, the evidence suggests that the Gülen movement is more self-assertive in the US, whereas the Mormons are less direct in their missionary activities in Turkey, where such activities are subject to state control. The Gülen movement is still in the process of establishing a foothold in the US, so it would be premature to make generalizations about their behavior in a liberal public sphere. Similarly, the LDS Church had a longstanding practice of talking indirectly about its presence in Turkey, calling the Mormon missionaries there "volunteers."[11] This reluctance to publicly acknowledge a church presence in Turkey also applies to church activities, which seem to be coordinated from one of the neighboring Balkan countries.[12] While the LDS Church shows clear signs of strategic ambiguity and reluctance about its public identity in Turkey, the Gülen movement is arguably at its most visible and transparent in the US than anywhere else in the world. In less than a decade, the movement has demonstrated that it can, indeed, utilize the opportunities a liberal public sphere affords in order to promote their goals. Compared to the other Turkish Islamic groups who came earlier and tried

11. "The Church Statement on Volunteers in Turkey," *Mormon Newsroom*, July 27, 2016, http://www.mormonnewsroom.org/article/church-statement-volunteers-turkey.

12. My inquiries to the Public Affairs Department between 2007 and 2008 were inconclusive. They were very vague about missionaries or places of worship in Turkey. The official website gives a brief history of missionary work, concluding that there are 221 members and no "concerted effort to proselytize" in the country (http://www.ldschurchnews.com/articles/58669/Country-information-Turkey.html). Some officials I have spoken to have served in various European countries, and they all mentioned they visited Turkey on what appeared to be a regular basis. I also had similar impressions from my students at the University of Utah, who served their missions in Eastern European countries. Some members were reported to have opened English and computer courses in Izmir and Istanbul, along with apartments dedicated for worship.

to create "little Turkey's" in the US, complete with ethnic mosques, grocery stores, and restaurants, the Gülen movement affiliates have made a greater effort to interact with other social groups, establish comparable social institutions, and carve out a niche within the existing pluralist American public sphere.

The LDS Church missionaries have identical messages, methods, and rituals throughout the world, yet, to advance their mission, they do acknowledge the local context. For example, they engage in dialogue and develop cordial ties with bureaucrats, politicians, local leaders, and they work with local institutions. The LDS Church Public Affairs officials seemed to be aware of such flexibility in working in more republican or authoritarian settings.[13] The bureaucratic hurdles and requirements to register with state authorities to do missionary work or open places of worship are alien notions to most Americans, yet the LDS Church officials understand the importance of being able to work within the limits of the political-legal context. This is another parallel between the LDS Church and the Gülen movement, as each religious group has adopted a similar attitude and doctrine toward their relations with the same political structure. They both refrain from the confrontational strategies or contentious politics of other human rights groups or religious groups. Their social activism is more mission or service based. This flexible strategy gives researchers tremendous opportunities to observe how social groups make sense of the political settings and adapt accordingly, allowing scholars a unique perspective on the larger dynamics of the existing political context. Studies on more established social movements like Greenpeace or Amnesty International tell us more about the movements than the contexts in which they operate. Indeed, this is another reason why the cases in this study are especially well suited to gauge the impact of external factors, such as the political context.

Although not the main focus of this study, the subsequent chapters also discuss additional control cases from Turkey and the US in order

13. Author's interview with public affairs specialists in December 2008.

to investigate the influences of the identical political culture on various religious groups. The Christian Right in the US and the Islamists in Turkey are examined comparatively to provide insight on the effect of political culture. In spite of their different goals, orientations, and ideological friction with one another, the Christian Right and the Mormon Church in the US, on the one hand, and the Islamists and the Gülen movement in Turkey, on the other hand, demonstrate key similarities in their internalization of the liberal and republican norms of engagement in their respective public spheres.

Conclusion

This chapter discussed the conceptual tools and theoretical assumptions of the study. The unified approach of social movement theory with its focus on motives, means, and opportunities offers a useful investigative framework relative to the numerous factors identified in the literature on religion and politics. Treating religious groups as actors whose public engagement and claims have bearing on other political actors' interests sets the stage for the foundations of this synthesis between scholarship on social movements and scholarship on religion and politics. The Gülen movement and the LDS Church have interacted with the public sphere in their respective polities to develop their political preferences, organizational and discursive strategies, and forms of representation. The following chapters will demonstrate those linkages, with an analysis of the public sphere in Turkey and the public sphere in the US, and offer a discussion of the changes and continuities in the two groups' public activism strategies.

PART ONE

Religion and the State

2

The Republican Public Sphere and Religion under State Tutelage in Turkey

This chapter explores the controversial role of religion in Turkey and identifies the key aspects of the republican public sphere concerning democratic governance, political representation, and national identity. In order to put the Gülen movement's public behavior into perspective, a brief historical overview of these factors is followed by a discussion of relevant issues, such as secularism, freedom of religion, political liberties, and the rule of law in modern-day Turkey. As such, the chapter will first dissect the issues surrounding the politics of religious representation and shed light on the sources of the uneasy relations across three domains of the polity: the state, political society, and civil society.

Kamusal Alan: Public Sphere Lost in Translation?

At the height of Turkey's secularist-Islamist tensions in the 1990s and early 2000s, the term *kamusal alan* (public sphere) itself became a source of controversy surrounding the limitations on public representations of religion. The controversy was largely related to how the Kemalist elite and non-Kemalists, such as liberals, conservatives, and Islamists, differently construe the public sphere. The Kemalist understanding was in line with the republican model, emphasizing the state's central role for public virtues and the public will. The Kemalists idealized the republican public sphere and closely guarded the state's authoritative claim as the sole source of legitimation of representation in the public sphere. This legitimation claim was both discursive and visual, in effect excluding the nonsecular practices of some private citizens as legitimate manifestations of the public good and national identity. For the Kemalists, any toleration of non-Kemalist lifestyles, public visibility, and discourse would amount to public legitimation and would thereby challenge the republican ideals of secular-rationalist modernity.[1] This Kemalist-republican perception of the public sphere as a place of only public, shared virtues and nonprivate identities made any alternative public displays of identity unacceptable (Çınar 2005; Göle 2000).

The Kemalist republican position drew opposition chiefly from two groups. One was the assertive Islamists and Kurdish nationalists, who were quite aware of the sensitivity of the republican elite to alternative representations of modernity and national identity. These groups simply wanted to challenge the Kemalist monopoly over the public sphere and contested the secular Turkish nationalism that defined the ideological foundation of the republic. Therefore, some Islamists, too, had the same conceptualization of public sphere along the lines of the republican tradition (Kadioglu 2005). Other opposition to the Kemalist, republican public sphere came from a group of non-Kemalist societal groups who largely promoted the liberal model of the public sphere. Among them were the pragmatic Islamists, who developed a less combative tone than the traditional Islamists (and called themselves Muslim conservatives), liberal intellectuals who wanted to expand the individual rights and civil liberties, and the liberal Kurds, who wanted to find accommodationist ways of reframing issues in order to overcome the deadlock and ideological tension surrounding their claims for increased autonomy. This constellation of opposition forces argued that the public sphere is not a place to discuss the good life or find consensus on moral questions and beliefs; according to them, those issues belong to the private realm, and they

1. For an examination of social and ideological bases of Islamism and Kemalism, see Gulalp 2001; 2003.

can only be invoked in public debate to empower individuals and groups vis-à-vis the state. These groups adopted the liberal strategy of leaving moral and religious matters to the private sphere as much as possible, narrowing the scope of public debate and public regulations to focus on liberty, justice, and public interest. Viewed from this perspective, religious issues, such as wearing the headscarf, should be seen as a matter of individual freedom, rather than a public discussion of whether certain clothing is in line with the national identity, modernity, or public order. The argument embraced by these assorted forces claims that if everything visible in the public sphere was not seen through the prism of the public good and conceptions of public identity, and, thus, was not subject to regulation by the public authority, then the society would be better off. Namely, society would bypass the futile struggles over whose definition of social order and the good life should be given the upper hand. Even though the Gülen movement's conservative roots gave birth to a pro-state, nationalist outlook with an emphasis on public virtue in its formative periods in the 1970s and 1980s, it disapproved of the Islamist-secularist tensions and gradually positioned itself within the latter coalition for a liberal conception of public sphere. Chapter 4 will discuss the roots and evolution of the movement's approach to politics in detail.

These conflicting understandings of the public sphere are related to the different significance each side attached to the public display of diverse identities, values, and beliefs. This prevented meaningful communication, further reinforcing the distance between the two positions and resulting in unproductive accusations by each side toward the other.

The historical evolution of the public sphere in the late Ottoman Empire and the early Turkish Republic reveals the roots of the crisis of Kemalism in regards to the public sphere. In particular, Kemalism struggled to adapt to increasing mobility and diversity of the society and the political demands to uphold individual freedoms, recognize multicultural roots, and create a robust and transparent human rights regime in line with global trends. The post-1983 discussions around the autonomy of the civil society, identity politics, and issue areas like regulations on women wearing headscarves tell the story of the struggle between the state and the society over the public sphere in order to influence public opinion and become the dominant force in the public sphere.

The Ottoman Modernization and the Emergence of the Public Sphere

The history of the public sphere in Turkey involves quite a different story than its European equivalents. As indicated in the previous chapter, according to Habermas the public sphere first emerged in eighteenth-century Europe as a result of the rise of the bourgeois society. The industrial revolution, the Reformation, and the Enlightenment all played decisive roles in the specific form of the public sphere that emerged in European societies. While the economy moved away from an exclusive focus on the necessity realm of the household and to a public matter of concern and debate, religion was affected in the opposite manner as it was pushed away from its public roles. Religious identity was supposed to become primarily a private identity eventually. The Enlightenment ideals of rationality and experimental science influenced the mindset of the society, trickling down from the elite to the middle class. Consequently, a new social class sought the rationalization of public policies in economic matters in an environment freed from absolute monarchs and the social domination of the church.

In contrast, the social forces that aligned the socioeconomic interests, societal identities, and public institutions together were either absent or ineffective in the eighteenth-century Ottoman Empire.[2] Nonetheless, the Ottoman polity had to come to terms with its decline vis-à-vis the Europeans and took an interest in the social, economic, and political transformations in Europe, seeing these dynamics as potential remedies for their own situation.

2. For a comparison of the Ottoman and western European institutions, see Mardin 1969.

Modernization efforts in the Ottoman Empire began primarily in the military and technical areas, followed by the educational system. By the end of the nineteenth century, the Ottomans and the Europeans maintained significant contacts as a result of diplomatic and military training endeavors. Thanks to the technical and economic modernization efforts, more general modern ideas and practices were transmitted to Ottoman society. Political reforms ushered in more concrete developments toward the emergence of the public sphere. The Tanzimat era (1839–76) reforms included changes to citizenship, bureaucracy, administration, and diplomacy.

Access to modern education abroad and, later, within the empire led to the formation of a new class of intelligentsia who had faith in modernity. Political reforms were carried out in order to respond to the twin pressures of the European penetration into the Ottoman territories and the challenges to the patrimonial Ottoman state from domestic reformist groups, such as the Islamic-modernist Young Ottomans and the Western-modernist Young Turks.[3] Many of the reformists came from within the bureaucracy and the Islamic scholars (ulema). They were focused on the goals of saving the Ottoman state from collapse, as well as helping the state catch up with Western standards of representative politics. In contrast to the public sphere that arose from the civil society of European polities, the Ottoman public sphere remained ideological and state-centric. The modernizing role of the bourgeoisie in Europe was largely played by the new class of intelligentsia in the Ottoman Empire.[4] In that sense, the Turkish

3. Both the Young Ottomans and the Young Turks pushed for constitutionalism and modernism using different frames of reference. Their names might suggest a monolithic platform; however, in reality both groups were loose coalitions of reformist and conservative opposition forces in post-Tanzimat Ottoman politics. Their ideas and politics played a formative role in the modern Turkish Republic. For an extensive analysis of the Young Ottomans and Young Turks, see Hanioglu 2008 and Mardin 1962.

4. For an analysis of the impact of the lack of a bourgeois influence on the formation of the Ottoman/Turkish public sphere, see Yilmaz 1998.

experience lacked a natural social base and remained more state-driven and elitist. The reformist group of intellectuals, the ulema, and the military-bureaucratic establishment came to believe that they needed to introduce a top-down process of modernization and reform since the society lacked the necessary incentives and organization to push the state to embrace change. The Committee for Union and Progress, which came out of the Young Turk movement to dominate the Ottoman state between 1908 and 1918, was inspired by the French Enlightenment ideals of rationality, positivism, materialism, and secularism and promoted a top-down modernization. The founding fathers of Republican Turkey followed a more radical form of this state-led, top-down modernization and embraced a republican form of the public sphere with a strong hegemonic state at its center.

Political reform was not an easy task. The proclamation of a constitutional monarchy in 1876 did not bring a significant change in the political system, due to the regime's short life. The second constitutional regime was declared in 1909; in the interim, the Young Turks had exerted significant pressure on the government in response to the absolutism of Abdulhamid II.[5] The opposition made itself heard through newspapers, journals, and European diplomatic channels. This period marked the rise of public consciousness in the higher echelons of Ottoman society. In spite of the sultan's policies of censorship and containment, this period witnessed the emergence of a fairly vigorous public debate regarding the ideological orientation of the state. The state was ruled by a hereditary monarchy at the time and the society was organized around ethnoreligious communities, known as *millets.* As European territorial expansion and economic penetration undermined the sultan's control and facilitated ethnonational agitation, Ottomanism, Islamism, and Turkism were the solutions offered by different groups of intellectuals to prevent the imminent breakup of the empire (Akcura 1976); policies consonant with each of these mindsets were put into practice by different administrations and

5. On the nature of the Young Turk opposition, see Hanioglu 1995.

sultans. However, even this "public" debate was effectively confined to a small class of intellectuals and statesmen living in Istanbul, and, to a lesser extent, in other provincial capitals.

The *millet* system, the organizing principle of the late Ottoman polity, arranged society according to communal identities. Religion was the main source of communal identity, but the *millet* system also involved ethnic and proto-national identities, organizing the Christian Orthodox populations of Armenian, Greek, Bulgarian, and Slavic origins under separate communities. Muslims and Jews were treated as separate and unitary, with little regard for ethnic or linguistic differences within each community. The Ottoman state granted a certain level of autonomy to every community, especially regarding religious practice and the jurisdiction of the ecclesiastic or rabbinical court systems in Christianity and Judaism, respectively. This was a pluralist—but not an egalitarian system. Though hardly monolithic, Muslims constituted the majority of the population, owned majority of the land, and dominated the imperial economy until the nineteenth century, owing to the agrarian nature of the economy. The power of the political center progressively deteriorated between the seventeenth and nineteenth centuries (Lapidus 2002, 489–97). The declining state capacity was accompanied by economic problems and foreign debt, which, in turn, made the Ottoman state vulnerable to foreign influence. By the nineteenth century the Ottoman Empire, as the "sick man of Europe," had to grant trade concessions to most major European powers. The non-Muslim population of the empire became a channel of influence for foreign powers seeking an increased presence in the Ottoman Empire. These communities benefited from this expanding European involvement, whether by sharing in the newly extracted economic capitulations or by gaining allies in their efforts to obtain political rights and equal citizenship. In fact, during this period, the non-Muslim population became economically dominant due to the rising European influence (Karpat 1973). For example, Greeks, sailing under the Russian flag, controlled naval transportation. Likewise, a large number of non-Muslims became "privileged merchants" under foreign protection (Hanioglu 2008, 26–28). The

Tanzimat era was marked by reforms that ensured rights to life, property, and honor and provided for the equality of all before law. However, owing to the socioeconomic class structure, which overlapped with the ethnoreligious communal divisions in Ottoman society, a unified national public never developed.[6]

The modernizing Ottoman Empire had a "fragmented public sphere" lacking the proper means to form a unified national public sphere (Mahcupyan 1998). The non-Muslims of the empire, especially Armenians, Jews, and Greeks, became influential in the state bureaucracy, parliament, and, most importantly, trade and finance. The rise of nationalism and the subsequent dissolution of the empire reduced the size of the non-Muslim population, who made up a significant portion of the capitalist class. The new Turkish state that emerged after the War of Liberation (1919–22) would enact a process of nation-state building, suppressing non-Turkish ethnic identities, and disestablishing Islam. The absence of a powerful middle class at the onset of the republican Turkey made *étatisme* an attractive, if not a necessary, economic policy for recovery and development. In turn, this facilitated the continuation of a powerful state tradition in the subsequent years of the republic.

The Early Years of the Republic: State Hegemony over the Public Sphere

In Turkey, religion in the public sphere has been a controversial issue since the establishment of the Republic in 1923. There has long been tension between the secular state and the religious sectors of the society. The containment policy of the state toward religious groups has, paradoxically, led religious groups to both detach from the public sphere due to a sense of alienation as well as to adopt strategies to

6. Some historians, such as Cemal Kafadar, argue that Ottoman society was much more integrated than is suggested by conventional understandings of the fragmented nature of the *millet* system. Kafadar bases his argument on the demographics of Istanbul neighborhoods (*mahalle*) and the intermingling between different ethnoreligious groups in coffee shops, the nascent (secular) public sites in Ottoman society (interview by Nuriye Akman, *Zaman*, April 11, 2004).

enhance their presence in the state apparatus and the political system. Islamic groups strived to survive the restrictive state policies toward religious organizations while looking for ways to bring religion to the public sphere. The Gülen movement was one of the most prominent and influential Islamic movements in modern Turkey, with a significant presence in other parts of the world. The movement's reluctance to embrace a transparent public identity, coupled with its active role in building public dialogue and supporting community organizations, is an instructive case with which to examine the relationship between religious groups and the republican public sphere.

With the establishment of the Republic of Turkey, the emerging critical public sphere—largely the product of the modernist intelligentsia—was curtailed and the scope of public deliberation was limited by the state. This was done for the sake of the "safe" and "effective" modernization of the country so that potential "backward" forces would not thwart the modernization process. The state adopted a new ideology, later referred to as Kemalism.

Based on the twin pillars of nationalism and secularism, Kemalism created its own modernity shaped by the enlightenment ideas of positivism, rationalism, and elitism (Yavuz 2003a, 37–58). The goal was to create a modern secular Turkish society through a number of cultural and political reforms. Since the society did not share the same ideals, the Kemalist elite also felt themselves responsible for educating the society so as to instill appropriate values. The mindset of the Kemalist elites was significantly influenced by French republicanism. Much like the Reign of Terror instituted by the Jacobins after the French Revolution, Kemalist elite adopted ruthless and radical measures against the enemies of the new republican regime—perceived or real. Due to a fear of counterrevolution, prominent Kurdish and Islamic figures were executed, imprisoned, or exiled based on their varying levels of opposition to the radical reforms introduced by the state.

The six principles of Kemalism, which formed the basis of the party platform of Ataturk's Republican People's Party (CHP), were laicism, nationalism, populism, statism, reformism, and republicanism. The lack of any reference to democracy—not even in a perfunctory manner—is an indicator of how the Republican government functioned as a one-party authoritarian regime. The government understood modernization in technical, economic, and administrative terms. During the one-party system (1923–46), the Kemalists promoted the earlier secularist-modernism of the Young Turks and silenced alternative perspectives. For example, the Islamic modernists, represented by the Young Ottomans in the latter part of the nineteenth century, felt the brunt of the government's efforts to promote its vision at the expense of other viewpoints.

As a result of the Kemalist hegemony, the public sphere became less critical and more illiberal, assuming an authoritarian republican form. Indeed, the constitutional monarchic periods of the Ottoman Empire witnessed a more liberal public sphere than was present in the formative years of the Republican period. The communal basis of Ottoman subjects, exemplified by the *millet* system, was replaced by a homogenous concept of citizenship whose virtues were centered around the Kemalist ideology. The state treated the public sphere as an exhibition site for the ideals modern Turkish citizens ought to espouse. It therefore undertook an ambitious social transformation through cultural reforms in dress, alphabet, and education; legal reforms in civil law and the constitution; and political reforms whose goal was to produce a republican system of government. The Kemalist revolution necessitated the shift from a traditional system of loyalty and social organization toward a civic one. For the Kemalist elite, the ultimate aim was to form a homogenous secular society with the desired republican-citizenship virtues.

This type of a republican mindset saw the public sphere as a place to socialize the masses to these new citizenship virtues and responsibilities. This approach to the public sphere comes close to Hannah Arendt's concept of an "agonistic public sphere." The existence of a republic meant that the people were the presumed sovereigns of the country, yet the state would ultimately define its own ideal public that would carry the attributes of Kemalist modernism. The "official" domain of the state dominated the public sphere during this era; people were denied space in it unless they complied with the Kemalist standard of good citizenship by embracing a secular Turkish Sunni Muslim identity.

In addition to the state hegemony in the public sphere, parts of the society associated with those the Kemalist state deemed to be "others" were silenced, leaving individuals in these groups with no hope or motivation to participate in public life and no desire to "unveil" their identities. Despite the seeming uniformity of the new Turkish public sphere, the fragmented nature of the public sphere continued to exist, at a more ideational level, divided by the values of the center versus the values of the periphery. The state under Kemalist hegemony claimed to represent the general will of the people, but it treated critical voices as obscurantist, backward, and antirepublican. In terms of its functionality, there was not an autonomous, legally protected, and inclusive public sphere where rational and critical political deliberation could be conducted in the Habermasian sense.

The Multiparty System (1950–1980): State Control over the Political Society

Turkey was not a combatant in World War II, yet the war still wrought changes to the country. The National Defense Law of 1940 and the Capital Tax Law of 1942 had further increased the state's power over the society. After the war, the Kemalist party in power at the time, the CHP, initiated political and economic liberalization. These reforms were both a gesture toward the Western alliance balancing against the Soviet threat as well as a response to the opposition platform of the nascent Democrat Party (DP). The political reforms had their intended effect. After the 1946–50 liberalization of the electoral system, Turkish politics became competitive, as illustrated by the rise of the DP. Despite some commonalities between the platforms of the RPP and the DP, large segments of the urban and rural electorate had grown wary of the RPP's party-state and favored DP for change: the DP won the first free and fair elections in 1950.

The DP had run on a platform of empowering the people against the "tyranny of the state" and claimed the mantle of the "national will" (Ahmad 2008). The DP had effectively challenged the hegemony of Kemalist ideology in the Turkish body politic. The passive opposition forces in the society became more visible, owing to a new hope that the expanded public sphere might now welcome their authentic value systems.

The DP's policies initially led to economic growth largely driven by agrarian reforms based on the modernization of existing agricultural practices and the distribution of state-owned land to peasants (Pamuk 2008). The DP capitalized on this initial success, subsequently consolidating its support among the rural electorate through state subsidies and networks of patronage. The DP also made symbolic gestures to its conservative base by ending the ban on the Arabic call to prayer (*ezan*) and easing restrictions on religious instruction.

Even though the DP's rule offered more room in the public sphere to conservative critics of the Kemalist reforms, CHP allies were better represented among the intelligentsia and the bureaucracy: the military and the judiciary, university professors, and journalists remained as a strong opposition bloc against the populist policies of the DP government. As a result of economic problems and social change in the latter part of 1950s, Turkish politics became increasingly polarized. Driven by rumors of a conspiracy inside the military against the government, the DP went on the offensive to detain military officers, initiate an investigation regarding the CHP's ties to the conspiracy, and clamped down on the critical press, universities, and the secular intelligentsia. This political conflict ultimately ended with military intervention in 1960. Under the DP, the parts of society that had acquiesced to the Kemalist reforms without necessarily internalizing them had found a window of opportunity for the representation of their socioeconomic interests and traditional values in the public sphere under the DP government. However, the "guardians of the Republic" were in charge of the civil service, the military, and the judiciary, all of which played a critical role in the 1960 coup d'état. The state once again asserted its primacy over the public sphere and institutionalized its guardian role by ushering in a new order. The following two decades were marked by an illiberal electoral democracy, where the power of the appointed was superior to the power of the elected. This division between the state and the government remained as a significant feature of post-1960 Turkish political culture. The scope of acceptable policies that elected governments could enact was closely guarded by the unelected bureaucracy, who formed the basis of the Kemalist state establishment.

After a short period of military rule, a new constitution was written and control of the government was handed back to civilians. The 1961 constitution extended freedom of assembly and gave autonomy to the public broadcasting institution (TRT) and the universities. This legal framework offered the potential for the society to forge a public sphere relatively independent from state influence. The autonomy of public radio and television would be especially helpful in this regard. Further, by loosening restrictions on associational life, new means and platforms for the expression of public opinion and new sites of public discussion began to flourish. However, these associations were mostly founded on ideological bases rather than around substantive public policy matters. As a result, a culture of coexistence between individuals on the opposite ends of the political spectrum never developed, and the public sphere was once again characterized by partisan contestation. When this ideological struggle escalated into violence, the military intervened again on the basis of restoring peace and order. The aim of the 1980 junta was to depoliticize a society that had been polarized along ideological, religious, and ethnic lines. The experiences of the 1960s and 1970s gave the military and bureaucratic elites an excuse for more restrictions on political liberties. Indeed, the 1982 constitution reflected diminished liberties compared to the 1961 constitution.[7]

Post-1980: Depoliticization, Civil Society, and the Struggle over the Public Sphere

Despite some significant illiberal measures regarding associational freedoms in the constitution, the 1980s were marked by an evolution of the

7. For a comparative historical view on politics of constitution-making, see Özbudun and Gençkaya 2009.

ideological public toward a more civil public.[8] Prime Minister Turgut Özal's (1983–89) twin policies of economic and political liberalization created a fertile environment for the birth of a pluralist public sphere.[9] The rise of a new class of Anatolian bourgeoisie paved the way for the construction of alternative media for public discussion. This included new private media networks, educational foundations, private schools, and business associations. Additionally, the military's depoliticization strategy was quite successful: the ideological fault lines of the society seemed to be fading after two decades of conflict. As a result of this depoliticization and the subsequent neoliberal economic policies of the government, identity politics emerged as the new source of activism. Privatization of the economy was followed by the "privatization" of the public sphere: individuals and groups sought more open representation of particularistic private identities, including ethnic, religious, professional, and, to a limited degree, sexual identities.

During his tenure, Özal tried to shift the Turkish public sphere away from its French republican mentality toward an Anglo-Saxon liberal-individual outlook. As the society became relatively more affluent and the political environment became relatively freer, groups within the society began to search for public visibility and representation. As a result, a growing vibrant civil society attempted to balance the power of the state. Gender issues, ethnic identities, and environmental concerns appeared in public discussions to an unprecedented degree. Islamic conservatism and Kurdish nationalism also tried to benefit from this favorable environment. Saturday Mothers (*Cumartesi Anneleri*),[10] A Minute of Darkness for Permanent Light (*Sürekli*

8. For more on the "civil" public sphere, see Çaha 1998.

9. See Onis 2004 for the legacy of Ozal's neoliberal reforms.

10. Saturday Mothers started in 1995 as a movement to raise awareness of "disappeared" family members from the 1980 military coup onward. These "disappearances" are similar to the fate of political opponents in the hands of Latin American military regimes. The activities of Saturday Mothers were a protest against the state and its policies of torturing and silencing political opponents, especially Kurdish activists and nationalists.

Aydınlık İçin Bir Dakika Karanlık), and Headscarf Protest (*Türban Eylemi*) are examples of slogans and names of civil platforms formed around ethnic and religious identities and the pursuit of civil liberties.[11] These acts made claims about desired rights and freedoms; the public sphere became the ground for promoting and asserting these rights and freedoms. However, the bureaucratic establishment did not have any intention of surrendering its privileges, and a struggle for control of the public sphere marked the 1990s.

Explaining the Transformation

There are competing interpretations of what happened in the 1980s and 1990s in Turkey concerning the convoluted relationship between the state and civil society in the public sphere. Nilüfer Göle (1994) portrays the 1980s as a period in which public discourse was rationalized and diversified and became less confrontational. Relations between social movements moved away from zero-sum state-focused politics to more constructive interactions, showing elements of conflict and cooperation. People of opposing political leanings began to listen to one another in a shared public space. However, this retreat of the state can also be seen as a new strategy. Namely, the state's actions can be interpreted as co-opting certain sectors of the society while directly struggling against other sectors that challenged the state's autonomy most. Yael Navaro-Yashin (2002), for example, disagrees with Göle's analysis of the increasing visibility of identity groups in the public sphere as an indicator of a growing symbiotic relationship between the state and the society. She points to some of the repressive measures taken by the state to control the autonomy of the civil society and to use civil society groups as a vehicle for reproducing and enhancing state power in the face of "self-generating" or "spontaneous" protest

11. A Minute of Darkness for Permanent Light started as a movement to protest the illegal/questionable activities of the state and the state's links to criminal organizations. This web of relationships surfaced after an apparent traffic accident, popularly known as the Susurluk incident of 1996, which uncovered connections between the armed forces, politicians, and organized crime.

activity (Navaro-Yashin 2002, 132). However, even those who, like Navaro-Yashin, are skeptical about the withdrawal of the Turkish state from the public sphere admit that there was an evident transformation in Turkish society: it was no longer possible to control the society by conventional repressive means or by hegemonic state measures. This change was also related to global trends toward rights and identity discourses as well as the interaction among transnational advocacy networks. These international connections were made possible by globalization and Turkey's increasingly integrationist policies on trade, diplomacy, and cultural relations.

The new terms of the relationship between the state and the society challenged some of the fundamental underpinnings of the Kemalist ideology. The rise in visibility of Islamist and Kurdish nationalist symbols intensely offended Kemalist establishment. The Kemalist elite perceived the promotion of images and differences vis-à-vis the public gaze as a power play, rather than a question of cultural, religious, or political freedoms. Through visual representations, such as images, displays, and performances, as well as through discourse and speech, everyday life was subject to different forms of intervention, contestation, negotiation, and constructed meanings (Cinar 1998). In that context, the boundaries of identity were reinforced and prioritized through the lens of public visibility: a female lawyer wearing the headscarf was seen first as a Muslim rather than an attorney, as a result of the categorizing effect of visibility in the public eye. Similarly, the secular gaze perceived the headscarf as a political symbol and a challenge to the secular republic. Ironically, public representation does not necessarily improve the status of excluded groups and identities; increased public presence can reinforce the social status of these excluded groups. Members of the larger society may engage in selective perception, focusing on the identity that reinforces preconceived notions about the excluded group, even though an individual associated with an excluded group may have multiple defining identities. Regardless of a veiled woman's intention or lack thereof to highlight her Muslim identity over her professional identity or other social roles, selective symbolization by the media and other social perceptions constructed a political meaning that became attached to women wearing the veil. In essence, the Kemalist argument that saw the headscarf as an Islamist political symbol became a self-fulfilling prophecy. In other words, the claims of symbolism attached to the actions of individuals constructed a public gaze that caused others within the society to view defining identities selectively. This symbolic narrative and these attached meanings became the basis for the production of public hierarchies, for claims concerning access to the public sphere, and for justifications regarding inclusion or exclusion from the public sphere.

Secularism and the Public Sphere according to the Kemalist Ideology

A full understanding of the controversy over the Turkish public sphere requires an understanding of its relationship with secularism. The republican way of organizing social life is subject to a certain view of secularism that has particular implications for the public sphere. Simply put, the generic meaning of secularism is the separation of "religious" and "mundane." This separation has multiple dimensions and meanings in a polity. As it pertains to the domains of the polity, there are three possible dimensions of this separation in theory and practice:

- Institutional separation (between religion [church] and the state)
- Ideological separation (between religious principles and political discourse)
- Value separation (between religious morals and the civil public sphere)

Any combination of the above three forms of secularism can be found in today's modern societies. The particular blend of these dimensions of secularism underscores the key historical struggles in a given society, which, in turn, result in the development of political traditions and institutional designs. In the US the secular regime comprises of core principles at each dimension with an overlapping consensus. On the first dimension, the First Amendment of the US Constitution unequivocally rules out governmental establishment of religion and upholds freedom of religion. On the second dimension, even though intermixing of religion and politics receives a great deal of skepticism from the liberals, the right of religious institutions to have representation in the political arena and the ability of the pious to bring their religious ideas to inform political discourse are widely acknowledged. On the third dimension, religion, whether a civil-generic religion or the particular Protestant worldview, has played a significant role in the American public square. In this sense, religion has become an integral part of the political socialization of citizens, providing a source of morality, patriotism, and integrity, that contributes to the national identity.[12] What is most controversial in the US is not these basic principles, but their application in particular laws, regulations, and practices that cross over the intersection of these three dimensions. In particular, school prayers, public displays of religious symbols, accommodation of religiously based practices in workplaces, and legal and public policy exemptions for religious institutions have become legal battle grounds between conservatives and liberals, making the US Supreme Court the key arbiter of disputes on secularism.

It is common to compare the Anglo-Saxon and French models of secularism—what Ahmet Kuru (2009) called "passive" and "assertive" secularism, respectively. These different models are significantly influenced by the dominant types of the public sphere along the liberal and republican models. In a republican country like Turkey, the state often treats secularism as a part of the state ideology and lifestyle that encompasses all aspects of community life. On the first dimension of secularism, rather than neutrality or institutional separation the Turkish state aims to keep the tabs on religious organizations and control its message. For the majority Sunni Muslims, the state appoints imams and religious personnel to all mosques in the country. The Directorate of Religious Affairs, Diyanet İşleri Başkanlığı, trains all the imams and centrally controls the religious teachings, including Friday sermons. The non-Sunni Alevi Muslims, who make up about 15 percent of the population, lack such state support and are

12. For the origin of the concept of civil religion, see Bellah 1975.

denied exemption from religious education courses in public schools. The only officially recognized minorities in Turkey are non-Muslim minorities who were identified in the Lausanne Treaty (1923): Greeks, Armenians, and Jews. As with Sunni Islam, these recognized minorities have been subject to state control over their places of worship, seminaries, and leadership. All other religious organizations outside of the officially recognized religious groups are required to register for their organization and activities, which are subject to limitations. On the second dimension, the Kemalist state establishment used secularism as a pretext to exclude Islamists from politics and periodically closed down Islamist political parties on grounds of challenging the secular nature of the state. On the third dimension, the Turkish state placed restrictions on religion's public role in the civil society. According to the Kemalist ideology, religious symbols and identities would have to be confined to the private sphere and not carried into the public realm.[13] The Kemalist secularism has been softened under the first two AKP governments (2002–11) and the state policies toward religion have since moved away from strict separationism toward de facto establishment of Islam. However, as explained in chapters 4 and 6, despite this shift, the republican mentality endured in terms of continued government control over religious teachings and organization, and restrictions over the civil society religious groups.

The Politics of Religious Symbols

Wearing the Islamic headscarf in public institutions was a major form of polarization in Turkey in 1990s and 2000s. Discussions about the headscarf issue were framed around representation in the public

13. For a relatively recent example of the Kemalist understanding of secularism, see Gürüz 2004. The paper highlights secularism, nationalism, positivism, and a sense of political and economic developmentalism as the pillars of a modern Turkish aspiration to "achieve the contemporary level of civilization." Kemal Gürüz was the head of the semiautonomous state organ the Higher Education Council, overseeing affairs of higher education in Turkey. In his eight-year tenure, he became the symbol of the strict application of the headscarf ban at universities.

sphere. Female university students were not allowed to wear headscarves because the Kemalist state establishment making the policy understood universities to be public institutions in which no religious symbol was permissible. Similarly, the wives of the Turkish prime minister and the speaker of the parliament were excluded from some official ceremonies and invitations because these women chose to wear headscarves.[14] These were striking examples of the tension around the interpretation and practice of secularism in Turkey. In these debates, the Turkish notion of *kamusal alan* (the "public sphere") was vaguely used on legal and political grounds—but the abstractness of this concept made the issue even more complex.

The Republican Public Sphere and Headscarves

On the issue of veiling in universities and other public institutions, the concept of the public sphere was invoked by the Kemalist elite to signify that the public domain has a functional relationship with public authorities. Thus, the public institutions, which belonged to the public, had to be fittingly overseen by the state. Therefore, the state reserved its right to intervene whenever the public and neutral nature

14. This incident is quite illustrative regarding the ideological, exclusionary, and mostly arbitrary restrictive boundaries created between public and private in Turkey. Abdullah Gül, who was the eleventh Turkish President between 2007 and 2014, used a double reception system during his early years in office to accommodate the "sensitivities" of the Kemalist state. For example, to celebrate Turkey's national day a reception would first be held during the day for the military generals so as to avoid involving the headscarf-wearing wives of political leaders. Then, everybody else, including spouses, would attend a second reception in the evening. This way, the generals would not have to shake hands with the headscarf-wearing wives of the president, prime minister, and the speaker of the parliament, for such a scene would legitimize the place of headscarves in the public (read: official) space. Some military generals went to great lengths to avoid such a scene, including turning their backs to pretend that they were having conversation with others, not attending events, and even fleeing the event through the back door of the reception hall. See, for example, "Resepsiyonu Arka Kapıdan Terkettiler" (They Left the Reception from the Back Door), *Akşam*, October 30, 2010.

of a site or an institution was called into question by the behavior of its staff or by those it served. The public sphere was, in this case, interchangeably used with the official sphere. The Turkish equivalent of the term public sphere is *kamusal alan*: the word *kamu* here comes closer to the meaning of the word *devlet* (the state) rather than the meaning of the word *amme* (the public).[15] In this linguistic shift, those who give public service and those who receive it are not differentiated.[16] Moreover, the state was not consistent in applying the restrictions on religious symbols in all public places and did not include all forms of public service, but only those that were perceived as symbolic and sensitive by the state. As recipients of public services, a university student and a patient in a public hospital should face similar rules regarding the acceptability of religious symbols when receiving their respective public benefits. However, being a veiled student was deemed unacceptable while being a veiled patient was generally acceptable in the eyes of the state bureaucracy.

The state establishment also felt uneasy about certain symbolic situations. After the pro-Islamic AKP came to power by winning the majority of the seats in parliament in 2002, Kemalist elite within the state once again shifted into high alert. Most members of parliament, including the prime minister and the speaker, had pious backgrounds and their wives wore headscarves. Receptions in Parliament, the presidential buildings, and at the military institutions as well as diplomatic protocols became a tricky issue, requiring Turkish leaders to go to great lengths to sidestep the public presence of headscarf-wearing wives.[17] The president and the military used a dual invitation system

15. Murat Belge, "Kamusal Alana Nereden Girilir?" (Where Do You Enter the Public Sphere?) *Radikal*, July 16, 2004.

16. Eser Karakaş, "Kamu Hizmeti ve Kamusal Alan" (Public Service and the Public Sphere), *Zaman*, November 12, 2003.

17. For example, during the June 2004 NATO Summit in Istanbul, the Turkish president did not invite the Turkish prime minister's wife to the formal dinner. Oddly enough, among all the spouses of the leaders of the NATO countries, only the Turkish prime minister's spouse was not in attendance. Similarly, the president did not

for the members of parliament and the government. The invitations sent to individuals whose wives wore a headscarf were directed only to the male, whereas the invitations sent to individuals whose wives did not wear a headscarf included both people. It was not permissible to wear headscarf in ***kamusal alan***. Even those places that are not directly related to the presidency become kamusal alan whenever there is a formal event in presence of the president. Practically everywhere the president went became the "public domain," and was thus subject to the Kemalist limitations on visibility and acceptable representation.

In the late 1990s and early 2000s, the Turkish state began to define the kamusal alan quite broadly by including practically every state institution, with no distinction between the public servant and the recipient of the service. The people who were denied the right to a public education started to conclude that the state did not accept them as full members of the nation—the very nation the state existed to serve. The republican mentality of an ideal society created by the state through education and standard-setting in the public sphere is evident here. Challenges to the Kemalist notion of a modern, homogenous society were not tolerated. Rather, the state chose to redirect the course of change or to prevent change, if possible. The growing chasm between the mentality of the state and the mentality of the society prevented the state from following and responding to societal change: the society became more diverse and tolerant of pluralism, but the state was reluctant to take any corresponding actions to acknowledge this pluralism.

These debates on the nature of the public sphere in Turkey in the 1990s and early 2000s demonstrated two things. First, different sectors of the society started to use the public sphere more effectively with the help of emerging non-Kemalist public intellectuals. Secondly, the state, cognizant of its symbolic and ideological significance, started to use different tactics to better control the public sphere or, at least, to avoid losing its place in the public square entirely.

---

accept an invitation issued by the prime minister for the following day because the prime minister's wife, who wears a headscarf, would be in attendance at that event.

1. *The lady with headscarf in a public bus says: "Let me get out before we come to a public sphere?!"* Latif Demirci, *Hürriyet*, November 11, 2003.

Some public institutions wanted to take the rationale of the public sphere as it pertained to the university dress code and presidential ceremonies and use this as precedent to restrict benefits from individuals receiving other public services. For example, during the height of this tension, a defendant was denied access to the court—and thus could not offer testimony on her own behalf—on the grounds that she wore a headscarf, which was unacceptable in the public sphere.[18] The caricature in figure 1 cleverly alludes to both the confusion associated with the state's approach and the society's perception of the official mentality regarding the public sphere and everyday life.

Some of the advocates of these regulations in the public sphere tried to come up with a functional definition of the public sphere. The

18. "Özkaya: Mahkeme, Kamusal Alan" (Özkaya: The Court is a Public Space), *Radikal*, November 7, 2003.

president of the Higher Education Council, Erdoğan Teziç, argued that when an issue concerns public order, the encounter between a public servant and a citizen creates a public domain; therefore, the citizen is expected to follow the regulations of that institution regarding the public service. He gave the example of a police officer checking the identity of a lady in a park, asserting that the officer has the right to ask the lady to take off her headscarf if he is having problems identifying her.[19] In addition to endorsing broad powers to the state with a function-based definition of the public sphere, the idealized homogeneous character of the public sphere is also apparent in Teziç's approach. Republican-secular motifs are also quite evident in other statements by Teziç, which reveal the mindset of the Kemalist intelligentsia regarding representation in the public sphere: "In the place called public [sphere], everyone has to express themselves with undifferentiated representation."[20] According to this perspective, religious or ethnic identities are seen as displays of symbols of difference in public, a domain in which Turkish citizenship should be the only form of operational identity for individuals and groups alike.

This restricted understanding of the public sphere, with its strong reference to nationalism and secularism, creates tension between the autonomy and the pluralism of the public sphere. If the categorical difference between the people and the public is not maintained, then the public sphere becomes an arena for homogenization and national identity formation. As a result, the space between the state and the people is blurred and the public sphere cannot serve as a neutral intervening discursive and dialogical space between the state and the society (Baban 1999). When national discourse dominates and colonizes the public sphere, national identity becomes the only legitimate mantle for actors in the public sphere, forcing other identities to the private sphere or to form counterpublics.

19. "Teziç Tanım Yaptı" (Teziç Made a Definition), *Radikal*, July 11, 2004.

20. "Kamu denilen yerde, herkes eşit görüntüsüyle kendini ifade etmek zorundadır." Erdoğan Tezic's statement reported by Taha Akyol, "Kamusal Alan, Liberalism, Demokrasi," *Milliyet*, July 14, 2004.

Questions of identity and the public sphere are important in any discussion of religion in public life in Turkey: the Turkish state tried to exclude religion from the public sphere and replace it with an exclusionary secular national identity. An ideal Turkish citizen would be secular-Sunni-Turkish-Muslim. This definition of the idealized citizen excluded pious Muslims, non-Sunni Muslims, non-Turkish ethnic groups, and non-Muslims. It is thus not a surprise that conservative Sunni Muslims, Alevis, Kurds, Greeks, Armenians, and Jews all had their share of problems with the Turkish state. Such an exclusionary system, serving a small minority of privileged elite, sometimes referred to as "white Turks," endured because of the lack of cooperation among other social groups, who had real or perceived enmity toward each other.

The Legal Status of the Headscarf Issue

The ban on wearing headscarves was based on the 1989 and 1991 rulings of the Constitutional Court. The 1989 decision overruled legislation passed in parliament that allowed individuals to cover their head and neck because of religious beliefs.[21] The 1991 decision was the dismissal of a case brought by the opposition party of the time, the Social Democrat Populist Party (SHP); the case sought to overturn a legislation that gave freedom of dress to individuals as long as such dress did not violate any of the laws in force.[22] This created a very complicated situation. On the one hand, in 1989, the court rejected the freedom to wear headscarves at universities. On the other hand, in 1991, the court refused to abandon a provision that recognized freedom of dress in higher education institutions, provided that it did not violate any effective law.

The wording of the law was not the real culprit—but the interpretation of it was critical for the headscarf question. One might approach the issue with consideration for the constitutional provisions ensuring

21. The Higher Education Law, no. 2547, 16.

22. The Higher Education Law, no. 2547, 17.

inviolable rights to education and religious beliefs. Alternately, as the constitutional court did, one might approach the issue with a secular-public neutrality point of view. In essence, those who are in favor of lifting the ban on wearing a headscarf generally based their argument on the liberal vision that involves freedom of religious practice and the right of an individual to an education regardless of his/her religious or ethnic affiliation. The proponents of the headscarf ban made their arguments on the basis of the right of the state to enforce laws and regulations in matters of public order and perceived threats to the secular character of the regime.

The lack of legal clarity gave discretionary power to the university presidents in terms of their implementation of the dress code. Until 1997, the climate was quite tolerant of wearing a headscarf. However, after the Islamist Welfare Party (RP) came to power, the Kemalist elite were alarmed by what they interpreted as a daring challenge to the secular regime. The ambiguity of the legal status of the issue led to its politicization. The highest administrative court, the Council of State (Danıştay), later rejected other appeals, citing the two decisions in 1989 and 1991 as sufficient. After the National Security Council directives of 28 February 1997, it became impossible for students wearing the headscarf to attend school. The headscarf issue reflected some ironies associated with modernization. On one hand, the existence of the issue itself was a ramification of the quest for modernization by the traditional sectors of the society. The women from traditional backgrounds sought education, employment, and visibility in public and did not wish to be confined to the private realm. On the other hand, the Kemalist state perceived the effort to retain their headscarves while pursing modern goals and engaging in modern behaviors as being against the very modernization ideals of the regime. The traditional sectors of the society were effectively squeezed in between their households and the Kemalist public sphere.

The European Court of Human Rights (ECHR) became an actor in Turkish domestic matters after Turkey granted its citizens the right of individual petition in 1987. As a victim of the strict implementation of the post-1997 ban, a Turkish medical student, Leyla Şahin, brought the issue before the ECHR. She claimed the Turkish state violated her religious freedoms and right to an education when she was denied the opportunity to sit in the exams and to enroll in Istanbul University. The court ruled that the headscarf ban, motivated by a desire to maintain the separation of church and state, could be justified under the European Convention on Human Rights in order "to prevent certain fundamentalist religious movements from pressuring students who do not practice the religion in question or those belonging to another religion."[23] This decision of ECHR disappointed those who framed the headscarf issue as a human rights matter. A sense of betrayal by and disillusionment with Europe grew among most Islamist groups, including the members of the ruling AKP, who adopted a strategic patience approach between 2004 and 2008.

The initial solution to the headscarf controversy came not as a result of legal liberalization, but through bureaucratic accommodation. In 2008, the AKP and the opposition Nationalist Movement Party (MHP) jointly initiated legislation that would amend the constitution to prevent anyone from being deprived of access to higher education for reasons not openly mentioned in the law. The amendment passed by a large majority (411 to 103) and was later approved by the president. In response, the main opposition party, the CHP, petitioned the Turkish Constitutional Court to overturn the amendment, contending that the new amendment violated the secularism article, marked as being among the unchangeable articles in the constitution. The Constitutional Court struck down the amendment in 2008; later that same year, this amendment was cited by the state prosecutor as evidence of the AKP's efforts to undermine secularism. That claim provided grounds for the state to outlaw the party and ban party leadership from politics. The party escaped closure after a close vote in the Constitutional Court in which the court ruled to fine the party, but allowed it to remain active. After this close call, the AKP

23. European Court of Human Rights, *Leyla Şahin v. Turkey* (No. 44774/98). Judgment on June 29, 2004.

leadership became convinced of the need to bring the judicial and higher education bureaucracy under control before taking concrete steps to ease the ban on headscarves. One of the party's founding leaders, Abdullah Gül, was elected president in 2007. Gül appointed Yusuf Ziya Özcan as the chief of Turkey's Higher Education Council (YÖK), a former bastion of the secularist establishment. Özcan did not initially take steps to relax the headscarf ban as the Constitutional Court struck down the 2008 legislation—and when he did so, he did it through an internal memorandum to universities. Most universities quickly complied. Despite some initial resistance by faculty members, college deans, or university presidents, the headscarf ban quietly ended at Turkish universities, public and private.[24] Between 2013 and 2018, the AKP government gradually repealed restrictions against the wearing of a headscarf in the civil and military services. As the next chapter demonstrates, 2010 was the critical year, as it brought the dismantling of the Kemalist establishment and freed the AKP from ongoing confrontation on the headscarf issue.

Conclusion

This chapter offered a broad picture of the Turkish political context concerning the role of religion and religious groups in the public sphere. One of the pillars of the Kemalist ideology was secularism, which took the form of state control of religion rather than a complete separation of religion and the state or a practiced neutrality between the two. The Kemalist state's emphasis on regulating the public arena and requiring individuals to act exclusively as national citizens in the public sphere were in line with Rousseau's general will and the French republican tradition. The existence of an officially mandated state Islam and the dissolution of private religious foundations and institutions left little room for open representation of religious symbols and discourse in the public sphere. This forced most Islamic movements

24. "Iste Universitelerde Basortusu Haritasi" (Here Is the Map of Headscarf Regulations at the Universities), *Radikal*, October 5, 2010.

to adopt a strategy of organizing informally with an emphasis on collective religio-national (*milli*) interests as opposed to particular group interests.

The headscarf question is the quintessential manifestation of the intricate relationship between the dominant form of the public sphere and the limits of religious representation in Turkey. However, it was not the only controversial issue in—and on—the Turkish public sphere. Another major source of public debates has been the status of Islamic movements in the public sphere. This chapter offered an analysis of the political context concerning religious representation in Turkey, and chapters 4 and 6 will situate the Gülen movement in this context as one of the most influential and controversial Islamic movements in modern Turkey. Unlike the Islamists and liberals, the movement remained much less assertive on the headscarf issue and opted for a strategy of appeasement and passive resistance toward the Kemalist establishment. This attitude toward the public sphere and its sociopolitical profile make the Gülen movement one of the most instructive cases with which to study the contours of the Turkish republican public sphere.

3

The Liberal Public Sphere and Religious Dissent in the United States

Religion was never marginal to the public sphere in American history and deeply molded its national narratives and myths. Politics of majority-minority relations were especially critical in the foundation and evolution of the liberal public sphere. Core Mormon beliefs and doctrines concerning constitutional patriotism, civil religion, and millennialism were shaped in relation to the salient issues of their time, from moral order to assimilation of immigrants. America's "Mormon question" can only be understood by uncovering the mutually constitutive role of the social forces that were external to the church and doctrines that were internal. This chapter explores the foundations of the liberal public sphere in the US and situates the rise of Mormonism in its historical context of religious revivalism, industrialization, capitalism, and the frontier conditions of the territorial expansion.

The Origins of the Liberal Public Sphere

The United States is a pluralist and liberal republic today with a robust regime of religious freedoms and a wall of separation between church and state. Despite disagreements over the meaning and boundaries of separation and freedoms, as stated in the First Amendment to the US Constitution, Americans overwhelmingly agree on the core principles.[1] A pluralist liberal regime, however, was not historically inevitable and emerged as a result of competing visions of and interests in social and moral order, civil rights, and political representation. For Puritans of the seventeenth century, the radical reformers who fled persecution in England, religion was not only a guide toward individual salvation, but also a blueprint for a social moral order that would make such salvation and divine favor possible. As John Winthrop, the Puritan governor of Massachusetts put it, America was destined to be the city on a hill, an exemplary model for the world, in the hands of God's elect. The success in building the new Israel would be the surest sign of being the elect. Divine favor required lifelong dedication, perseverance, self-discipline, and conformity to the teachings of the Bible. Puritans established the Congregational Church in New England colonies of Massachusetts, Connecticut, and New Hampshire. Their Protestant beliefs were radical in challenging the authority of the Catholic Church; however, they were not radical enough for the next generation of Americans who sought to claim individual relationship with God without any mediation from their clergy as they grappled with the question of salvation and men's sinful nature. The ensuing religious revival that emphasized the individual born-again experience in the eighteenth century, known as the First Great Awakening, fundamentally transformed the landscape of American religion and politics during the Revolutionary period and the formative years of the Republic. The shifting landscape brought tensions between the established religions of the colonies, such as Congregationalism in New England and Anglicanism in the South, and the dissenting denominations, such as the Quakers, Catholics, Baptists, and the Methodists. The middle colonies of Pennsylvania, Delaware,

1. Opinion polls consistently show strong support among Americans for the First Amendment in general and religious freedoms in particular. According to Newseum Institute's State of the First Amendment Study, about two thirds of Americans supported extending religious freedoms to all faiths (http://www.newseuminstitute.org/wp-content/uploads/2017/06/FAC_SOFA17_report.pdf).

Maryland, Rhode Island, and New Jersey had no official established church and became home to the dissenting denominations.

Popular preachers like Jonathan Edwards and George Whitfield went on revivalist expeditions across the colonies and formed a popular evangelical base for the American religion. By 1760, an antiestablishment popular movement had gained strength and portrayed the Congregational and Anglican Churches as remnants of the old colonial aristocratic order. Freedom from British rule not only meant freedom from economic subjugation, but also religious subjugation under the old order, thus adding a religious-moral dimension to the rationalist arguments advanced by the political leaders of the revolution. The evangelical opposition to state funding for established denominations paved the way for their unlikely alliance with the rationalist elite, which included James Madison and Thomas Jefferson, who advocated for religious freedoms for the dissenters and disestablishment of churches. This evangelical-rationalist coalition came to play a critical role in how the Constitution and the Bill of Rights dealt with church-state relations.

Many of the founding fathers were influenced by ideals of the Enlightenment and were clearly against religious control over the state. Yet they did not want to completely do away with organized religion, which they believed was a key source of moral conduct and social order in a polity that relied on popular sovereignty. Benjamin Franklin, John Jay, and George Washington were disinclined but not necessarily opposed to the continuation of colonial practice of state funding to established churches. This moderate Enlightenment position and pragmatism during the formative years of the Republic made them amenable to the supporters of established religions (religious republicans) and their opponents. Religious republicans mainly included the nonevangelical religious elite and some of the founding fathers, like John Adams. Evangelicals were even more zealous about the importance of Christianity to the moral order, yet they naturally opposed state establishment of religion that favored the traditional denominations, like the Congregationalists, Episcopalians, and the traditional Presbyterians. Among the founding fathers was a key group of Lockean liberals who were more concerned about freedom of conscience than social moral order and pushed for a wall of separation between church and the state. These Lockean liberals included Thomas Jefferson, who drafted the Declaration of Independence (1776), and James Madison, who similarly led the drafting of the Constitution (1787) and the Bill of Rights (1791). The coalitions formed during the drafting and ratification of state constitutions and the federal constitutional convention were fluid. The shifting alliances among Christian republicans, civic republicans, evangelicals, and the Lockean liberals explain the final status of church state separation and freedom of religion in the US Constitution and the Bill of Rights (Sehat 2011).

The Constitution prohibited religious test for office and contained only a symbolic reference to God. This "godless constitution" was problematic for the Christian republicans of the established denominations and the evangelicals. The lack of any reference to freedom of conscience—or any other individual freedoms, for that matter—was problematic for Lockean liberals, like Jefferson and Madison. When the first Congress convened, these concerns with the Constitution were addressed in the First Amendment. Rather than providing the federal government powers to enforce freedoms, as Madison initially preferred, the Bill of Rights limited its powers and paved the way for the nineteenth-century moral establishment (Sehat 2011).

The freedom established by the First Amendment was not *freedom from religion*, as in the French and Turkish republican *laïcité* models, but *freedom of religion*. The founding principles of the Bill of Rights were strongly influenced by the British philosopher John Locke's ideas on the inalienable rights of individuals to life, liberty, and property; the basis of government authority and legitimacy resting on the consent of the governed; and toleration of religious minorities. This ideological dimension was combined with the quintessentially American obsession with government taxation. This meant that mandatory taxes would not be collected for religious functions, an act that could be seen as a violation of the liberty of conscience.

From its very beginning, the core of the American political system was limited government based upon the consent of the governed.

Such a bottom-up approach to nation-state building was quite different from its contemporary French counterpart—and the subsequent Turkish state-formation process—which resulted in stronger, ideological, and more assertive states in their respective polities. The limited US conception of government resulted in a public sphere that gave the civil and the political society a great deal of autonomy from the state. In such a system of *negative freedoms*, the society was ensured autonomy and protection from undue state interference, yet the weakness of the state in enforcing *positive freedoms* would also later lead to discrimination against certain minorities at various levels.[2] The Catholic immigration from Ireland and eastern Europe in the nineteenth century would be one of the early challenges to the limits of pluralism in the liberal American public sphere.

The Protestant De Facto Establishment as Nonsectarianism

The issues surrounding the public education system in the United States illustrate the substance of the public debate and the structure of the prevalent public sphere in the first half of the nineteenth century. The republican elite saw the educational system as a tool for national integration. The public school system was seen as a necessary institution to deal with both urbanization and the changing demographics of the American society. The elite felt it was quite important to "domesticate" the new working class, so that the republic would not descend into populist democracy (Feldman 2006). State-funded public schools were also attractive to the vast majority of Protestant Americans, since such schools were a free alternative to church schools and emphasized moral education. As a result, the public education system appealed both to the ruling elite and the Protestant majority as a tool for promoting a common national identity as well as a place to teach moral values to the younger generation. The particular moral values reflected in the public school system were those that had been deeply engrained in the dominant Protestant culture. The

2. On positive and negative liberty, see Berlin 1958.

nondenominational claim of the public school system in the US was less than satisfactory for Catholics, who saw moral education within the public school system as an imposition of Protestant sectarianism (Feldman 2006).

The reading of the Bible, prayers, and the teaching of morals at public schools were a battleground for the Catholic minority as these practices were nonsectarian, yet clearly Protestant and often anti-Catholic. Protestants preferred students' direct reading of the King James translation of the Bible, which was unacceptable for the Catholic Church. Catholics unsuccessfully tried to receive government funding for private Catholic schools to educate their children. After failing to secure state funding for private schools, Catholics sought to get exemptions from religious instruction and practices in common schools, again unsuccessfully. The next strategy for Catholics would be demanding an end to Bible reading altogether, which would lead to Bible riots in many big cities like Philadelphia and New York with polarized Catholic and Protestant constituencies. The Catholic struggle for exemption coincided with the increasing nativism and economic anxieties of working-class Protestants, who blamed the waves of Irish Catholic immigration in the 1840s and 1850s for their economic misfortunes. Catholic leadership was skillful in utilizing the principles of nonestablishment and religious freedom to challenge the common school practices, and their activism was influenced by a broader Catholic intellectual revival. Catholic priests were assertively challenging the liberal Protestant understanding of individual freedom as autonomy of the self and feasibility of moral education without a creed. For this movement to establish "Catholic control of Catholic institutions," mass, prayer, and devotional experiences were at the core of cultivating a moral and virtuous self (McGreevy 2004, 49–50). In this struggle, Catholics were seeking protection from majoritarianism and were striving to build communal autonomy by utilizing the core principles and mechanisms of the ideal American liberal public sphere.

The Catholic-Protestant battle around public education subsided in 1860s during the Civil War (1861–65). However, another fault line in the public sphere emerged during this time, around serving in the army. Many Irish Catholic men protested against the conscription in what came to be known as draft riots. After the Civil War, the public education struggle once again heated up and culminated in widespread state laws banning funding for private schools and a near success for a nation-wide ban through a constitutional amendment, known as the Blaine Amendment. The anti-Catholic sentiments also significantly shaped the Temperance Movement in the 1870s, which blamed the new wave of Catholic immigrants from Ireland, Germany, Italy, and other European countries for their perceived cultures of heavy drinking. For many Protestant churches alcohol replaced slavery as the next evil to eradicate, and the anti-Catholic sentiments and nativism continued to influence struggles in the public sphere.

Mormonism would also face a similar struggle against an unfriendly social environment during its formative years. Like Catholics, Mormons would be subject to the claim of being "un-American." At the time, being American was defined largely along the lines of Protestant ethos. Nativism and anti-immigration sentiments shaped the state policies toward minority religions and the courts often sided with the state on restrictive policies aimed at assimilating and "Americanizing" the non-Protestants. Aside from the Victorian outrage toward the Mormon practice of polygamy, the hierarchical church governance and the strong tendency of Mormons to vote as a bloc were often invoked by the Protestant majority to question the Mormons' conformity to basic American values and loyalty to basic American political institutions, much as the same accusations were used against the Catholics.

The strategies used by Mormons and Catholics to achieve exemption or accommodation in the American public sphere can best be summarized as minority politics. Although the Catholic Church officially condemned secularism, liberalism, and democracy until the 1960s, Catholic Americans were active in pushing for a more secular public education system that was in their community interest. Despite winning some battles, by the 1920s the Catholics seemed to have lost the larger war in the public sphere: no Catholic exemption in common schools, no public funding for parochial schools, and some state laws for compulsory public education that went as far as criminalizing sending children to private schools instead of public schools (Abrams 2009).[3] Despite this adversarial backdrop, Catholic assimilation in the United States was well on its way by the mid-twentieth century, and was epitomized by the election of Catholic John F. Kennedy to the presidency in 1960. For Mormons, assimilation began after officially discontinuing polygamy in 1890 and gradually easing the church's control of Utah politics during the first half of the twentieth century. Arguably, the nomination of Mormon Mitt Romney as the Republican Party's presidential candidate in 2012 symbolizes a similar turning point for Mormons to that of Catholics with Kennedy's presidency. Both the Catholic and Mormon experience underscore the limits of pluralism in the American liberal public sphere in the nineteenth century and the assimilationist imperatives for the minorities.

Certain parallels to the Turkish case are evident in this overview of the evolution of minority-majority relations in the American public sphere. The imperatives of nation-state building are present even in a liberal public sphere. Likewise, one can argue that the American case in this period also demonstrates elements of republicanism, which could explain the political pressures on the Mormon community. Two cautionary notes are merited here, however. First, the American public sphere during this period was based on strong liberal characteristics, such as the guarantee of individual liberties and religious freedoms from government encroachment. The application of liberal principles were meant for different Protestant denominations that made up the majority of the population. Second, the contours of the public sphere were more society-driven than state-driven. Namely, the national government in nineteenth-century America was significantly weaker than the Turkish government in the early twentieth century and responded to majoritarian impetus from the society. Nevertheless, it is clear that

3. Oregon's 1922 Compulsory Education Act was the culmination of this anti-Catholic public school movement. The law required all school age children to attend only public schools. The Supreme Court struck down the law as unconstitutional in 1925 (*Pierce v. Society of the Sisters*, 268 US 510).

the Mormons were pressured to conform to the common republican values, defined by the mainstream Protestant majority, within the "nondenominational" liberal public sphere.

The LDS Church in the Nineteenth-Century American Public Sphere

In a liberal public sphere, like that of the United States, social groups organize in civil society and compete for influence and power in politics through pressure groups, lobbies, and political parties. Political power is a result of organization in the civil and political realms, and is also reflective of the resources that groups possess and utilize. The most important tools for outsiders as they seek to access these political and social processes are the constitutional protections for freedoms and the principles of liberty and local autonomy. The Mormon strategy during the unfavorable social and political context of the nineteenth century took shape against this backdrop.

A unique combination of the principles of religious liberty and federalism were at the center of the Mormon approach to religion and politics. Accordingly, the Mormons' right to freely exercise their nontraditional religious beliefs and practices would be under the protection of the First Amendment to the US Constitution. Federalism would add another protective layer to the autonomy of Mormon communities to establish their political institutions in parallel to their religious institutions. This early Mormon approach treated the First Amendment's freedom-of-religion clause as an absolute and rejected the application of its separation clause outside of the federal government. Consider the early experiences of the Mormons under the first prophet, Joseph Smith, in Nauvoo, Illinois: the 1840 Nauvoo Charter granted the combined powers of mayor, commander of the military, and president of the church to Joseph Smith. An additional example of the embrace of both religious liberty and federalism can be seen in the failed attempt to create the State of Deseret as well as the theodemocracy that persisted in Utah until 1890. It was only after Utah was admitted to the Union that the church initiated a process of disestablishment.

During the antebellum period, evangelical fervor was at its peak as a result of the Second Great Awakening; there was a movement toward promoting Protestant Christianity as the guiding moral force of the nation. Mormonism developed within the context of the Second Great Awakening, and it quickly became a victim of majority-led social and political discrimination.[4] It was during this time that the Mormons made ready recourse to the free-exercise clause of the First Amendment. Paradoxically, their actions ran counter to the establishment clause when they had the opportunity to create their own government in Nauvoo and later in territorial Utah. Arguably, Mormon-controlled governments were more sensitive to the issue of freedom of religion as a result of their past experience of being a religious minority with unconventional beliefs and an atypical lifestyle. Yet these same unique characteristics also led them to insist on their right to self-govern with minimal interference from the federal government.

In much of the nineteenth century, the LDS Church continued emphasizing the freedom-of-religion clause of the First Amendment, and was reluctant to accept that the nonestablishment principle could be applicable to state or local government. Although the move to disestablish religion was complete at both the national and state level by 1833[5], there were still obstacles for the free-exercise clause in the form of blasphemy laws, religious requirements for office, and religious overtones associated with jury duty. In 1868, the Fourteenth Amendment extended the provisions contained in the Bill of Rights to state governments vis-à-vis their populations. Yet cultural change took time. Indeed, some scholars argue that there was a de facto Protestant establishment in the US until the liberal-rationalist turn in academia and the judiciary during the first two decades of the twentieth century (Kuru 2009). It was not until the 1960s that all of the archaic state

4. For an excellent study that debunks myths about the existence of a complete disestablishment and the freedom of religion related to the First Amendment, see Sehat 2007.

5. The year 1833 is the date when Massachusetts disestablished congregationalism. It was the last state to rid itself of an established religion.

laws restricting the freedoms of conscience and expression on the basis of public order were removed from state constitutions, finally firmly setting the parameters of the current church-state regime.

The Supreme Court would interpret the separation of church and state through several landmark cases. The first time the court interpreted the free exercise clause of the First Amendment was in *Reynolds v. United States* (1879). Faced with antibigamy legislation and the prosecution of polygamy, the Mormons appealed to the Constitution, in which they had a great deal of confidence. They made their arguments on the grounds of religious freedom. The court, however, ruled unanimously that the Constitution protected freedom of belief, not all religious practice. In this case, Mormons would be free to believe what their religion teaches them, but not to engage in any religious practice they wished. Otherwise, the court alleged, everyone would become a law unto themselves and crimes ranging from human sacrifice to bigamy could become exempt from the law.[6] In the wake of this decision, the federal government would enforce the antipolygamy laws with more rigor.

Civil Religion, Legal Secularism, and the Christian Right

Despite the importance of the First Amendment in shaping the understanding of religion and the state, its meaning and implications were anything but clear during much of the nineteenth century. The federal government and the Supreme Court refused to apply it to cases that involved states and individuals on the basis of federalism and dual sovereignty. The court considered and ruled on the *Reynolds v. United States* case because Utah was not a state at the time and federal government alone had jurisdiction. The distinction between states vs. federal territories and freedom of belief vs. freedom of practice were for the most part lost on the public, leading to a discord between the popular constitutionalism of the public and the technical constitutionalism of the legal establishment (Gordon 2010). This gap between the

6. *Reynolds v. United States*, 98 US 145 (1879).

popular and the technical understanding of the law would be gradually bridged in the next six decades after the 1879 *Reynolds v. United States* ruling (Hammond 1999).

The Supreme Court tackled the very question of exemption on the basis of religious freedoms in a series of cases. In *Minersville School District v. Gobitis* (1940), the court rejected an exemption sought by the minority dissidents, Jehovah's Witnesses, from pledging allegiance to the US flag.[7] The court based its ruling on the need for national unity and cohesion during times of war. The lone dissenting voice of Justice Harlan Fiske Stone, who, as a Jew, was also a minority, would signal the subsequent turn the court would take regarding the protection of dissent and minority rights. In fact, a month after rejecting the exemption claim by Jehovah's Witnesses in the *Minersville School District v. Gobitis*, the court would rule in favor of a religious discrimination claim by another member of the Jehovah's Witnesses in Connecticut. In this landmark case, the Supreme Court applied the First Amendment's free-exercise clause to the states.[8] The Supreme Court would eventually emerge as the fundamental protector of civil liberties, especially after *Brown v. Board of Education* (1954).[9]

The nineteenth-century understanding of religious diversity as diversity within Protestant denominations (nonsectarianism) evolved into the early twentieth-century understanding of religious diversity that allowed for more varied religious beliefs. This change would be completed with a move toward recognizing the diversity of and liberty for the nonaffiliated and the nonreligious. The 1965 extension of the conscientious objection exemption from military service to citizens who do not subscribe to a comprehensive religious doctrine yet cite their belief in a Supreme Being as the basis of objection underscores this change.[10]

7. *Minersville School District v. Gobitis*, 310 US 586 (1940).

8. *Cantwell v. Connecticut*, 310 US 296 (1940).

9. *Brown v. Board of Education of Topeka*, 347 US 483 (1954).

10. *United States v. Seeger*, 380 US 163 (1965).

In most of the nineteenth century, religious neutrality as a legal practice and public policy principle was applicable toward different Protestant denominations while minorities, such as Roman Catholics, Jews, and Mormons faced exclusionary practices. A socially acceptable difference was largely within the boundaries of Protestant Christianity: during this time, being different—while still deserving of legal protections—was a privilege accorded mostly to those from different Protestant denominations. This mindset was modified with the construct of the Judeo-Christian heritage, which added the Jews and the Catholics as religious minorities worthy of inclusion in the mainstream. This made good political sense during the early phases of the Cold War in the fight against what many conservatives defined as godless communism. The new civil religion would be a collection of generic religious symbols that would offer a sacred basis to American patriotism. In 1954, the Pledge of Allegiance incorporated "one nation under God," giving a civic patriotic ritual a semireligious basis. At the height of this monotheistic civil religion, President Dwight Eisenhower famously said that "our form of government has no sense unless it is founded in a deeply felt religious faith, and I don't care what it is."[11] Similarly, in 1952, the Supreme Court declared that "we are religious people whose institutions presuppose a Supreme Being."[12] This was an important turn from the 1892 characterization by the same court of the United States as a "Christian nation."[13] In 1956, Congress would officially declare "In God We Trust" as the national motto. These shifts were not only related to Eisenhower's personal relationship with popular evangelical preacher Billy Graham, but were also a byproduct of the emerging Christian-capitalist alliance in reaction to Roosevelt's New Deal policies (Kruse 2015). Energized by the Cold War, this conservative religious-business alliance

11. Address at the Freedoms Foundation, Waldorf-Astoria, New York City, New York, December 22, 1952. https://www.eisenhower.archives.gov/all_about_ike/quotes.html.

12. *Zorach v. Clauson*, 343 US 306 (1952).

13. *Church of the Holy Trinity vs. United States*, 143 US 457 (1892).

would rigorously challenge the liberal turn in the judiciary and the intelligentsia.

As the national ideology moved toward a more inclusive form of Judeo-Christianity, the Mormons were already securing their place in this patriotic mainstream by diligently participating in World War II and then doing their duty in the fight against what the thirteenth president of the church, Ezra Taft Benson, called "evil communism."[14] Benson had served as the secretary of agriculture for both Eisenhower administrations and was also closely involved with the ultraconservative anticommunist John Birch Society in the 1960s and 1970s, prior to his church presidency. He is reported to have addressed the participants of the semiannual LDS Church General Conference in 1961 with the admonition that "no true Latter-day Saint, and no true American, can be a socialist or a communist, or support programs leading in that direction" (Fox 2006, 1–2).

As the public discourse was becoming more religious and moving toward making the national ideology more inclusive by using generic religious symbolism and discourse, there was also an emerging countermovement. This discontent was expressed by legal secularism, which wanted to disentangle religion altogether from government. This was different from the more elitist secularist movement of the late nineteenth and early twentieth centuries, which had been more direct in its rejection of religion and embracing of modernity and science. Legal secularism was more sophisticated, as it acknowledged that people could be religious, but held that the government needed to be secular; this push for secular government was especially important given the increasing diversity of the nation (Feldman 2006).

The secular turn in Supreme Court decisions—a shift that would overturn some aspects of the civil religion—became apparent in the 1960s. The court found school prayer[15] and reading the Bible as part

14. Ezra Taft Benson, "Prepare Yourself for the Great Day of the Lord," https://www.lds.org/new-era/1982/05/prepare-yourself-for-the-great-day-of-the-lord?lang=eng

15. *Engel v. Vitale*, 370 US 421 (1962).

of the public school curriculum to be unconstitutional.[16] In *Lemon v. Kurtzman* (1971), the court required legislation to have secular reasoning to obviate the "entanglement of church and state."[17] Accordingly, the constitutionality of legislation concerning religion depended on criteria outlined by the court in this ruling, criteria that came to be known as the "lemon test."

A second countertrend in response to the more inclusive civil religion came from conservatives. Conservatives became uneasy with what they perceived to be the overly generic and almost empty rhetoric associated with the changes to the civil religion and the newly emerging legal secularism. The rise of liberal popular culture, the civil rights movement, and the legalization of abortion were additional grievances fueling the subsequent rise of the Christian Right, supporters of which felt that the country that they once knew was eroding under their feet. The LDS Church in this period would generally side with the conservative bloc, but was also less activist overall and more selective with respect to its involvement in particular issues. This distance was due to the continued revelation and presence of other authoritative sources in Mormonism besides the Bible. This makes the Mormon doctrine both less rigid than its evangelical counterparts, but also brings more skepticism toward Mormons' claim to being a Christian church in the eyes of the evangelicals. Chapter 7 will discuss these issues and church policies in more detail. First, however, a discussion of the relevant aspects of Mormon doctrine will provide context for understanding how the Mormons made sense of the American political system and their position as a religious minority in that system.

Mormon Doctrine on the State and Patriotism

The church teachings on the nature of an ideal political regime reveals two mindsets. On the one hand, the basic articles of the Mormon faith emphasize the importance of freedom of religion and

16. *Abington Township School District v. Schempp*, 374 US 203 (1963).
17. *Lemon v. Kurtzman*, 403 US 602 (1971).

conscience, for Mormons and non-Mormons alike, and characterize Mormons as law-abiding citizens, respectful of the law of the land (even if the law prohibits proselytizing).[18] On the other hand, the raison d'être of Mormonism is its millennial outlook. As the church's proper name, The Church of Jesus Christ of Latter-day Saints, suggests, Mormonism claims to be a present-day restoration of the true Christian Church in order to prepare the world for the Second Coming of Christ and his personal rule during the millennial era.[19] The Mormons thus call themselves Latter-day Saints in order to distinguish themselves from earlier saints. There is a strong emphasis on the special mission of the Latter-day Saints to create a virtuous community, a safe haven, and a new Zion in America for the Kingdom of God to be built on this earth, as stated by President Joseph F. Smith: "Without doubt the time will ultimately come when every man-made institution will be arrayed against the Church and kingdom of God-the only institution of divine origin on the earth, and the only institution that will stand and remain unmoved, while all others will fall, disintegrate, and decay" (Bergara 2007, 245).

18. Joseph Smith, "The Articles of Faith of The Church of Jesus Christ of Latter-day Saints," *Times and Seasons*, March 1, 1842.

19. The Mormon thought on millennialism evolved over time and carries elements of premillennialism and postmillennialism. During the very early years, in the 1830s, Mormons believed the return of Christ was imminent and identified Independence, Missouri, on the American frontier, as the new Zion—the gathering place and the center of the Kingdom of God. They interpreted the hostilities and persecution as signs of the latter days. Since this immediate anticipation did not materialize, the leadership identified Utah territories as the gathering place. An anticipation of an apocalyptic confrontation between the Church and the federal government over polygamy continued until the practice was officially abandoned in 1890. After the admission of Utah to the union, the literal understanding of Zion gave way to more symbolic interpretations and the LDS doctrine turned more postmillennialist, believing that the Second Coming will be after the Kingdom of God is established on earth. This requires more of an active waiting during which the world is prepared for the return of Christ and necessary institutions are built in preparation for the millennium through missionary and temple work.

Mormons believe that prior to the Second Coming of Christ in the millennium, every nation or tribe must have heard the Mormon message and the Zion in the US will be the safest place to gather and take refuge. With respect to politics, there are two important points among these beliefs. First is the expectation that governments around the world are going to fail to sustain a just, virtuous, and peaceful order in the face of moral decay and violent conflicts. Second is the answer to this chaos: the Mormon alternative with a system of laws, government, and organizations will fill in the void with great vigor and legitimacy. According to Mormon theology, the Kingdom of God is believed to be righteous and consists of correct principles. There will be freedom of conscience, albeit a very limited one, since God will dictate matters for the welfare of His people and for the establishment of a righteous kingdom.[20]

Mormonism incorporates elements of restorationism, covenantalism, and dispensationalism, resulting in a unique eschatology that lends itself to a Christian American patriotism.[21] The millennial

20. An 1848 official statement defines the limits of freedom as follows: "The Kingdom of God consists in correct principles; and it mattereth not what a man's religious faith is whether he be a Presbyterian, or a Methodist, or a Baptist, or a Latter-day Saint, or 'Mormon', or a Campbellite, or a Catholic, or Episcopalian, or a Mohammedan, or even pagan or anything else, if he will bow the knee and with his tongue confess that Jesus is a Christ, and will support good and wholesome laws for the regulation of society, we hail him as a brother, and will stand by him while he stands by us in these things; for every man's religious faith is a matter between his own soul and his God alone; but if he shall deny the Jesus, if he shall curse God, if he shall indulge in debauchery, and drunkenness, and crime; if he shall lie and swear and steal; if he shall take the name of the great God in vain, and commit all matter of abominations, he shall have no place in our midst, for we have long sought to find a people that will work righteousness, that will distribute justice equally, that will acknowledge God and all their ways, that will regard those sacred laws and ordinances, which are recorded in that sacred book called the Bible, which we verily believe and which we proclaim to the ends of the earth" (Bergera 2007, 246–47).

21. Dispensationalism divides the history into distinctive epochs ("dispensations") each with different plans of salvation, differentiates between the Jews of Israel and the Christian church, and applies biblical prophecies separately. This was

outlook in Mormon theology provides a particular lens through which to view American history; this interpretation of events supports Mormon patriotism. The church sees the US Constitution as a special document that was inspired by God. Religiously based American exceptionalism attributing special meanings to historical events are not unique to the LDS Church. Puritans, dating to the earliest settlements in seventeenth-century America, had attached such meanings to the existence of America or to particular events in American history. The new land was not just a place to exercise religious freedoms, but also a new beginning, much like the biblical story of exodus and the reaching to a promised land, a new Israel. The new world would not be an ordinary place, but a city on a hill in the New Testament image. To realize this ideal, Puritans emphasized strong social mores and discipline to establish order and promoted civic engagement to build community. Even though the Puritan settlers had emancipated themselves from the religious persecution of the old world, the establishment of their Congregational Church was in no way a model for individual religious liberty. The Methodist and Baptist preachers challenged the role of the established clergy and church-state relations with a revolutionary idea of validity of individual spiritual experience for salvation and the need for being born again. The populism and evangelism of the First Great Awakening in the seventeenth century would not only unleash a wave of religious revival in colonial America, but also create a popular foundation for rejecting state establishment of a particular church and upholding individuals' right to religious

---

a radical departure from the Covenantalism of the mainline churches, such as the Presbyterian and Methodist, which maintained that promise was fulfilled and passed onto the Christian church after Jesus. The dispensational method of biblical interpretation emerged from the nineteenth-century conservative evangelical Plymouth Brethren movement in England and was popularized by the teachings of the Anglican priest John Nelson Darby. Even though Darby and Joseph Smith were contemporaries, they developed their ideas independently of each other and with different implications for American Christians, restoration of Jewish rule in Israel, and the Second Coming (Yorgason 2016).

liberty. Puritanism, pluralism, populism, and evangelicalism were the key formative forces of religion in the colonial and early Republican America (Fowler et al. 2010). The intersection of the Puritans' covenant theology, the ethos of self-governance and congregationalism, and the social contract theory that called for a limited government laid the foundations for the liberal public sphere in the US. One can argue that these religious and popular forces have been pervasive in American political culture to this day, with admittedly more secular tones since the turn of the twentieth century, feeding into different manifestations of American exceptionalism and civil religion.

American patriotism is very much shaped by a belief in the unique history of the political system of the US, including the Constitution, the system of checks and balances in its political system, and the Bill of Rights. Manifest Destiny, the fight against communism, and the promotion of liberty and democracy abroad have all been used as a justification by the government for American foreign involvement with recourse to a sense of America's special historical mission. Despite—or perhaps because of—their unsettling historical experience with the government and people of the US, contemporary Mormons are in general very patriotic Americans, and they identify very strongly with America's special role in the world.[22] One can argue that much of Mormon history revolves around questions of Mormon loyalty to the US, and the "Americanness" of the Mormon people. Even today, the church strives to promote its signature activities, such as the Mormon Tabernacle Choir and the Mormon Helping Hands, as recognizable national brands in service of Americans and American values. Many Mormons carry their ethos of serving for their church to serving their countries and are well represented in the country's capital.[23]

22. In a 2008 survey, 72 percent of Mormons agreed that the "US has a special role in world affairs" ahead of all other American religious groups in the study (National Survey of Religion and Politics, 2008, University of Akron, cited in Guth 2012, 78).

23. Dan Gilgoff, "With or without Romney, DC a Surprising Mormon Stronghold," CNN Belief Blog, May 12, 2012, http://religion.blogs.cnn.com/2012/05/12/hfr-with-or-without-romney-d-c-a-surprising-mormon-stronghold/.

Mormons are closer to the American mainstream public culture than ever, so their presence in government and civil service should not be surprising. Many Christians also carry similar convictions about American exceptionalism. What is unique about the LDS Church, however, is that church teachings *sacralize* this patriotism, thereby offering a truly American religious outlook.[24] For Mormons, the civil religion has a central place in church theology.[25]

The Mormon Story and the American Polity

The Book of Mormon is based on the story of ancient tribes in Central America whom Mormons believe migrated from Jerusalem, carrying with them the Old Testament teachings. The Book of Mormon is essentially the biblical work as recorded by an American prophet named Mormon, finished and buried as gold plates by his son Moroni. Moroni later appeared to Joseph Smith and gave him the golden plates, and Smith then translated the biblical work into English. In the Mormon version of the Christian story, Jesus appeared in the New World to teach the Gospel after the crucifixion and resurrection. Mormons

24. Mormon theology directly addresses some of the tensions between historical Christianity and modernity. It rejects the doctrine of original sin, celebrating human free will and intelligence and embracing unlimited human potential and progression. In that sense, there is no categorical difference between man and God; it is a matter of perfection and intelligence. As Church President Lorenzo Snow put it, "As man now is, God once was; as God now is, man may be." The Mormon doctrine also radically solves the issue of the nature of God and the Trinity. God is believed to have a body with flesh and bones, and the three personages of the Trinity are separate beings. Compared to the centuries-old doctrinal debates in Christianity, this is a very radical position, devoid of nuance or complexity. In a way, the Mormon doctrine offers a more straightforward, rational, and simple solution to vexing theological questions as a result of its continued revelations and prophethood. The church is historically and scripturally American, in line with the American dream (of potential growth and progress with disciplined work) and the American outlook (a material-rational explanation for many intricate theological issues).

25. For an analysis of the theology and outlook to make this connection, see Givens 2004, 1–58.

believe the Second Coming will also occur in the new Zion on the American continent when the millennial reign begins. One can thus easily see the special place of America in the Mormon plan for salvation. Likewise, the formation of the US was inspired by God in order to pave the way for the restoration of the gospel in the latter days. The Book of Mormon describes the promised land as

> . . . choice above all other lands, which the Lord God had preserved for a righteous people . . . and whatsoever nation shall possess it shall be free from bondage, . . . captivity, and from all other nations under heaven, if they will but serve the God of the land, who is Jesus Christ.[26]

The US Constitution—especially the First Amendment—had a special significance for the new religion, allowing it to form and flourish in face of enemies and challenges. In an 1839 testimony from the Liberty Jail in Missouri, Joseph Smith maintained:

> The Constitution of the United States is a glorious standard; it is founded on the wisdom of God. It is a heavenly banner; it is to all those who are privileged with the sweets of its liberty, like the cooling shades and refreshing waters of a great rock in a thirsty and weary land. It is like a great tree under whose branches men from every clime can be shielded from the burning rays of the sun. (Bergera 2007, 98–99)

Even during the conflict between the federal government and Utah in the latter part of the nineteenth century, the church did not lose its faith in the Constitution; rather, church leaders saw themselves in a unique and critical position to defend the higher constitutional principles. The third church president, John Taylor, warned:

> We have rights under the Constitution, and however much these may be denied to us, it is still our bounden duty to contend for them, not only in behalf of ourselves, but for all our fellow citizens

26. Esther 2:7; 12, *Book of Mormon*, 1981.

> and for our prosperity, and for humanity generally throughout the world. Were we do less than this, we would fail in performing the mission assigned to us, and be recreant to the high trust which God has reposed in us. (Bergera 2007, 98)

A common belief among Mormons dating to the early days of church history is that a time will come when the Constitution will be in danger of complete destruction. According to Joseph Smith, the Constitution would be so weakened that it "would hang as if by a thread," and the Elders of the Church would save the Constitution from utter destruction; this is also known as the "White Horse Prophecy." Mormons of different generations have interpreted this prophecy differently. The first Mormons, still residing on the East Coast, anticipated the Civil War and expected to play crucial roles in the resolution of the conflict. The earlier Utah generation saw the tension between the federal government and the Mormons over the constitutional provisions of freedom of religion and federalism as an indication of larger dangers to the existence of the Constitution. Some in the current generation see the debates on same-sex marriage, prayer in public schools, and religious symbols in public as the new threat to the basic principles of the Constitution and the nation's integrity. The White Horse Prophecy in which the Constitution is saved only by the efforts of the church provides Mormons with a source of motivation for their involvement in public issues. It also helps believers integrate this activism in their religious narrative, offering a form of meaning creation for the members (Bringhurst 2008). In its formal messaging the church keeps such subjective accounts out of their public discourse. This is a good example of the constraints of the public sphere that push religious groups to adopt more rational language in their public representations.

Speculation regarding the White Horse Prophecy gained momentum around 2006, when Mitt Romney competed in the Republican Party's presidential primaries.[27] An independent scholar of Mormon-

27. "Media Focus on Romney's Faith—and Underwear," *Sunstone*, December 2006, 74–75.

ism, Newell Bringhurst (2008), identified ten Mormons who have run for the presidency since Joseph Smith declared his candidacy in 1843. Their political ideology ranged from far-right to very liberal left, and they ran on Democratic, Republican, and third-party tickets. Even for candidates who were not active members of the church, their Mormon background often hurt them, as was the case with candidate Morris King "Mo" Udall in 1976 and the black vote. Mitt Romney was the first Mormon nominee on a major party ticket. He initially chose not to address the issue of his religion, hoping to prevent his campaign from being defined by it; as the campaign wore on, Romney ended up addressing the issue in a similar fashion to how John F. Kennedy had spoken of his Catholicism. Romney assured Americans of his loyalty to the nation without lessening his commitment to his religion. His message carried strong elements of American patriotism, emphasized religious liberty, and conveyed a conservative outlook on the role of religion in public life.[28] Moreover, even the church's official position on the issue of public manifestations of religious beliefs and practices is comparable to other conservative groups in the US. For example, a 1990 church news release held that religion should have an honorable place in the public life of the nation, and "the name of Almighty God" should have a sacred use in its public expressions.[29] The church has also stated that, in order to ensure the protection of and respect for "the spiritual and religious heritage" of the nation, it may be necessary to resist "the forces that would transform the public position of the United States from the constitutional position of neutrality to a position of hostility toward religion."[30]

Although Mitt Romney does not represent the church as an institution, his ideas about the role of religion in the public sphere are

28. For a transcript of his speech at the George Bush Presidential Library in College Station, Texas, see "Transcript: Mitt Romney's Faith Speech," NPR News, December 6, 2007, http://www.npr.org/tablet/#story/?storyId=16969460, April 24, 2011.

29. Church News, October 27, 1990, cited in Bergera 2007, 83.

30. Church News, March 17, 1979, cited in Bergera 2007, 84.

shared by many other Mormons. Mitt Romney and other prominent Mormon politicians from the Republic Party, such as Utah Senator Bob Bennett, opposed Donald Trump's candidacy. Even after Trump secured the party's nomination, Evan McMullin, an independent Mormon from Utah, emerged as an alternative to those Mormon conservatives who rejected Trump's populist, anti-immigration platform. The populist anger directed toward minorities reminded many Mormons of their painful historical experience as a persecuted minority religion and made them feel the need to uphold the constitutional protections.

The contemporary Mormon outlook is marked by an idealism rooted in the American experience. From this perspective the Constitution of the US is not only uniquely attractive to and beneficial for Americans, but it carries some universal appeal and should be extended "for the rights and protection of all mankind."[31] One of the reasons for the almost-identical missionary work carried out by Mormons in vastly different corners of the world is this confident faith in "the American way." It would be simplistic to reduce Mormon global presence to promotion of Americanism, yet the clean-cut, idealistic Mormon missionaries in over 145 countries comes very close to the federally funded Peace Corps in representing American ways of life and commitment to service abroad. This combination of patriotism and a service mentality makes Mormons natural recruits for most government programs and professions. These circumstances have even led some Mormon skeptics to contend that the LDS Church encourages its members, especially returned missionaries, to work for the government in the Foreign Service and intelligence positions to influence and gradually take over the American government.[32] Whether motivated by religious, patriotic, or professional reasons, Mormons are well represented—if not overrepresented—in American government

31. LDS First Presidency message, December 15, 1969, cited in Bergera 2007, 97–98.

32. See, for example, Heinerman and Shupe 1985.

and maintain strong professional networks and solidarity bound by religious ties.[33]

In part, Mormon history is the story of a fringe religious community that had been driven toward the remote American wilderness, then transformed into a mainstream faith filled with thriving professionals with access to centers of power and influence. Mormons have gone from the bearded, polygamous people who tried to establish a theocratic political system with a closed communal economy to clean-shaven, striving, middle-class Americans who believe in the separation of church and state, take part in the two-party system, thrive in Wall Street capitalism, and search for a legitimate place in mainstream society.

How did the Mormon transformation take place? The Mormon political identity was transformed by the convergence of two essentially conflicting forces in American political history: political liberalism and the Protestant moral establishment. Although the extent and limits of the constitutional principle of separation of church and state have been the subject of much debate since the founding of the US, one thing was clearly unacceptable inside the American system of government: theocracy or politics under the shadow of a church hierarchy. A second common point of agreement between the liberals and conservatives was that polygamy was un-American, and that American political institutions would not tolerate such lifestyles. All three branches of government took steps to prohibit polygamy: Congress through legislation that outlawed polygamy and punished the LDS Church, the federal government through federal appointees who implemented the federal laws regarding polygamy, and the Supreme Court through upholding related legislation and in its interpretation of the limits to the First Amendment.

33. Dan Gilgoff, "With or without Romney, DC a Surprising Mormon Stronghold," CNN Belief Blog, May 12, 2012, http://religion.blogs.cnn.com/2012/05/12/hfr-with-or-without-romney-d-c-a-surprising-mormon-stronghold/.

Today, the more limited but apparent suspicion toward Mormons still reflects this combination of liberal and conservative forces (Stack 2008). Many liberals are reluctant to trust a hierarchical church with what they see as continuing authoritarian and secretive practices against its members. In particular, the way disciplinary councils have been employed against liberal intellectuals and nonconforming members is especially troubling for liberal critics. Many conservatives are still reluctant to accept Mormons as (Protestant) Christians, despite the efforts of the LDS Church to minimize the discussion of unique Mormon doctrines and emphasize the church's Christian roots and practices.

Conclusion

In the nineteenth and early twentieth centuries, Mormons, like other religious minorities in the US, experienced a certain level of societal and political discrimination. Mormons today are more integrated into American society and have largely benefited from the opportunities provided by the liberal public sphere in the US. Thus, Mormons have become very active in government institutions, such as the US Department of State, the military, and the intelligence community, as well as in American political society and civil society.

The evolution of the public sphere in the US was closely related to minority-majority relations, as well as to public discussions on the source of public morality and patriotism. This is quite different from Turkish public sphere where the key struggle was primarily between the state and the society, rather than between different sectors of the society. Both the Mormons and the Gülen movement have very closely identified their religious traditions with their respective national stories and symbols. In spite of this, both groups would find their loyalty to the nation called into question. Chapter 5 will analyze this interesting contradiction and discuss Mormon strategies to survive, transform, and flourish in the American public sphere.

PART TWO

Religion and Politics

4

The Gülen Movement and Politics of Religious Activism in Turkey

As demonstrated in chapter 2, religion in the Turkish public sphere has been a controversial issue since the establishment of the Republic in 1923. A tension existed between the secular state and the religious sectors of the society under the Kemalist model. The containment policy of the state toward religious groups led them in the direction of alienation and paradoxical strategies of penetration into the state apparatus and the political system. By 2011 the Gülen movement's network, organizations, and influence reached its zenith, making it one of the most powerful Islamic movements in Turkey, with a significant global presence in other parts of the world. The movement's hesitance to declare a transparent public identity, on the one hand, and pioneering an activist role in promoting public dialogue, on the other hand, is an instructive case for uncovering the relationship between religious groups and a republican public sphere.

This chapter starts with an anecdote of the movement's approach to activism and authority as a civil society organization. Subsequently, it will discuss Fethullah Gülen's evolving views on the ideal form of government and state-society relations. The rest of the chapter will trace the stages of the movement's development in parallel to its forms of engagement with politics, and conclude with an account of the impact of the structure of the public sphere over the movement's evolving public strategy.

"Islamic" Civil Society Actors

Since its founding, the status of the Gülen movement in the Turkish public sphere had remained ambiguous. For one thing, it avoided a publicly declared formal identity or officially recorded status. Clustered around private organizations, such as foundations, schools, and media outlets, it functioned through personal and social networks. However, it also became one of the most talked about, enigmatic, lauded, feared, and, hence, controversial public groups in Turkey.

A quick description of the Gülen movement's attitude toward politics would be "cautious engagement." During most of its existence, it remained conflict-averse and preferred engagement to withdrawal from public life or to confrontation with the state even under the strong limitations it imposed on the movement's functions and institutions.[1] From the beginning Fethullah Gülen advised his associates to develop cordial ties and cultivate trust with bureaucrats, politicians, and community leaders while not committing political support or becoming financially dependent. This attitude was meant to protect the burgeoning movement's functions and organizations from state repression and stemmed from a firm belief that if the statesmen and political leaders were well informed about the positive contributions of the movement in the areas of education, trade, and social integration, they would appreciate their service to their country. This cautionary approach is a stark contrast to some other religious groups, who are more vocal about their political activism and challenges to established authorities and the status quo. The cautious engagement attitude is responsible for the movement's reluctance to endorse civil disobedience and contentious politics. As an example, Gülen's surprising critique of the Gaza Flotilla and the Mavi Marmara incident in 2010 was instructive for drawing the line between what one may call an "assertive/contentious civil society activism" of some Islamist

1. For an analysis of the engagement between Islamic movements and the Turkish state, see Turam 2007.

groups in Turkey and the "nonconfrontational/accomodationist civil society" modus operandi of the Gülen movement.

"Palestine is our destination, humanitarian aid is our load" was the slogan used by the peace activists to describe the mission of the Gaza Flotilla of 2010. Seeing this as an attempt to break the naval blockade imposed on Gaza since 2007, Israeli special forces seized the passenger ship in the international waters and diverted its route to an Israeli port in Ashdot. Although the operation was successful in keeping the blockade intact, Israel received strong condemnation for the operation's toll: nine killed, and dozens injured.[2] All of the dead were Turkish citizens; among them was also a dual US citizen. This incident ended up adding fuel to the already tense relations between Turkey and Israel, two longtime US allies in the Middle East.[3] Israeli authorities disputed the peaceful nature of at least some of the organizers and participants, especially the Humanitarian Aid Foundation (IHH) of Turkey, arguing that they had links with Hamas. IHH is considered a legitimate charity by the Turkish government and is not on the US State Department list of terrorist organizations. IHH rejected the allegations and blamed Israel for brutally murdering civilians whose only goal was to alleviate the suffering of the Gaza people living under the restrictions imposed by the Israeli blockade. One thing in the IHH discourse was striking: the double strategy of appropriating inclusive secular/humanist language to describe the mission of the flotilla and Islamic language in public demonstrations. The IHH chairman pointed to the diverse background of participants from different religions, nationalities, ideologies, and professions, emphasizing that the aid flotilla was a humanitarian mission, rather than an exclusively Islamic one. The organizers also played down their political motivations, maintaining that IHH was an independent Non-Governmental Organization (NGO). A close examination of the

2. "Deadly Israeli Raid Draws Condemnation," *New York Times*, June 1, 2010.

3. "After Flotilla Raid, US Is Torn between Allies," *New York Times*, June 2, 2010.

slogans and symbols used by the protesters in this event reveals that religion was fused with humanism and nationalism.

As the Turkish public was rallying around the flag, mourning for the dead with heightened emotions, a different, surprising interpretation of the incident came from Pennsylvania. In an interview published by the *Wall Street Journal*, Gülen—who has resided in the US since 1999—carefully criticized the approach taken by the peace activists and expressed his disapproval of the confrontation.[4] He went as far as suggesting that the organizers should have secured the approval of the Israeli authorities or worked with them rather than pushing the two US allies onto very thin ice. He did not condone the way Israeli forces handled the situation, but, at the cost of going against a very strong current in Turkey, he attempted to come forward with the unpopular task of self-reflection. In response, he received a great deal of critique from some of Turkey's Islamists, who saw his reading of events as that of an outsider not understanding how the process worked before the unfortunate confrontation.[5]

The puzzling difference between two civil society groups, IHH and the Gülen movement, both carrying some sort of Islamic identity can be explained by two main factors. One is the ideology or the worldview of the two groups, which is a key factor in understanding variation of group strategies in the same public sphere. The Gülen movement emerged as a service-based civil society network that emphasized building educational, civic, cultural, and humanitarian organizations rather than political agitation against Turkey's staunchly secular establishment at the time. Gülen deliberately distanced himself from political Islam's worldview, as well as the Islamist parties and identity movements, which IHH has been part of. Islamic movements in Turkey—and across the Muslim world for that matter—have been pretty diverse in their goals, strategies, and functions. Mr. Gülen

4. "Reclusive Turkish Imam Criticizes Gaza Flotilla," *Wall Street Journal*, June 4, 2010.

5. Hakan Albayrak, "Hocaefendi'ye Acik Mektup" (Open Letter to Hocaefendi [Fethullah Gülen]), *Yeni Safak*, October 5, 2010.

had surprised the Turkish public before, during some other critical junctions. When the coalition government led by the Islamist Welfare Party was forced to resign in 1997, Mr. Gülen publicly encouraged the leadership of the ruling party to be responsible enough to resign rather than resist an obviously undemocratic demand by the military.[6] This was a total shock to most Islamic groups, as they were preparing for an enduring struggle against the authoritarian and draconian measures proposed by Turkey's National Security Council, which was dominated by the military at the time.

Turkey underwent a series of significant legal reforms after the 1997 military intervention, to reform its political system under the European Union membership requirements, and, by most accounts, it was a freer and more democratic country by the end of 2010.[7] Both the Gülen movement and the IHH benefited from the expansion of civil liberties and the strengthening of the autonomy of the civil society vis-à-vis the state during this process. IHH became one of the biggest Islamic charities in Turkey, providing humanitarian aid worldwide, from Palestine to Haiti. The Gülen movement also achieved greater access to power and a greater level of institution building—for example, of business associations, federations, private schools, hospitals, and civic platforms.

However, it is clear that the IHH and the Gülen movement have different understandings of the role of the civil society. IHH wants to see a civil society that is autonomous from the state, can have mutually beneficial relations with political groups, and can be assertive of its religious identity. The Gülen movement emphasizes broader goals of contributing to the well-being of Turkey as a nation, supporting

6. Fethullah Gülen's interview with Yalcin Dogan on Kanal D TV, April 16, 1997.

7. In its annual report in 2011 the Freedom House generally praised the political, economic, legal, and constitutional reforms enacted under the AKP governments since 2002, while raising critical questions about the due process in the ongoing Ergenekon investigations and limitations on Kurdish cultural and political rights (https://freedomhouse.org/report/freedom-world/2011/turkey).

broader issues of human rights and democracy, and promoting a moderate, benign, modern, and less confrontational face for its Islamic identity. This philosophical difference is key in making sense of the different reactions witnessed in light of the Gaza flotilla raid. IHH does not only believe in peace but also approves of civil disobedience or nonconventional means of challenging authorities and the status quo. If this requires confrontation, that is seen as an acceptable consequence. In the end, the regrettable loss of life was the reason why the organizers or their cause enjoyed so much publicity. There are even indications that they may have achieved a certain level of success in bringing the Gaza blockade to the attention of the world public as an unproductive and untenable policy with clear negative humanitarian consequences.

The Gülen movement also emphasizes peace and is aware of the precarious humanitarian conditions in Gaza, yet starkly differs in its proposed method to alleviate it. The movement affiliates tend to be pacifists but not necessarily activists. The humanitarian aid agency associated with the Gülen movement, *Kimse Yok mu*, was reported to have delivered aid to Gaza, but under the permission and guidelines offered by the Israeli government.[8] Gülen preferred coordination between governments and civil society organizations and tried to minimize confrontation between them. He was apparently disturbed by some of the footage released by the Israeli Defense Forces (IDF), where activists were resisting against the Israeli commandos on the deck of the ship before it was seized (the "ugly scene"). This is not unlike when he asked his followers to keep off the streets and encouraged female college students not to prefer their headscarf to their education when they had to choose between the two in the aftermath of the February, 1997 "soft" coup (Gülen 2007, 162–65).[9]

8. "Reclusive Turkish Imam Criticizes Gaza Flotilla," *Wall Street Journal*, June 4, 2010.

9. Gürbüz 2007 reads this as a deliberate strategy of nonviolent "moral opposition."

Evidently, there is diversity when it comes to religious groups and their modes and levels of public activism. The Gülen movement has differentiated itself from other Islamic groups that utilize religion more openly for political mobilization and agitation. As chapter 7 will demonstrate, the LDS Church has also acted similarly to the Gülen movement in terms of their modes and levels of political activism, compared to the Christian Right. Similarity in this key aspect is important to reemphasize here, as this constitutes the basis of the "comparability" of the two cases under study in this book; how similar philosophies take shape under different contexts is the main purpose of this study. The political context, then, is key in understanding social movements, their public identities, and organizational and discursive strategies. This chapter will now proceed to situate the Gülen movement in the republican Turkish public sphere.

Organizational Profile of the Movement

The Gülen movement started as a restorationist community initiative at the Turkish periphery in the early 1970s and experienced a tremendous growth spurt and transformation in the 1990s and 2000s. The bulk of the service activities remained locally based in their nature, but the direction by the movement elders and the coordination between its participants made it a transnational movement with a considerable global presence. At the height of its global reach in 2010, there were more than 1,000 schools operated by the movement in more than 100 countries. Adding cultural centers and business associations active in countries without movement schools, the total number of countries where the movement was active approached 150.[10]

The movement combines elements of a congregational organizational structure with concentric circles of activism. There is a core cadre of devotees around Gülen who have functioned as transmitters of

10. See Ergil 2010 for a worldwide list of schools and cultural centers affiliated with the movement. See also Turgut 2010 and Knowlton 2010 for a journalistic account.

his ideals, passing along the know-how to others for building schools, opening cultural centers, and teaching language courses. They also shaped movement's relations with other civil society actors, politicians, and governments. Built primarily on a face-to-face form of interaction, the movement leadership relied on frequent trips and mobility to link the outer concentric circles of its participants to the core. Such coordination contributed to the effectiveness of the movement, making it a coherent and collective entity, while the movement's everyday activities and projects have been run by associates in the outer circles. The idea of volunteering and committing one's time, talent, and money plays a key role in the activities of the group. The estimates of the size of the movement participants at the peak of its popularity was eight to ten million (Ebaugh 2009, 4).

Most Islamic movements in Turkey are rooted in the Sufi tradition. This is not only an intellectual and spiritual affinity, but also an informal continuation of the well-established Sufi orders and networks during the Ottoman Empire. Shortly after the Republic of Turkey replaced the Ottoman Empire, the state dissolved the Sufi orders, closed down their lodges, and formally banned them in 1925. Most of these orders initially went underground and later continued informally around mosques and private residences. Thanks to modernization and the resulting social change, especially urbanization, networks of urban professionals, intellectuals, and students emerged as a modern alternative to the traditional role of the Sufi networks, such as offering a sense of community, belonging, and social purpose. The failure of the state to sufficiently integrate individuals through institutional networks and infrastructure and address economic and social inequalities had created a vacuum during Turkey's modernization process (Özdalga 2005, 433). The new Islamic movements were well positioned to fill in this vacuum. They are colloquially known as *cemaatler* (communities), and they became active in a whole host of public sectors and issues, such as education, publishing, and the print media. At first, they offered an alternative to the officially sanctioned form of modernity, which largely excluded their traditional values.[11] Reading circles, social networks, and civic institutions constituted a form of counterpublic, and an alternative form of modernity. Later on, the Sufi networks adapted to the imperatives of modern polities by becoming suppliers of social services, including health care, relief and humanitarian aid, and human rights advocacy.

Islamic movements have been very flexible and pragmatic in terms of their discursive and organizational strategies. Turkey's exclusionary republican public sphere was a key factor for the transformation of the traditional popular Sufi networks into nebulous private institutions and networks. The Gülen movement's decision to remain informal and not to claim any collective ownership of property or institutions can be seen as a form of necessity, survival instinct, or an "organizational strategy" (Agai 2005). As Turkey underwent a process of economic and political liberalization between 2003 and 2011, the civil society enjoyed more autonomy vis-à-vis the state. During this period, the Gülen movement became more assertive thanks to this structural change, but it also faced the imperative to become more transparent as state control over its organization eased. During its first four decades, between 1970 and 2010, the movement was quite shrewd in reading the "logic" and "spirit" of the political contexts under which it operated. This helped the movement to survive and grow under adversity, faced with constant state pressure and surveillance. That the movements organized as an informal network of institutions, constructively engaged with democratic, market, and global forces, and worked with liberal intellectuals and the European Union as influential allies suggest that its leadership was capable of reading the zeitgeist. However, the post-2013 confrontation with the ruling Justice and Development Party (AKP) reversed its achievements, which took decades to accomplish. As of 2018, the movement had lost all of its schools, business

11. See Yavuz 2003b for a description of this alternative modernity and the passive opposition of the Islamic movements against the state-imposed modernization project

ventures, and community organizations inside Turkey and its participants faced an unprecedented crackdown by the Turkish government. This dramatic story of Gülen movement's rise and fall have unfolded parallel to the evolution of the public sphere in Turkey.

The bulk of the movement's public activities focused on the civil society in areas of education, business associations, and cultural events. Such activism and high-profile visibility in the civil society inevitably brought the movement in contact with not only other civil society organizations, but also with politicians, bureaucrats, and interest groups. The movement maintained a veneer of political neutrality and distance from everyday politics and direct political involvement in terms of openly endorsing candidates or political parties. However, in reality, the movement diligently cultivated strategic relationships and assumed for itself the role of a moderate, reasonable, and modern Islamic actor in the public sphere. During the peak of its power in 2000s, the movement worked behind the scenes to forcefully communicate its preferences and fiercely promote its interests and agenda. Through the media associated with the movement, such as the (now defunct) Samanyolu TV network and the *Zaman* daily newspaper, one could see how those preferences were articulated and promoted in support of preferred policy options by the movement followers and circles of influence. The movement's expressed motive behind such preferences appeared noble: the empowerment of the civil society, carving more autonomous space for the political society, and balancing the power of the preeminent state in the Turkish public sphere. However, its growing influence in bureaucracy, business, mass media, and education came at the expense of other factions and eroded the credibility of its stated goals.

As the movement built and accumulated financial resources and one of the largest infrastructures in Turkey's civil society, the earlier strength of its informality under Kemalist state pressure became a liability. Interestingly, since there was no official collective legal status to the movement, there was also no agreed-upon name. There were various different designations that entered into usage in Turkey and abroad, with each wording signifying a certain connotation and politics behind it. *Cemaat* (community) is a generic term, but in the Turkish political context it came to exclusively refer to the Gülen movement ("the cemaat") by 2010.[12] There were also more pejorative terms, such as *Fethullahçı* (a cultic follower of Fethullah), *F-Tipi* (F-type organization, insinuating suspicion and sectarian favoritism and conspiracy),[13] parallel state, and FETO.[14] Gülen himself regularly used the term *gönüllüler hareketi* (volunteers movement) to describe the movement. He seems not to approve of the movement being called after himself, which is likely to be influenced by his Sufi philosophy of being humble and modest,[15] but also for countering the appearance of a cult-like organization.[16] Gülen justifies this by underscoring the fact that he does not know a vast majority of the people in the movement and has probably only seen a small minority of institutions built by them. There has also been an emerging trend among the Western scholarship, and a visible effort on the part of the movement affiliates, to refer to the movement as the "Hizmet movement."[17] The term was largely endorsed in two conferences organized by the movement supporters in Los Angeles (2009) and Chicago (2010).[18] *Hizmet* is

12. For an examination of the use of the concept and its implications, see Eyup Can, "The Cemaat," *Hurriyet Daily News*, August 29, 2010.

13. See, for example, Murat Yetkin, "Mesut Yilmaz: Emniyet Istihbarati F-tipi" (Mesut Yilmaz: The Police Intelligence Is F-type), *Radikal*, January 15, 2009.

14. Parallel state and FETO have been used by the AKP government after 2013, when the alliance between the two fell apart. Parallel state refers to a sinister organization of Gülenists in the state bureaucracy, who are loyal to Gülen, rather than to the state institutions. FETO is short for Fethullahist Terrorist Organization, a name Turkish government has predominantly used after it blamed the July 2016 coup attempt on the movement.

15. Rather than a popular folk Islam, Gülen's Sufism can be better understood as a spiritual and doctrinal approach to the Islamic scripture and tradition. For more on Gülen's theology and spiritual outlook, see Saritoprak 2003.

16. For his own account of the name of the movement, see Gülen 2009.

17. There is a blog maintained by Gülen sympathizers in the US: http://hizmetmovement.blogspot.com/.

18. For the background of this shift, see Kurucan 2010.

a Turkish word that loosely translates as "service." This was in fact the way it was symbolically referred to by its own practitioners since its very early years. It offers a description based on the substance of the movement rather than its charismatic leader. *Hizmet* signifies the movement's engagement in a series of social service projects, including education, health care, and relief, among others.

The politics of its name aside, what keeps this decentralized, informal, and loosely connected network a coherent movement is the shared worldview and philosophy of social activism of its members. Therefore, understanding the ideational roots of the movement is as important, if not more important, than its organizational structure and its resources. When asked about the movement and Gülen's role in it, most participants would repeatedly say that he is the "inspiration" behind the activities in its quintessential public discourse.[19] Nevertheless, in understanding the ideational background of the Gülen movement, it is crucial to examine Gülen's speeches and writings, since the movement's intellectual capital largely stemmed from his sermons and writings.

Gülen on the State, Nation, and Patriotism

The bulk of Gülen's speeches and writings revolve around questions of belief, spirituality, and social-ethical practice. A relatively smaller portion deals with political issues.[20] This section will mostly draw on the relevant segments of the latter.

Gülen subscribes to a vision of an esteemed Turkish-Islamic civilization and statehood. He believes that Turks played a significant role in Islamic history, not only by defending the Muslim world militarily, but also by producing a remarkable civilization based on

19. Even the DC-based, semiofficial representative of the movement in the US, Alliance for Shared Values, calls itself inspired by Gülen, and not his formal representatives (http://afsv.org).

20. There was a significant increase between 2013 and 2018 in the proportion of speeches touching on Turkish politics after the movement's confrontation with the ruling AKP.

Islamic principles. He argues that by the tenth century Turkish Muslim scholars in central Asia were able to understand the "universality" and "spirit" of Islamic teachings and use new methodological tools for interpretation and inference.[21] Accordingly, the Saljuk and Ottoman Empires benefited from this comprehensive jurisprudence to freely borrow from other civilizations and legal systems to make their sharia-based rule more flexible and in touch with sociological realities. Gülen's worldview on the special historical role played by Turkish peoples and civilization in advancement of Islamic identity colors his view of how Islam should be interpreted and lived in the modern era, amounting to a form of Turkish Islam.[22] As he openly praises the Turkish understanding and practice of Islam, he offers it as an alternative to *Salafism* and political Islam. Similar to the Mormon belief in the special status of the US in world history, the Gülen movement displays elements of patriotism in its emphasis on the special historical role played by the Turkish states in defending and spreading Islam with a strong commitment to justice. From this historical account, the Turkish interpretation and practice of Islam is tacitly presented as a civilizational alternative to the more literal *Salafi* Islam that originated in the Arab world.

Gülen's treatment of political authority carries tones of the classical Sunni ulema's emphasis on social order, whose absence would lead to a Hobbesian state of nature: "Very negative propaganda would sabotage the state. The state means authority. It is the final point where a community's diverse trends are united. Therefore it is important; without it anarchy arises."[23] In the 1980s and early 1990s, Gülen had continued to emphasize the centrality of the state in educating the public and inculcating public virtue and morality. Here is an example of his approach to government:

21. "Türkiye Müslümanlığı," journalist Hulusi Turgut's interview with Gülen, *Sabah*, January 23, 1997.

22. For a conceptual analysis of "Turkish Islam" and the "Turkish model," see Ugur 2004.

23. Nuriye Akman's interview with Fethullah Gülen, *Sabah*, January 1995.

> While a republican government allows individuals broad rights and freedoms, it must educate them as people of elevated morality and virtue, and sound thinking and strong will. The republic needs people who identify fully with its principles. Its governing body should be dignified and wise, and its works should be fair and just. (Şahin 1990, 32–33)

Gülen believes in politics of virtue rather than interest, rejecting a mundane and utilitarian view:

> Those who understand politics as political parties, propaganda, elections, and the struggle for power are mistaken. Politics is the art of management, based on a broad perspective of today, tomorrow, and the day after, that seeks the people's satisfaction and God's approval. (Şahin 1990, 34)

Such early quotes hint at the influence of republicanism on Gülen's approach to politics. He described ideal institutions in connection with ideal traits of people who govern them, in a similar fashion to Socrates's guardians, who can escape temptations of attachment to worldly pleasures, wealth, and comfort (Carroll 2007). After the movement became more transnational and Gülen himself lived in the US, his opinions have been tamed with a more liberal outlook, including more emphasis on negative freedoms, democratic rule, and individualism. Drawing on his decade-long experience in the US, he stated unequivocally that Muslims can practice their religious beliefs there more fully than in most Muslim countries, thanks to the strongly established principle of religious freedom (Gülen 2008). On a more practical front, the fact that most supporters and institutions of the movement have benefited from economic and political liberalization in Turkey and globalization in the world cannot be ignored and may have been a key factor for the movement to support such policies. From the 1980s to the 2000s, the newly emerging middle- and upper-middle-class businessmen—also known as the "Anatolian Tigers"—benefited from privatization, competition and new opportunities in the market (vis-à-vis the former state-supported Istanbul-based bourgeoisie), the rule of law, and political stability. The movement-affiliated journalists, intellectuals, and media benefited from expansion of freedom of information and expression during this period. Turkish Islamic movements scholar Hakan Yavuz (2003a, 201) argues that without adopting a principled liberal outlook and by virtue of these benefits, the movement reconciled itself with democracy and secular life without becoming truly secular, liberal, or even democratic. In a way, liberal policies were in the very best interest of the majority of the movement's associates, and their attitudes were influenced by such interest calculations.[24] This includes opting for a more liberal practice of secularism as opposed to the illiberal/Jacobin practice.[25]

Gülen's approach to democracy underscores another key motive of the movement: reconciliation of Islam and modernity. According to him, there is no inherent contradiction between Islam and democracy. He argues that the Quran does not specifically prescribe a political system, rather emphasizes some key principles, such as the accountability of the ruler to the ruled, importance of consultation, and a form of social contract based on rights and responsibilities. He maintains that democracy is the best system that humanity has achieved so far, and he goes further to say that democracy should fulfill the spiritual needs of people and consider not only the welfare of believers in this world, but also in the hereafter (Gülen 2001). It is not clear how democracy can fulfill the spiritual aspirations of citizens, whether through more freedoms and opportunities to live a spiritually fulfilling life, or accommodating their religious beliefs in everyday life. Such ideational ambiguity is not uncommon to the Gülen movement, which is more practice oriented than theory based. An analysis of the practices and activities of the movement will provide some clues to its ambiguous philosophy and politics.

24. For a detailed examination of the movement with respect to the question of liberalism, see Kilinc 2007.

25. Walton 2009 observes in the Turkish case an emerging "liberal piety," as opposed to a pious liberalism. Ahmet Kuru (2009) also similarly looks at conflicting interpretations of secularism as "assertive" and "passive."

Public Activism of the Gülen Movement

The Gülen movement became increasingly successful in expanding its grassroots support, educational and business networks, and associational life in the 1990s and 2000s. The social growth translated into a greater presence of movement sympathizers in government posts and the civil service. Combined with the resurgence of Islamists in the political arena, the increasing penetration of Islamic movement sympathizers into the bureaucracy alarmed the Kemalist establishment, who had controlled the state institutions throughout much of the republican period through a combination of co-optation and coercion tactics. The Gülen movement was pivotal, if not critical, in this change. While most other Islamic communities were busy mobilizing pious Turks to create distant parallel Islamic sectors to the secular state in education, publication, and social services, the Gülen movement encouraged its followers to be present in every sphere of social life, including secular state institutions. Gülen sought to persuade his followers to send their children to not only Imam Hatip schools, which specialized in religious instruction, but also to other high schools and colleges, where they would receive education in sciences and technology. This prepared them for better-paying jobs in the private economy and made prestigious civil service positions more accessible. Many of the movement recruits were from low-income families, and the movement's resources and networks offered them opportunities for upward mobility. Gülen aimed to create a new generation of Muslims intelligentsia, business owners, and professionals who would challenge the hegemony of the "white Turks" in the society and the state. To balance the power of the traditional Istanbul-based big businesses that supported the Kemalist establishment, he advised small-business owners in Anatolia to combine their resources and become competitive nationally, and, later on, to enter the global market. The movement sought to turn Islam and Islamic networks into social capital to be used for promotion of Islam in the public sphere.

In less than three decades, the movement's public strategies helped its participants to become part of the reformist coalition that gradually undermined the status quo and dismantled the coalition behind it. A new generation of highly educated, ambitious, and confident urban dwellers challenged the previously dominant economic class, the intelligentsia, and the media. Istanbul-based Turkish Industrialists and Businessmen Association (TUSIAD) lost its overwhelming economic control, having to share it with the newly rising conservative Anatolian Tigers. Thanks to the support from pro-Islamic bourgeoisie and the AKP government, the secularists lost their hegemonic control of the media. The new bourgeoisie, who carved a space for their conservative values within everyday practices of modern life, became critical for the power struggle and subsequent transformation of Turkey's political system.

The Turkish political system went through a remarkable transformation during the 2000s. Liberalization of the Turkish economy was underway starting in the 1980s, but the country had suffered from periodic high inflation, persistent high unemployment, large public deficit, and a currency crisis in the 1990s, ultimately leading to a major economic crisis in 2001. Even though the coalition government undertook much-needed reforms in the banking sector and implemented an IMF stabilization program, the economic crisis led to a major shake-up in the Turkish political scene in 2002. That year the reformist wing of the Islamists, who reorganized under the Justice and Development Party (AKP) in 2001, won a sweeping electoral victory and came to power. In addition to the continuation of the IMF economic program, the AKP government undertook major political and legal reforms to meet the membership criteria of the European Union. As a result, the bastion of the Kemalist establishment, the military, gradually lost its power over civilians (Cizre 2007), tipping the balance of power for the political society vis-à-vis the state bureaucracy.

These economic and political reforms were very strongly supported by the Gülen movement, which became part of the reform coalition made up of the ruling conservative AKP, other Islamic communities, liberal intellectuals, and the Anatolian Tigers. It is at this juncture that the Gülen movement's decades-long efforts to get its participants in civil service became more critical. The Kemalist establishment were alarmed at what they saw as Islamists attempting to capture or infiltrate the state; they argued that the Gülen movement was becoming too powerful in the bureaucracy, especially in the judiciary, the police, and the army.[26] The Gülen movement dismissed the accusations as defamation, arguing that, unless there are actual cases of wrongdoing, corruption, or abuse of power, those broad allegations were nothing but fearmongering by those who are trying to cover up their own wrongdoing or have lost their privileges in government. Gülen stated that "citizens do not infiltrate their own state," emphasizing their constitutional rights to be employed without discrimination.[27] The AKP allied itself with the pro-Gülen bureaucrats to eliminate the Kemalist opposition inside the state; however, the two Islamic allies fell apart after 2013. The infiltration issue would be a major setback for the public relations of the movement, and it ultimately led to widespread purges and the dismantling of its entire social organization in Turkey.

The infiltration issue is very instructive for understanding the political context in Turkey. There are a number of beliefs and assumptions about the ideal state-society relations in a republican political culture—first, that the state is clearly the most important and powerful actor in the public sphere. There is an ideological basis for the state, whether it is secular Turkish nationalism under the Kemalist regime or Islamic nationalism in the post-Kemalist era. The civil society is seen with a suspicious eye, and the state spends considerable resources for monitoring civil society activism. Such conceptions of the state would not be possible in a liberal public sphere, where a minimalist, nonideological state is the norm. The Gülen movement's strategy of bringing Islam to the public sphere was carved within the republican political culture. The experience of top-down modernization that offered both opportunities and constraints for conservative sectors of the country

26. For an insider's account of the infiltration narrative by a career police chief, see Avci 2010.

27. "Gülen: Citizens Do Not Infiltrate State Posts," *Today's Zaman*, October 12, 2010.

is critical in understanding how the Gülen movement both engaged with secularism and aimed to transform it. While building modern institutions of education, civic organizations, media networks, and business ventures, the movement also aimed to increase its access to power. Most Gülen sympathizers hid or downplayed their ties to the movement. For some, participation in a social circle was at best irrelevant, at worst an unnecessary complication for their career goals in the state bureaucracy. For others, especially in the military and judiciary, it was a liability they could not afford to openly display, and hence they strived to hide their piety from the extensive secular vetting and clearance process for admission and promotion. For others, their presence and organization in the state bureaucracy was part of a long crusade against the Kemalists, who discriminated against conservative people. In this crusade the conservatives' ends of unsealing state institutions justified their means of reticent penetration. Ultimately, the movement's ambitious project of a wholesale transformation of the public sphere ended up effectively promoting a Janus-faced image for the movement: a progressive cluster of social organizations that promoted access, upward mobility, and opportunity for its participants, along with a vision of globally connected democracy, pluralism, and dialogue, on the benign side; and a carefully guarded coordination of bureaucratic recruitment and factionalism on the sinister side.

To ensure the survival of its social organizations and increase access to resources, the movement walked a fine line in its politics. Gülen and the leadership of the movement cultivated relationships with politicians and statesmen from the center-right and the center-left, yet refrained from open endorsements and partisan politics. Even where a large share of its participants overlapped with a political party's support base, the movement remained circumspect about partnership with the political party. Between 2002 and 2011, the movement became allies with the AKP on most key political issues; nonetheless, it went to great lengths to publicly distance itself from the ruling party, arguing that they have supported the reforms, not the particular political party who promoted them. Acting under the constraints of the republican Turkish public sphere with the ambiguity and lack of a monolithic voice in public intensified the public skepticism toward its intentions and backdoor politics.

The Gülen Movement and Public Issues

Similar to the "political neutrality" principle of the LDS Church, the Gülen movement repeatedly maintained that it does not have and never has had a practice of endorsing any political party or candidate—in the past or the present.[28] Gülen described the movement being "equally close" to all political parties, modifying the more conventional term "equal distance" in a more ostensibly positive way.[29] As the critics of the movement would swiftly point out, though, this does not mean it does not get involved in politics in any way, shape, or form. Similar again to the "moral issues" twist of the LDS public affairs, the movement claimed to get involved in issues that fall under the broader concept of "democratization, human rights, and social harmony," often with a reference to Turkey's EU process and the requirements for accession, known as the Copenhagen criteria.[30] Consequently, the movement was very vocal and active in the 2010 referendum on amending twenty-four articles of the Turkish Constitution of 1982 and the legal process known as the "Ergenekon trial," which was dubbed at the time by its supporters as Turkey's "operation clean hands" against its own *Gladio*.[31]

28. "Evet'i Desteklememiz, Kişileri Değil Yapılan İşi Takdir Meselesidir" (Supporting "Yes" Campaign Is Not Supporting Politicians Behind It, Rather Appreciating the Substance of the Work Done), *Zaman*, August 24, 2010.

29. Hüseyin Gülerce, "CHP, Cemaat, AK Parti," *Zaman*, May 14, 2010.

30. The Copenhagen criteria include stable institutionalized democracy, rule of law, protection of and respect for minority rights, a functioning market economy, and ability to take on the obligations of the membership and adherence to the aims of the union ("Accession Criteria," European Commission, http://ec.europa.eu/enlargement/enlargement_process/accession_process/criteria/index_en.htm.

31. Gladio is the code name for NATO's stay-behind operation in Italy. It was formed as a paramilitary force to be used against a possible communist takeover. However, it was also used to prop up "friendly" governments, sometimes engaged in internal subversion and "false-flag" operations, and undermined influence of the

Forcing the Genie Out of the Bottle: The Ergenekon Trials and the 2010 Referendum

The Ergenekon trials revolved around an alleged illegal ultranationalist organization accused of planning to oust the democratically elected AKP government. The organization was blamed for planning and engaging in false-flag operations against secular intelligentsia and bureaucrats, in targeted assassinations of non-Muslim minorities, and ultimately aiming to destabilize Turkey and provoking and justifying a military takeover. The prosecutors' indictments went to great lengths to implicate the Ergenekon network with a number of attacks that took place between 2006 and 2007: the assassination of judges from the council of state (Danıştay), grenade attacks to the secularist Cumhuriyet newspaper in Ankara, the murder of an Italian Catholic priest in Trabzon, the torture and murder of Christian missionaries in Malatya, and the assassination of Armenian journalist Hrant Dink in Istanbul. The indictment also claimed that some of the major militant groups, including the rival Kurdish separatist PKK and Islamist-Kurdish Hizbullah, were in effect controlled by the Ergenekon network. The prosecutors widened the investigation and attempted to portray Ergenekon as a wide underground network of secular ultranationalist (*ulusalcı*) cabal and their extensions in the military, intelligence, and police force. This was an attempt to uncover the ever-speculated Turkish "deep state." The case became quite confusing, as it unfolded and targeted alleged military and "civilian lobby" wings, including retired army generals, university professors, politicians, journalists, and businessmen (Unver 2009; Balci 2010).

The indictments maintained that the organization was more than a set of marginal disgruntled ultranationalist groups, but had taken concrete steps, including coup plans, some of which were publicized in the diaries of the Admiral Özden Örnek, published by the weekly

communist parties (Willan 2002). Similar organizations existed in other NATO countries in Europe, and parliamentary investigations on the matter were carried out in Italy, Belgium, and Switzerland (Ganser 2005).

Nokta. A separate investigation and trial called Balyoz ("Sledgehammer") ensued in 2010 after a set of classified documents about purported destabilization and coup plans within the military was published by the daily *Taraf*. The Balyoz trials targeted hundreds of active military officers, as well as retired generals. As the secularist opposition blamed the Ergenekon and Balyoz trials as being politically motivated and questioned the authenticity of the documents admitted by the court, Prime Minister Erdoğan staunchly defended the trials as a necessary part of the democratization process, to remove the rogue elements within the state (Cagaptay 2009). The AKP very seriously put its weight behind the trial after being convinced that they came to the brink of military and judicial coups, a danger they had frequently and secretly contemplated during their first term in office. Liberals were initially supportive of the trials on the basis of transparency and democratic control of the Turkish Armed Forces, but became more critical after the trials turned into a witch hunt against secular intelligentsia.

The Gülen movement was the strongest supporter of the trials, as the revealed documents in *Taraf* newspaper seemed to suggest that they were also the target of the alleged subversive activities of the Ergenekon network. Movement activities and organization would almost certainly suffer under an eventual Kemalist military rule. Critiques of the trials cited the lengthy detentions, wire-tapped private conversations, and fiercely contested authenticity and legal admissibility of the evidence for the Balyoz and Ergenekon cases presented to the court (Jenkins 2009). The targeting of a prominent police chief, Hanefi Avcı and an investigative journalist, Ahmet Şık, in 2011 added more weight to the arguments that the trials were politically driven to silence the opponents of the AKP government and the Gülen movement.

The movement's strong emphasis on the importance of the Ergenekon trials for Turkey's democratization added to an already growing myth about its growing power and influence.[32] Mustafa

32. Mehmet Ali Birand, "Gülen Movement Becoming Victim of Its Own Legend," *Hurriyet Daily News*, October 5, 2010.

Akyol, a liberal Turkish writer, likened the popular discourse about the movement at the time to the notorious anti-Semitic forgery the Protocols of the Learned Elders of Zion (Akyol 2010).[33] There was little doubt that the members of the judiciary and law enforcement who were affiliated with the Gülen movement were the principal actors in the process, and the AKP government retained the image of having been reluctantly pulled into it by the movement (Cagaptay 2009). Similar to how the LDS Church was singled out for its critical role among a coalition of different conservative groups for their support, involvement, and grassroots mobilization during and in the aftermath of the Proposition 8 campaign in California, as discussed in detail in chapter 7, the Gülen movement became a lightning rod for its role in the Ergenekon trials.[34]

The Ergenekon and Balyoz trials led to scores of detentions and purges, as well as the sentencing of many secularists in the Turkish Armed forces, by 2012. This offensive on the Kemalist establishment opened avenues for the AKP and the Gülen movement to bring in their loyalists in critical bureaucratic positions and eliminate the Kemalist hegemony. However, after a series of corruption investigations that targeted the higher echelons of the government, the AKP-Gülen movement coalition spectacularly crumpled in late 2013, and the two sides found themselves on a collision course. The AKP government called the investigations a "coup attempt" by the Gülen movement loyalists in law enforcement and the judiciary, moving to decimate the movement. Holding the Gülen movement responsible for the Ergenekon trials, the government opened the way for the collapse of the entire case and also moved onto a tactical alliance with some of the nationalist-secular factions (*ulusalcı*) in the civil

33. Journalist Suzy Hansen also likened some of the accusations to anti-Semitism: they run the media, they're rich, they stick together, they only help their own (Hansen 2010, 10).

34. "Mormons Tipped Scale in Ban on Gay Marriage," *New York Times*, November 14, 2008; "Mormon Church Draws Protest Over Marriage Act," *New York Times*, November 8, 2008.

and military bureaucracy, whose numbers had dramatically dwindled during the trials.

As the Ergenekon and Balyoz trials led to the detention and retirement of scores of high-ranking military officers, the mighty guardian of the Kemalist establishment, the military, had gone on the defensive. The next step for the AKP-Gülen coalition was to dismantle the remaining pillars of the Kemalist order by overhauling the judiciary. Erdoğan had realized his government's vulnerability when it came to the brink of closure by the constitutional court in a 2008 case and passed a package of constitutional amendments in the parliament.[35] Since the party lacked the required two-thirds majority, the measures were put in the ballot for a national referendum in September 2010.[36] Contrary to the modus operandi of the Gülen movement's indirect approach and behind the scenes lobbying efforts, Gülen also came out during the referendum campaign season to strongly endorse the

35. Much like its Islamist predecessors, the AKP faced charges of undermining the secular nature of the Turkish state in the closure case before the Constitutional Court. The court's ruling found that there was merit for the prosecutor's charge, but that it did not warrant closure, and ruled for limiting the funding the party received from the treasury. After the near escape, the composition of the high courts became a matter of political survival.

36. The package contained twenty-six amendments, including noncontroversial provisions on affirmative action for women, collective bargaining rights for public-sector workers, civil liberties, and personal privacy, and more politically consequential ones, such as the jurisdiction of civilian courts over coup plotters (including the generals of the 1980 coup), an expansion of the number of high-court judges, and an increase of the president's and the parliament's say over their appointment. The AKP framed the referendum on the basis of democratizing Turkey, preventing future military interventions and bringing the 1980 coup plotters to justice and ultimately a much-needed patch for a constitution that was drafted under a military regime. The opposition, however, maintained that the provisions on gender discrimination, civil rights, and collective bargaining were basically the Bubble Wrap in a package whose main objective was dismantling Turkey's secular establishment and further entrenching Erdoğan's power. The amendments were approved with a 58 percent yes vote. Most liberals supported the amendments, some finding them necessary but not sufficient ("evet ama yetmez").

constitutional changes and mobilize the movement resources for the "yes" campaign. The media outlets operated by the movement, such as the *Zaman* daily and Samanyolu TV, dedicated most of their editorials and coverage on a plain "yes" campaign.[37] At the grassroots level, volunteers were sent to knock on the doors and ask voters to turn out at the polls and support the amendments, as well as to serve on the ballot commissions, which were in charge of verifying and counting the ballots. The opposition parties, the secularist CHP, and the nationalist MHP fiercely condemned this active, if not activist, position of the Gülen movement, referring to them as "the cemaat" ("the" religious community) or the "other side of the Atlantic ocean" in their campaign propaganda, alluding to Mr. Gülen, who resides in Pennsylvania.[38] This way they also played into the nationalist fears of outside interference from Western powers with "ill intentions" against the "territorial integrity" and "political independence" of Turkey.[39]

Prioritizing Freedoms? Religious and Political Liberties

The headscarf question analyzed in chapter 2 is also important in understanding the Gülen movement's public-relations strategy. In line

37. They have employed a strategy of interviewing celebrities, intellectuals, and past victims of military rule almost every day. The pro-Gülen media was unusually blunt about its support for the proposed amendments.

38. "Bahçeli: Fethullah Gülen Türkiye'ye Gelip Oy Kullansın" (Bahceli: Fethullah Gülen should first return to Turkey and vote), *Hurriyet Daily News*, August 2, 2010; "Okyanus Ötesinden de Duyulsun" (Let It Be Heard from the Transatlantic), *Sabah*, September 7, 2010.

39. The secular nationalists in Turkey still talk about "Büyük Ortadoğu Projesi" (BOP), referring to the failed "Greater Middle East Initiative" of the Bush administration between 2002 and 2004. The purported goal was to promote a democratic Middle East. Turkey's experience with secularism and democracy as a Muslim majority nation was mentioned as a possible source of inspiration and lessons for other nations in the Middle East. The prolonged war in Iraq was a major reason for the failure. In spite of this marginal effect, the project stuck as a centerpiece of political rhetoric in Turkey and a source of "explanation" for whatever has happened in the Middle East since then.

with a continued emphasis on reconciliation and a strategy of avoiding direct confrontation, the Gülen movement adopted a more moderate and less vocal voice than the Islamists on the headscarf controversy. This was a very risky position, given that the supporters of the movement also overwhelmingly opposed the ban and the majority were in fact victims of the ban. During the zenith of the military's domination of politics between 1997 and 2002 (also known as the "February 28 process," or the "postmodern coup"), Gülen tried to appease the generals and soften tensions in society by advising his female followers to choose education over their attire, offering his religious interpretation that covering one's hair is not a part of the fundamentals of the Islamic faith (Gülen 2007, 162–65).[40] As a result, he was strongly denounced by the Islamist conservatives for failing to stand up against oppression. Most of the female Gülenists removed their headscarves or wore wigs when they entered the universities, unlike those who either quit education altogether or found ways of continuing their education abroad.

Although the AKP government was able to pass legislation liberalizing the dress code, the secularist-dominated Constitutional Court struck it down on the grounds of violating the secularism principle.[41] As discussed earlier, the party came to the brink of closure by the Constitutional Court primarily because of this attempt.[42] The Gülen movement cautiously supported the move by the AKP, and, after the court decision, suggested that the focus of the government should be institutionalization of democracy along the EU membership process rather than a piecemeal approach to liberty. Media outlets affiliated with the Gülen movement defended the view that without a new and more democratic constitution that may produce a more liberal and less ideological/activist judiciary, the efforts to deal with problems like the headscarf ban would simply be in vain.

40. See also Orhan Yurtsever's interview with Fethullah Gülen, *Aksam*, March 13, 1998.

41. The ruling can be accessed from the court's website, http://www.anayasa.gov.tr (case no. 2008/116, May 6, 2008).

42. See http://www.anayasa.gov.tr (case no. 2009/4, November 12, 2009).

A controversial issue in which Gülen took a clear, public position is the mandatory religion and ethics class taught from fourth to twelfth grade in public schools. The course was designed to cover world religions and focused on the moral aspects of Islam, but in practice the actual instruction depended on the teacher. Until 2011, most classes did not include the teaching of practical aspects of Islam, such as praying and fasting. After 2012, the government introduced new elective courses on the Quran, Life of Prophet Mohammad, and Basic Religious Knowledge, which in many cases became mandatory in absence of the availability of other nonreligious electives (Gürcan 2015). In the last decade, some Alevis[43] sued the Turkish government before the European Court of Human Rights for imposing Sunni Islam on other Muslim minorities.[44] Gülen was one of the pioneers of establishing better relations with the Alevi community. He proposed to codify the oral sources of the Alevi tradition, and in fact the Directorate of Religious Affairs (Diyanet) have compiled some early volumes. Gülen also took concrete steps to overcome the tensions between the Sunnis and the Alevis, by meeting in person with some leadership and standing against some popular stereotypes of Alevis.[45]

In spite of his apparent sympathy toward the Alevi community, Gülen has never called for the abolition of the religious instruction—or Diyanet, for that matter. Diyanet is one of the largest bureaucracies in charge of religious services in Turkey. The Turkish state is secular in the sense that it is not founded on religious principles or laws, but the state still wants to monitor religion and keep it under control. There

43. A heterodox, folk-based interpretation and practice of Islam that makes up roughly 15 percent of the populace in Turkey (Ocak 2000).

44. The ruling in 2007 called for accommodations from the government, which initiated some roundtable discussions with members of the Alevi community. Partly because of the conservative base of the AKP, and partly because of the divided nature of the Alevi community, there was no consensus on what should be done. For a detailed analysis of AKP's "Alevi Opening," see Köse 2010.

45. "Gülen: Mum Söndü Alevilerde İftiradır" (Gülen: The Candle Extinguish Is a Slander on the Alevis), *Taraf*, January 24, 2008.

are no private mosques in Turkey, and all imams are civil servants. In a way, there was a de facto established religion under the politically secular Kemalist system. When the AKP replaced the secular establishment, it continued to use the public education system and the mosques and pushed the de facto establishment into a more conservative direction. In the past Gülen praised the government officials who included the religion and ethics class in public education, and refrained from criticizing Diyanet until Diyanet leadership questioned the religious credentials of Gülen and his movement after the movement's coalition with the AKP collapsed in 2013.[46] This underscores Gülen's belief in the primacy of religion in the moral values of society. Even though he found past practice of Turkish secularism an excessive infringement on citizens' religious freedoms, he never proposed a separation in the American way.[47]

The movement's other positions have been very pragmatic on various controversial issues, including prayer in schools. The schools affiliated with the Gülen movement avoided open endorsement of release times for the daily Islamic prayers, yet most provided suitable lounges which faculty and students could use for prayer during recess times. Unlike the US case, the question of prayers in Turkey was not about actual joint school prayers, but rather individual prayers taking place on school sites. Some students, who wanted to perform one or two of their five daily prayers, used some rooms in basements in public schools, and they faced opposition from more secular teachers or

46. Mehmet Gündem's interview with Gülen, *Milliyet*, January 17, 2005.

47. Gülen's worldview is significantly shaped by the Ottoman model. He frequently refers to what he sees as the Ottoman tolerance of non-Muslims within the *millet system*, and the constantly evolving nature of the legal system, which combined sharia and secular law. Sharia functioned as the framework of general legal and moral principles, very much in line with the contemporary role of constitutions. In fact, there was no theocracy in Islamic history until the 1979 Iranian Revolution. Most Muslim states treated Islam as an established religion rather than subscribing to a rule by clergy. Naturally, very few Muslims prefer a complete secularization. For an excellent brief on this matter, see Feldman 2008.

families. The question was whether to designate a room in which such students could perform their prayer during the breaks, which seldom interfered with their attendance. Some students asked for accommodations to go to Friday prayer. There was no official law in favor of or against such accommodations, and the actual practice was largely based on the school and district administrators and the students in both public and private schools (Kuru 2009).

Some issues at the core of religion and politics controversies in the US, such as abortion, gay marriage, and euthanasia, were not major sources of debate in 1990s and 2000s Turkey. Therefore, the Gülen movement, or other public actors, did not have clearly elaborated attitudes on these issues. One shared issue of public debates in both the US and Turkey is minority rights, which is also crucial to understanding the movement's public attitude. One of the distinguishing characteristics of the Gülen movement compared to other Islamic groups was its sustained efforts to build good relations ("interfaith dialogue") with non-Muslim communities in Turkey and to support expansion of legal protections and easing of bureaucratic hurdles against them. In addition to routinized interfaith gatherings, the movement supported positions of minority communities in symbolic issues, such as the property rights of Assyrian Church of Mardin on Mor Gabriel Monastery, and opening of the Greek Orthodox theology school in Halkali, Istanbul. The movement participants were also quite supportive of the Armenian community when journalist Hrank Dink was assassinated.[48]

The Gülen Movement and Turkish Politics

Gülen has always been critical of movements that used Islam as the source of political ideology and identity. His opposition is based on a

48. The investigation of the Dink assassination has been largely shaped by the political atmosphere. The case first moved toward implicating the alleged ultranationalist Ergenekon network. After the Ergenekon case collapsed in 2014, the direction of suspicion turned to the Gülen movement. After many twists and turns, the trial was still ongoing in 2018.

belief that Islamists instrumentalize Islam, reduce it to political slogans, and in effect empty its spiritual and rich civilizational content. Accordingly, partisanship undermines the universality of Islam and makes it a source of conflict, rather than cooperation or unity. Gülen sees justice, security, and order as the basic functions of a government and defines politics as the art of conflict management and leadership to please the public and God.[49] Based on this definition, one of the early goals of the movement's politics was in line with upholding the authority of the state and preventing ideological conflict and bloodshed. These principles were broadly in line with the center-right political parties. For these objectives and the welfare of the movement, Gülen and his close associates developed cordial ties with politicians and statesmen, which created opportunities and access to power for the movement.

In the 1970s, anticommunism was the major driving force behind the movement's politics. Gülen's ideas were closer to the right-wing conservative/patriotic social groups, and he frequently spoke about the importance of maintaining state authority and advised those who listened to his sermons not to give into pressure by militant groups to close down their businesses.[50] Gülen's opposition to leftist agitation was combined with his belief that communication and outreach to radical youth groups would ease ideological cleavages and tensions in the society. After a decade of worsening ideological polarization and conflict, Gülen saw the 1980 military coup as a positive development toward overcoming the bloodshed on the streets, despite the junta's warrant against him.[51] During his time in İzmir as a public preacher, he developed close relations with Turgut Özal, who would come to power as prime minister in the first elections in 1983, despite opposition from the leading generals. Gülen's relationship with Turgut Özal

49. Fethullah Gülen, "Siyaset," *Sizinti*, September–December 1987.

50. "Fethullah Gülen'in Ogrencilerinden Aciklama," Dogan Haber Ajansi (DHA), March 27, 2014, http://www.dha.com.tr/fethullah-gulenin-ogrencilerinden-aciklama_634292.html.

51. "Son Karakol" (The Last Outpost), *Sizinti*, October 1980.

would prove quite helpful in surviving the aftermath of the military coup and escaping detention in 1986.[52] After he was cleared from the state's wanted list, Gülen quickly resumed his sermons in Ankara and Istanbul, mobilizing his movement to up their game in education, media, and publication. In the 1990s, after Özal's death, Gülen continued his strategy of cultivating relationships with the center-right politicians from Özal's ANAP and Prime Minister Tansu Çiller of the True Path Party (DYP). More important, Gülen expanded his outreach to some center-left politicians, such as Prime Minister Bulent Ecevit of the Democratic Leftist Party (DSP). The latter relationship was very surprising, given the opposing social values of the DSP and the conservative Gülen movement. Despite his secular politics, Ecevit was impressed by Gülen's moderate Islamic messages and the accomplishments of the movement schools in Turkey and abroad. This relationship would prove to be a great asset for the movement between 1997 and 2002, when the Turkish military once again intervened in politics and cracked down on Islamic movements, threatening the very existence of the Gülen movement. During this period, Gülen would come forward to criticize the Islamist Welfare Party (RP) for creating unnecessary tensions in the country due to its ideological politics.[53] Even such a public gesture would not be sufficient to appease the secularists, who orchestrated a media campaign against the Gülen movement in 1999. A state security court subsequently initiated a trial against Gülen, charging him of forming an organization to undermine the secular nature of the state. Gülen was acquitted of these charges in 2008.

The 1997 military intervention in politics inadvertently transformed Turkey's popular Islamist movement, Milli Görüş. After its

52. "1986'da Fethullah Gülen'le birlikte kimler yakalandı? O gün ne dediler? Şimdi neredeler?" *Hurriyet Daily News*, August 3, 2016, http://www.hurriyet.com.tr/1986da-fethullah-gulenle-birlikte-kimler-yakalandi-o-gun-ne-dediler-simdi-neredeler-40178992.

53. Fethullah Gülen's interview with Yalçın Doğan, Kanal D TV, April 16, 1997.

leader, Necmettin Erbakan, was forced to resign from premiership and banned from politics, the closure of the RP led to a split between the traditionalists and the reformers. This was during 1997–2001, when politics was still dominated by the military, as President Süleyman Demirel famously (mis)predicted that the February 28 process would last "a thousand years." The reformers created the AKP after failing to win the bid for RP's successor Virtue Party's (FP) chairman in the 2000 convention. The AKP dominated Turkish politics since then, winning two parliamentary elections in 2002 and 2007.

The Gülen movement's earlier relations with the AKP was in the form of encouraging them to move away from the contentious politics of Islamism, toward the center. The strategies of the new Islamists and the Gülen movement seemed to be in line for the first time in three decades as the AKP renounced Islamism, adopted a self-declared "conservative democrat" identity, and expanded its bases with some center-right politicians. In order to balance the military's power and influence, the AKP brought in influential domestic and international allies, such as liberal intellectuals, moderate Islamic groups, and the European Union. Focusing on EU membership had the crucial effect of undertaking much-needed political and economic reforms, as well as offering a common platform for political allies inside and out. The Gülen movement was at first cautious about supporting the AKP, but after 2007 the movement became more vocal and relatively open about their support for the AKP government. The alliance for the two Islamic groups was a win-win in their struggle against the Kemalist state establishment to expand their political access and influence.

There are three key examples for the movement's de facto support for the AKP. Compared to the aforementioned Ergenekon trial and 2010 constitutional referendum, the 2007 elections come closest to an almost direct endorsement of a political party.[54] To put it in

54. *Zaman*'s editor-in-chief Ekrem Dumanlı and columnist Hüseyin Gülerce justified their thinly disguised support for the AKP based on the "critical nature of the elections." Although there is no tradition of editorial endorsements in Turkey,

context, the parliamentary elections were held early as a result of the 2007 "e-memorandum" by the military against AKP's wishes to elect one of its key leaders as president. The chief of staff, Yaşar Büyükanıt, posted a warning message on the military's website the day after the first round of votes in the parliament. The Friday evening (April 27) message was based on what he saw as the erosion of Turkish secularism.[55] This was directly related to the presidential elections, which seemed to be destined to result in an Islamist president with a first lady wearing the much-ostracized headscarf. The AKP decided to stick to its popular politics against the military by coming out with a countermessage the next day, emphasizing the democratic nature of the Turkish political system. The presidential elections continued as scheduled, but the opposition party CHP allied itself with the secularist-dominated Constitutional Court to come up with a new requirement for a two-thirds majority quorum. Although the two previous presidents were elected by simple majority, AKP was denied the same opportunity. The response of the government was to call for early elections, which, for all intents and purposes, turned into a referendum on the political role of military and democratization. Having suffered from the military's militant secularism, the Gülen movement strongly came out to support the AKP. The movement saw this as a critical stage of the struggle against the establishment and for Turkish democracy with clear implications for their own future well-being.

The 2007 elections resulted in another sweeping victory for the AKP, and Abdullah Gül became president. Between 2007 and 2012, the AKP-Gülen movement coalition went on the offensive against the Kemalist establishment and undertook a series of judicial cases to

one does not need to be expert to understand the less than subtle leanings of the Gülenist Samanyolu TV in their dramatic coverage of the Ergenekon trials, the 2010 referendum, and the 2007 and the 2011 elections.

55. http://www.tsk.tr/10_ARSIV/10_1_Basin_Yayın_Faaliyetleri/10_1_Basin_Aciklamalari/2007/BA_08.html.

penetrate into the state bureaucracy. The Ergenekon and Balyoz trials resulted in the detention, purging, and sentencing of scores of military officers by 2012. The shackles of the Kemalist establishment seemed to be finally coming off.

As the old Kemalist order was falling down, it was not clear what would replace it. After the transformative four years of AKP's second term in office, the 2011 parliamentary elections were held on the basis of writing a new constitution to signify the political transformation that took place. The AKP had proposed a draft constitution overseen by a respected constitutional scholar, Ergun Özbudun, for public debate in 2007. However, this relatively liberal constitution was proposed under the military's pushback to forge a broad coalition, and the party by 2011 felt more secure in power and started drifting away from its earlier promises of a constitution that would expand political freedoms and civil liberties for all. Prime Minister Erdoğan was now less restrained in his ambitions to pass a constitution with an executive presidency and minimal checks and balances. All other major groups in the country were afraid of Erdoğan's increasing dominance and opposed his presidential plans. The AKP came short of the required qualified majority in the parliament to change the constitution. After the elections the parliament formed a constitution drafting commission with equal representation from all political parties represented in the parliament. The commission's work was poisoned by the presidentialism question and became political theater. The commission was dissolved in late 2013, citing lack of progress. It became clear for the opposition that AKP was derailing further liberalization and a new constitution because of its intentions to wait for a more opportune moment to further consolidate its power.

The years between 2011 and 2013 in effect changed the trajectory of Turkish politics away from the preceding reformist decade. Once the common enemy was weakened, divisions emerged and deepened among the anti-Kemalist coalition made up of the AKP, the Gülen movement, and the liberals. The Gülen movement and the AKP were skeptical of each other's ultimate goals and eventually found themselves in conflict. After a prosecutor attempted to indict Turkey's spy chief in 2012 on the basis of ongoing secret negotiations with the Kurdish guerrilla organization, PKK, the AKP government became skeptical of the Gülen movement loyalists in the judiciary. The relations between the two were further strained when the government's harsh treatment of the environmentalist-turned-antigovernment Gezi Park demonstrations in Istanbul during the summer of 2013 was criticized by the Gülen movement.[56] The rift became more visible with the movement's newspapers publishing stories about the government's plans to ban private tutoring, a major blow to Gülen movement's financial and human capital.

A corruption investigation against some members of the AKP government in December 2013 was the last straw. With predawn raids targeting bankers, businessmen, bureaucrats, local politicians, and the sons of three cabinet ministers, the country woke up to the news of an alleged scheme of money laundering, graft, and kickbacks. As the government reshuffled the cabinet, law enforcement, and the judiciary in order to halt the investigation, alleged recordings of Prime Minister Erdoğan's phone conversation with his son Bilal on the day of the police raids, about getting rid of large sums of cash from their house, was leaked on YouTube.[57] The AKP government quickly blamed the Gülenists in the judiciary and the police for the investigations, calling it a "coup attempt" by a "parallel state" in cahoots with sinister international powers. With the upcoming local, national, and presidential elections, the AKP quickly replaced the Kemalist state establishment with the "parallel state" as the enemy of the people and their national will. A sweeping purge affected hundreds of thousands of civil servants, police officers, judges, and prosecutors. The crackdown wasn't limited

56. "Gülen: Karınca deyip geçmeyin," *Cumhuriyet*, June 7, 2013, http://www.cumhuriyet.com.tr/haber/diger/426282/Gulen__Karinca_deyip_gecmeyin.html.

57. "The Erdoğan Tapes," *Al-Monitor*, February 27, 2014, http://www.al-monitor.com/pulse/originals/2014/02/supporters-deny-taped-conversation-erdogan-son.html.

to the Gülen movement, however, and the freedom of the press, the rule of law, political liberties, and democratic rule also deteriorated.[58]

After the stories of the government's plans to shut down private tutoring centers, the Gülen movement mobilized its network on social media.[59] The movement, known for its cautionary politics for decades, was joining forces with opposition parties and civil society organizations to undermine the AKP government's electoral hegemony. However, Erdoğan would survive every setback by utilizing a political combination of populism, polarization, and nationalism. After overcoming each setback, Erdoğan further undermined the Gülen movement's presence in the state and the society. Gülen community was one of the most popular and influential Islamic movements in Turkey around 2010.[60] In contrast, by 2016, membership to the movement was criminalized, and an overwhelming majority of the public believed that the movement was a danger for Turkey.[61]

Conclusion

The rise and fall of the Gülen movement in the Turkish public sphere is closely connected to the evolving nature of the public sphere and

58. "Democracy in Crisis: Corruption, Media, and Power in Turkey," Freedom House Report, February 3, 2014, https://www.freedomhouse.org/article/democracy-crisis-corruption-media-and-power-turkey#.Uu04YLTJUum.

59. Some high circulation twitter hashtags: #dersanemolamsaydı (if I didn't have my tutoring center); #dershanemiseviyorum (I love my tutoring center); #bencedershaneler (tutoring centers according to me).

60. According to one of the most comprehensive studies of religious movements and communities in Turkey, the Gülen movement was the most well known and most effective religious group, with the largest number of participants or sympathizers ("Türk Toplumunda Cemaat Algısı," Andy-AR Center for Social Research, 2011, http://andy-ar.com/turk-toplumunun-cemaat-algisi-arastirmasi/).

61. According to a survey by the same agency that conducted the 2011 study (Andy-AR), 77.7 percent of the respondents believed that sympathizers of Fethullah Gülen and the community were a danger to the existing order and the future of the country ("Türkiye Siyasi Gündem-Darbe Araştırması," Andy-AR, July 2016, http://www.andy-ar.com/wp-content/uploads/2016/07/Darbe-Araştırması-Temmuz-2016.pdf).

corresponds to different political strategies employed by the movement. Under the secularist republican public sphere dominated by the Kemalist establishment, the movement adopted a policy of cautious engagement rather than more assertive forms of human-rights advocacy or political agitation. The message of nonconfrontation, social reconciliation, dialogue, and modernism provided legitimacy for an ambitious Islamic enlightenment project (Yavuz 2013) alternative to the Kemalist secular modernity. After initial success in education, the activities of the movement expanded into a wide array of social sectors, including business associations, trade unions, health care, and humanitarian relief, amounting to a form of a parallel civil society or a public presence movement. Part of the appeal of the movement's organization was upward mobility and access. Unlike most Islamic communities who aimed to make the society and the state more in line with their Islamic identities, the participants of the Gülen movement compartmentalized their private religious identities and modern public personas. Whether this was a strategic ambiguity to evade the secular state and carve a niche in the neoliberal order (Hendrick 2014), a form of measured political engagement/circumspect activism (Balci and Miller 2012), or a transformative and ambitious Muslim enlightenment (Yavuz 2014), the movement's strategy was a response to the constraints of the republican public sphere and ensured its survival. As the Kemalist establishment weakened under AKP rule, the Gülen movement's influence and access to power increased. As the public sphere became relatively more hospitable to Islam, the movement became more assertive in its politics. As became apparent in post-2010 Turkish politics, the weakening of the Kemalist republican public sphere did not mean ushering in a liberal order. In the ensuing power struggle, the Gülen movement became the victim of its success. The tactics that helped the movement's loyalists survive and flourish while evading the Kemalist crackdown turned out to have alienated, angered, and alarmed many in the state bureaucracy. Moreover, the movement struggled with establishing credibility and transparency after decades of informal organization and habits of concealment, vacillating between a civil society organization, an interest group, and a secret fraternity.

The movement negotiates its public relations based on what is ideal and what is feasible. The movement's key public initiative, the Abant platform, offers a critical case study in understanding how the movement managed this trade off. Chapter 6 investigates the Abant platform and the movement's attempt to organize civil society.

5

The LDS Church and Politics of Religious Activism in the United States

Although early Mormon history is replete with the problems of integrating into the American public sphere, the Mormons are currently in a relatively more secure position in the American body politic as compared to the nineteenth century. In their public relations, Mormons regularly utilize the opportunities provided by the liberal public sphere in the US. The church has varying levels of activism in each of the three domains of the American polity: the state, political society, and civil society. The church is first and foremost a civil society actor, providing various social services to its members and to nonmembers, albeit to a lesser extent. The LDS Church carries considerable weight in Utah politics owing to the state's large Mormon population and the historical role played by the church in Utah's founding. Mormons have also played key political roles in other western states, such as California, Idaho, Arizona, and Hawaii. In particular, Mormons in these states have been politically active in electoral measures that concern what the church considers to be moral issues (Campbell and Monson 2007). Despite the church's continued engagement in moral and public policy issues, its overall involvement with government and politics is considerably limited compared to its earlier history in Missouri, Illinois, and Utah territory.

This chapter offers a general discussion of the church's relations with the public sphere. Understanding Mormon history from its inception is essential in order to explain the present situation. The

Mormon story is a crucial case study in understanding the structure, substance, and limits of the liberal public sphere as it existed in the US of the nineteenth and twentieth centuries. Therefore, this chapter begins with an analysis of the interactions of the church with the American government and political actors. In this nearly two-hundred-year history, both the American public sphere and the Mormons have gone through tremendous transformations. The LDS Church became more mainstream by ending polygamy and economic communalism, as well as by curbing the influence of its ecclesiastical authorities and dismantling its theodemocracy model. In the church's most recent major theological evolution in 1978, it reversed its policy concerning exclusion of blacks from priesthood. The American public sphere has also become more tolerant and inclusive by extending its pluralism to non-Protestants (including Catholics and Mormons), non-Christians (such as the Jews), and the nonaffiliated. With respect to the American public sphere, the LDS Church now acts as a confident representative of the well-integrated, increasingly middle-class-based, and predominantly conservative mainstream American Mormon community.[1]

1. Mormons are one of the most ethnically and racially homogenous religious groups in the US with 85 percent identifying as non-Hispanic white. "The Most and Least Racially Diverse US Religious Groups," Pew Research Center, July 2015, http://www.pewresearch.org/fact-tank/2015/07/27/the-most-and-least-racially-diverse-u-s-religious-groups/. Mormons are significantly more likely than the general population to have college education (61 percent vs. 50 percent). Mormons are slightly more likely to live in households within the middle income range ($50,000–$100,000 annually) than the general population (38 percent vs. 30 percent). Mormons are slightly less likely than the overall population (26 percent vs. 31 percent) to be in the lowest income bracket (less than $30,000), but they are almost as likely as the general population (16 percent vs. 18 percent) to make $100,000 or more annually. The income distribution of Mormons is in the middle of other religious traditions on the socioeconomic spectrum. "A Portrait of Mormons in the US," Pew Research Center, July 2009, http://www.pewforum.org/2009/07/24/a-portrait-of-mormons-in-the-us/#4.

The Four Stages of Mormon Public Identity

Parallel to the evolution of the public sphere in the US, the LDS Church faced challenges and, in turn, formulated strategies to ensure its survival, to promote the welfare of its members, and to advance its ideals. Both continuities and changes are identifiable in the long history of encounters and engagement between the LDS Church and the larger American society. The changes can be traced back to a few critical junctures in the church's relationship to the American polity.

At first, Mormons endeavored to build a self-governing community in which they could follow their distinctive beliefs and lifestyle. The very idea of forming a community with a strong sense of faith, identity, and solidarity inevitably led to tensions with the outside world. The larger community was simultaneously being reshaped by religious, demographic, and social changes. Questions of patriotism, common moral values, and assimilation conditioned how the society perceived the Mormons and vice versa. The underlying economic and political reasons for the conflict between the Mormons and the non-Mormons can be better understood by considering the context in which those interactions took place. The first critical juncture in the relationship between the Mormons and the larger society came when the founding prophet Joseph Smith was killed by a mob in his jail cell. The majority of Mormons concluded that living among the gentiles as a minority religious group was not possible for them; they decided to establish self-rule in a new land.

The second era opens with the Mormons beginning their westward migration to the Great Basin. To ensure their survival, the Mormon faithful decided to escape from public attention and the reach of the federal government. The dominant belief of the leadership, led by Brigham Young, was that the believers would have to become a self-sufficient and self-governing community. However, America's westward expansion, fueled by understandings of Manifest Destiny, would once again find the Mormons in Utah. The Utah Territory's petition for statehood would remind the nation of its "Mormon problem."

To the prevalent Victorian norms and lifestyle, Mormons embodied a particularly un-American outlook: no separation of church and state, a hierarchic church structure and conformity to religious authorities, plural marriage, and economic communalism. The aggressive economic, legal, and political measures on the part of the federal government would keep the pressure on the church and its members, resulting in another critical juncture for the survival of the church. In what appears to be a compromise, the church discontinued the teaching and practice of polygamy in its 1890 Manifesto, laying the groundwork for the eventual approval of Utah's statehood in 1896.

The third era is marked by the normalization of the relations between Utah and the nation as a whole. In this period, the Mormon identity was negotiated in the public sphere, resulting in more integration and assimilation. As the church discontinued polygamy, it also closed down the (Mormon) People's Party and withdrew from formal politics. This disestablishment of Mormonism was a gradual process in Utah. The years 1905–1907 are notable for being another painful period for church leadership: a congressional hearing on the question of whether to admit one of the church's general authorities, Apostle Reed Smoot, to Congress for the seat to which he had been elected. In this case, the church faced a public trial-like atmosphere (Paulos 2008); even the church prophet Joseph F. Smith testified in Congress about the allegiance of the members to the nation. Smoot's eventual seating in Congress was a victory for Mormons, moving them closer to the center of American society; it was also, arguably, a victory for the American political system (Flake 2004), showing that even groups with the least mainstream beliefs and values could become orderly citizens if provided with the right set of incentives.

The church strove to create a patriotic American image for the Mormons throughout the first half of the twentieth century. The diligent participation of Mormons in the two world wars, disaster relief efforts, civil service, and US diplomatic relations all contributed to the increasingly normalized place of Mormons in the American social compound. Utah was not an outlier in the national trends of this era, whether it was the establishment and repeal of Prohibition or the New

Deal, voting patterns were in line with national trends. This congruence with the national political mood occurred despite some efforts by church leadership to sway the politics of their followers in a more conservative direction.

After the era of normalization, the early decades of the Cold War witnessed another critical juncture for the LDS Church. The new generation of Mormons, who grew up during the decades of normalization, were more assertive about their identity and values; they sought to carve out a niche for the church in the anticommunist conservative coalition. Since the 1970s, Utah has remained one of the most conservative-leaning states: the Republican Party has regularly secured its largest electoral margins in Utah. The LDS Church became one of the major actors in the conservative coalition on moral issues, such as the Equal Rights Amendment and same-sex marriage.

Today, Mormons are seen as striving middle-class Americans, although perhaps with some different beliefs and values. The 2002 Winter Olympics and Mitt Romney's presidential bids in 2008 and 2012 also brought added publicity to the Mormons at the national and international levels. While the public face of Mormonism has continuously been negotiated since its very foundation, the trend has been unmistakably toward a more mainstream and more secure place in the American public sphere.

A detailed examination of these eras and their associated critical junctures offers valuable insights on the transformation of both Mormonism and the American public sphere.

The First Era: The Formative Years

In 1830, Joseph Smith brought a new revelation, known as the Book of Mormon, to an environment of religious fervor, evangelism, and rivalry among the many Protestant sects and denominations. His new revelation was met with a predictable reaction on the part of the religious establishment of the time. This was especially the case in New York and Pennsylvania. This religiously based tension was later complicated by other economic and political concerns when the Mormons started to evangelize to the Native Americans and appeared pro–Native American, believing the Native Americans to be the people whose forefathers were mentioned in the Book of Mormon. The ambivalent stance of the church on slavery raised additional suspicions toward the church among the slave-owners when Mormons moved to Missouri—a slave state (Arrington and Bitton 1980).

After achieving significant success in gaining new converts, the Mormons moved to Kirtland, Ohio, and later to Jackson County, Missouri, to start building the institutions of their first community. Joseph Smith then received a new revelation about the organization the Latter-day Church needed to prepare for the Millennium. He initiated missionary work as early as 1831, and the Mormon population reached three thousand by 1836. The followers of Joseph Smith were called "Saints" for the first time in this period. The community of the faithful dedicated the first temple in Kirtland, Ohio, in 1836. This was an important turning point for the church and marked its difference from other Christians: Smith's followers rejected the institutional historical Christianity and embraced a restoration of the primitive-original Christianity. In this era Mormonism sought to pave the way for the beginnings of a new order in what they anticipated would be the Kingdom of God and an imminent ushering into the Millennium. However, the conclusion to the Mormon's time in Kirtland was not as auspicious as their initial years there. The 1837 failure of the bank founded by Joseph Smith inflicted substantial debt on church members, and the rumors about Smith's inappropriate sexual conduct undermined trust in his leadership and brought turmoil to the church. Joseph Smith ultimately had to leave Kirtland; he fled to Missouri.

Opposition from the gentiles, as the Mormons called nonbelievers, to the newly founded church turned bloody in Missouri. A crucial moment came when Joseph Smith declared Jackson County, Missouri, as the new Zion—the gathering place for the Saints. Prior to this new revelation, dealings between Mormons and non-Mormons in Missouri had been largely peaceful. However, the designation of the very community in which they were living as the gathering place for all converts made local landowners uneasy, fearing that the Mormons would take over their lands. Tensions increased and armed Mormons clashed with the state militia. Mormons were eventually driven out of many towns in Missouri, losing property and the confidence that it was possible to live side by side with nonbelievers while pursuing their ambitious project to build the new Zion.

The larger society's repugnance toward Mormon religious beliefs was now complemented by fears of the Mormons' growing economic and political power. The Mormon response to these worsening tensions was not necessarily to turn the other cheek. Rather, they employed countermeasures in the manner of their opponents. The Mormons built an unsanctioned paramilitary force, the Zion Camp, to fight against outside threats. The Mormons also retaliated in kind to the burning of their homes. The Daughters of Zion (also known as the Danites) began as an active defense corps, but occasionally acted with vigilante-esque fervor, working as both a political action fraternity and a secret vengeance-seeking society (Arrington and Bitton 1980).

The raids carried out by Mormons and non-Mormons on each other's communities continued, with horrific scenes of violence. The governor of Missouri issued an executive order describing Mormons as in defiance of the laws and called for their forceful removal or extermination. Mormons fled en masse, realizing that, otherwise, they would face certain death. Declaring a religious group as the enemy of the public order was a first in the nation's history, which left a lasting imprint on the collective psyche of the Mormons and their perception of the outside world. Persecution has been an important force in building the historical Mormon self-identity. Paradoxically, persecution has also strengthened the Mormon sense of being a special and chosen people. This combination of insecurity and chosenness along with a lifestyle that promoted self-discipline, avoiding "vices" such as alcohol, premarital sex, and gambling, and the delaying of instant gratification may have been key for the subsequent success of Mormons in the twentieth and the early twenty-first century (Chua and Rubenfeld 2015).

As Mormons embraced the premise that all prophets and their followers throughout history have gone through similar challenges (Shipps 1985), their experience in the next two decades following their removal from Missouri would be characterized by continued persecution and exodus. The next Mormon settlement was Nauvoo, Illinois. Similar to the earlier years in Kirtland, the community started to flourish and take root. By 1844, the Nauvoo population reached twelve thousand, rivaling Chicago as the biggest city in Illinois. Mormons adopted a form of economic communalism with practices such as collective ownership of property and centrally organized resources to fund investments in crucial industries and in land development. The Nauvoo Charter granted extensive authority to Joseph Smith: he was the lieutenant general of the Nauvoo Legion's five thousand soldiers, a number second only to the national army; the self-appointed chief justice; and the elected mayor. Smith held these roles in addition to serving as the president of the church, meaning he was the religious seer, prophet, and revelator. The Nauvoo political order had a theocratic basis, but Mormons also understood the game of electoral politics. Thanks to the size of their population and their reputation for bloc voting, neither the Democrats nor the Whigs in the Illinois Legislature could afford to alienate Mormon voters. Consequently, the unprecedented Nauvoo Charter was passed unanimously.

In Nauvoo, the secretly practiced revelation of "celestial marriage," which authorized polygamy, was shared with the laity, creating reverberations inside and outside the church.[2] Owing to a combination of millennialist doctrine and political exigency, Joseph Smith established the Council of Fifty with the intent to build the political Kingdom of God. The council was comprised of church leadership and some non-Mormon allies; it started working discreetly to develop strategies to manage the political relations of the church. When Smith decided to run for president of the US in 1844, the Council of Fifty was in charge of his campaign; this was a fitting role for a group that had previously ordained Smith as "King, Priest and Ruler over Israel on Earth" (Quinn 1997).

2. For a detailed examination of the sources of the conflict in Nauvoo, see Hampshire 1985.

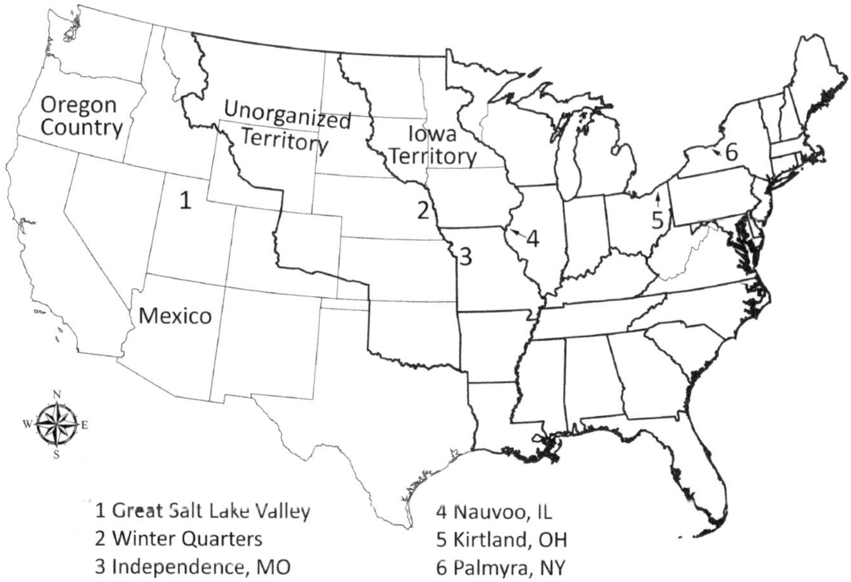

2. Mormon settlements between 1830 and 1847. Designed by University of Washington Librarian Kian A. Flynn.

Combined with their political ambition, the Mormon economic and social dominance not only agitated their neighbors, but also created cracks among the faithful. The *Nauvoo Expositor*, published by dissident Mormons, questioned Joseph Smith's introduction of polygamy and his ambitions to hold positions of political and military power and called for a return to the early teachings of Mormonism (Bushman and Bushman 2001). Smith did not take such criticism very well: he ordered the destruction of the press. Perceived as an assault on the freedom of media, this action outraged the public. It also served as one of the pretexts for the mobs that would kill Smith in 1844. Smith's death came after he had been charged with treason and was jailed in Carthage, Illinois. Despite the governor's promise to protect his life, Smith's murder in his prison cell solidified Mormon distrust of the "gentiles" (Ostling and Ostling 1999).

Joseph Smith had a chance to flee Illinois and considered going west of the existing US frontiers. Afraid of the disappointment of his followers for abandoning them, he surrendered. Losing the founding prophet of their religion was a critical juncture for the Mormons. Smith's followers would complete the westward migration that Smith himself contemplated but never took.

The Second Era: Finding a New Zion in the West

Contrary to the expectations of the anti-Mormon forces, the death of the founding prophet was not the end of Mormonism as a religious movement nor as a social movement. Smith became a martyr for his followers and ultimately strengthened their collective identity. In the immediate aftermath of the death of the Mormon prophet, Nauvoo burst into chaos. Mobs threatened Mormons and burned their houses. In addition to fearing for their earthly lives, Mormons faced spiritual uncertainty about who would succeed Joseph Smith. As the President of the Quorum of the Twelve Apostles that served under Joseph Smith's presidency, Brigham Young was able to rally support of the majority around his leadership and offered some order and purpose to the disoriented followers. In the meantime, the state of Illinois revoked the Nauvoo Charter and asked Mormons to leave. The Mormons felt wronged by the people and the government of the US once again and started their westward migration to find a place beyond its sovereign control. In the eyes of Mormons, the US government was founded on divinely guided, correct principles, but the political leadership had failed to abide by these principles. It was thus time to find a separate space for implementing the principles of God's kingdom on earth.

Brigham Young decided to lead the Saints to the Salt Lake Valley, which was under Mexican jurisdiction at the time. The Mormon exodus had begun. Joseph Smith's widow, Emma, and his son Joseph III decided to stay in Nauvoo. Joseph Smith III would later establish the Reorganized Church of Jesus Christ of Latter Day Saints (presently known as the Community of Christ) with the small remaining minority in the Midwest. The majority, however, had followed Brigham Young for one of the greatest mass migrations in American history.

The first group of Mormons left in 1846. After three months and one thousand miles on wagons and foot, the first pioneers arrived in the Great Basin. Brigham Young preferred this territory because it was isolated and would be less attractive for settlement by non-Mormons. The Salt Lake Valley and the Great basin represented an opportunity for the Mormons to build everything from scratch in the Mormon way (Berrett 1985).

After the Mexican War (1846–48), the western territories, including the Salt Lake Valley, were acquired by the US. Within a year of their escape from the reach of the American government, Mormons once again found themselves under its authority. In 1847, the Council of Fifty, acting like a legislature, quickly adopted a constitution and appointed Brigham Young as the governor of the new provisional Mormon state of Deseret (named after a word for honeybee found in the Book of Mormon). The US Congress refused to recognize Deseret and decided to create the Utah Territory as part of the 1850 Compromise. This political two-step allowed California to join the Union as a free state and created the New Mexico and Utah Territories without provisions for the legality of slavery. The State of Deseret petition was dead. President Fillmore appointed Young as the governor of the Utah Territory, but also required him to work with other non-Mormon federal appointees. Young contested the authority of the Congress and the power of the federal appointments, going so far as to organize the people of Utah to petition Congress to recognize the autonomy of the Utah government. Half of the federal appointees for the Utah Territory were selected from Mormons. These officials included Brigham Young, who continued to serve as the governor of the Utah Territory until the 1858 appointment of Alfred Cummings by the federal government. Mormons did not welcome the outside federal appointees; the appointees, in turn, departed for Washington, DC, with tales of complete church domination. Mutual distrust and suspicion would continue to fuel tensions during the next forty years.

Building the Beehive State under Watchful Federal Eyes

There was little demarcation between religious and temporal in the new western Mormon colonies, which stretched from northern Mexico to southern Canada. The main settlements in the new territories were built around sacred symbols. Following the arrival of the Mormons in the new land, temple construction quickly began at the center of Salt Lake City. During the first two years of Mormon settlement there was, in fact, no civil government: the church organized the full extent of colonization and settlement. The territory was divided into differently sized regional groupings, known as stakes and wards, along the lines of ecclesiastical divisions in church organization.

Church Economic Systems. The first settlements in the Great Basin exhibited a strong communitarian spirit. There were communal plots for farming and the land was allocated to maximize the community's development of resources. Property rights were conditional on the protection and development of the land. Each household had enough property to support a family; the surplus was placed in a common pool, known as "the Lord's storehouse." This practice was based on the Stewardship Revelation, which asks believers to exercise responsible ownership of resources with an eye to the needs of the community.[3] The necessary industries for development—iron, coal, lead, sugar, cotton, and silk—were built as communal enterprises without outside capital or dependence. Some communities also implemented the more radical and egalitarian Law of Consecration. With this approach, individuals dedicated their time, talents, and possessions to the church to create a system of joint ownership of property and communal inheritance.

The implementation of the principles of Consecration and Stewardship and the associated cooperative enterprises under church leadership are together known as the United Order. This collectivist approach was put into practice during different periods in the nineteenth century, when the church assumed a leadership role in creating self-sufficient communities during mass migrations and times of crisis. The first several decades of church history provide examples of

3. "Every Man Shall Be Accountable Unto Me, a Steward Over His Own Property" (The Church of Jesus Christ of Latter-day Saints, *Doctrine and Covenants*, D&C 42:32).

different communitarian efforts. Attempts to establish a United Order can be found in some early Mormon communities in the Midwest as early as mid-1830s; later, in the Great Basin, between 1855 and 1858; and, again, following the completion of the transcontinental railroad, which brought an influx of non-Mormons to Utah. In the latter case, Brigham Young emphasized the system in response to the economic threats of potential job losses and the erosion of capital as well as to address rising poverty in the Mormon community.

Challenged by American capitalism and congressional sanctions against the LDS Church, the "Mormon way" in Utah was increasingly weakened: ultimately, the communitarian economic system had limited overall success. It was gradually replaced with mainstream capitalism after the normalization of relations between the federal government and the Mormons around the turn of the twentieth century. Dedicating one's time, capital, and talents is still an ideal embraced by many Mormons, albeit now under different systems and structures. For example, responding to "calls" from the church leadership for lay priesthood, tithing, and contributing to the church welfare system are important pillars of present-day Mormon communities. These practices embody the earlier communitarian spirit and the associated pooling of resources (Arrington 1992, 435–41).

Theodemocracy. The Mormon pioneers first attempted to create a civil government in 1849. The State of Deseret claimed a good portion of the west, including the current states of Utah and Nevada as well as portions of Arizona, Oregon, Idaho, Wyoming, Colorado, New Mexico, and southern California. A constitutional convention for the state of Desert adopted a typical text that combined elements of the US Constitution and other established state constitutions, such as those of Iowa and Illinois. In order to satisfy the federal government's requirement of republican rule over all US territories, the constitution for the state of Deseret provided for the separation of powers between the three branches of government, freedom of religion, and full suffrage for white males—but the constitution did not mention the controversial issue of slavery (White 1996).

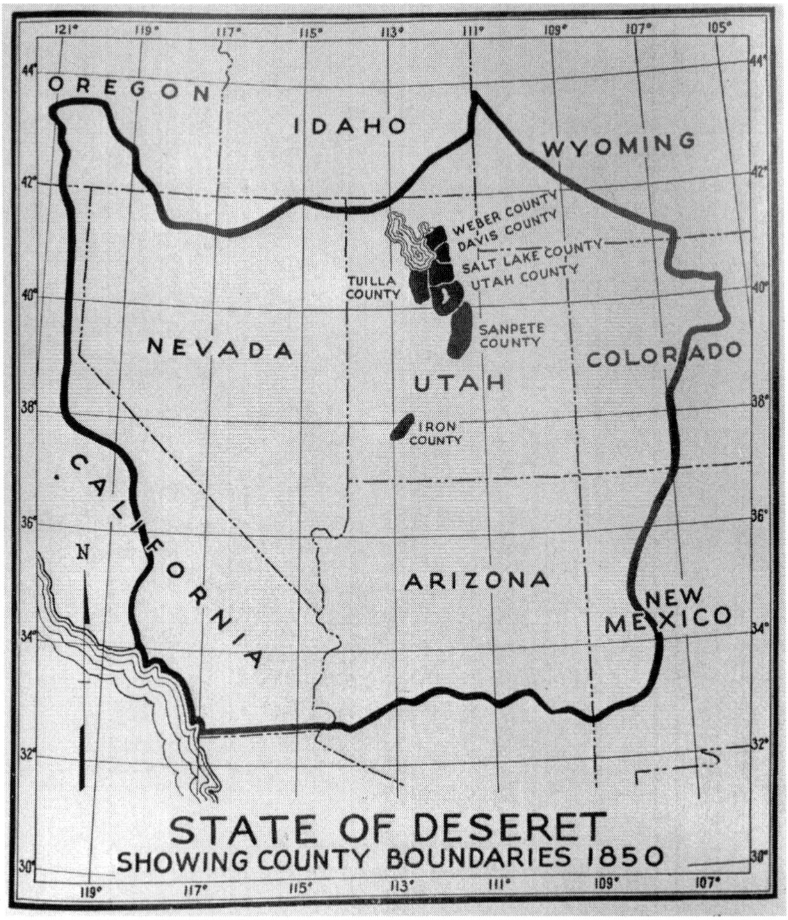

3. Proposed State of Deseret. Utah State Historical Society. Used by permission.

Brigham Young would remain the church president as well as being the governor of the state. Other officers from the church rank and file were "elected" to government positions, according to the wishes of Brigham Young and church leadership, by using the Mormon Church tradition of calling and sustaining. Consequently, a somewhat parallel civil government was formed alongside church administration. The practice of filling political offices with high-ranking church officials gave the ecclesiastic authorities hegemony over the civil government and further magnified the church's political power. Sacred and secular were integrated: there was hardly any demarcation of political and religious positions (Williams 1966). The territorial legislature immediately granted extraordinary legal powers to the church in terms of enacting marriages and acquiring and controlling property. The economy was under church control and management owing to the church's tight grip on land, infrastructure, agriculture, and industry (Gordon 2002, 26–29).

After the constitution was drafted, a petition was sent to Congress for statehood. The proposed state of Deseret did not receive the necessary political support in the nation's capital. President Taylor believed that Deseret was not fit for statehood, based on the immense size of the territory, its relatively small population, and its underdeveloped political institutions. In addition to the fact that issues related to slavery were occupying much of the national agenda, the widely perceived un-American ways of the Mormons were receiving renewed attention. The secret Mormon militia, the Daughters of Zion, were known as "Danites" and occupied the popular imagination of the violent fanaticism of the Mormon men. Polygamy represented the oppression of the Mormon women. Along with slavery, polygamy became a social crusader's cause in 1850s (Austin 2012). Popular novels in 1850s, such as Alfreda Eva Bell's *Boadicea, The Mormon Wife* (1855), Maria Ward's *Female Life among the Mormons* (1855), and Metta Victoria Fuller's *Mormon Wives* (1856) increasingly dramatized polygamy and invoked strong popular sentiments. The bid for statehood was further debilitated by this anti-Mormon and antipolygamy sentiment in the society and affected the representatives in Congress. In short, both the political climate and popular sentiment worked against the bid for statehood.

The question of polygamy and the petitions for statehood highlight the ongoing negotiation in the American public sphere regarding the principles of federalism and religious liberty. The thinly disguised Protestantism of the "nondenominational" religion and the morality lessons that were taught in public schools did not suit Catholic immigrants. Catholics tried unsuccessfully to get exemptions from this content for their children or to receive government funding for their private schools. In a similar vein, polygamy was beyond the limits of acceptable Christian morality; tolerance for behaviors contrary to the standard of Christian morality were not covered under the public standard of religious liberty at the time (Gordon 2002, 71).

Mormons had learned the bitter lesson that the national government was either unable or unwilling to help them against their persecutors in the 1830s and 1840s. With respect to government inaction, Joseph Smith reported that President Van Buren told him, "Gentlemen, your cause is just, but I can do nothing for you"; Smith would later retell this story as part of his presidential bid (Garr 2009, 51). Since the power of the federal government was relatively limited in the western territories at the time, Mormons expected the same deference toward local sovereignty and tendency to federal noninterventionism for their own government in Utah. However, the Civil War would paradoxically strengthen the national government and rule out secession for the states. The Fourteenth Amendment would then pave the way for the application of the Constitution and the Bill of Rights to the states. In the two decades following the Civil War, Mormon leadership felt pressure from the larger American society and the federal government to assimilate in order to receive the privilege of being under the protection of the Constitution and its guarantee of religious liberty.

Growing Tensions and the Eventual Confrontation

Brigham Young occupied the positions of church president and territorial governor between 1851 and 1857. He regularly clashed with the non-Mormon appointees serving as federal secretaries and federal judges in Utah. Many of the federal appointees returned to Washington without completing their full term of service out west. They harbored anti-Mormon sentiments and told stories of the church leadership's complete domination of territorial affairs. When the federal government finally decided to assert more control over Utah and appoint a non-Mormon governor, President Buchanan sent 2,500 US Army soldiers to escort the newly appointed governor, Alfred E.

Cummings. The Mormon establishment had long threatened that any attempt by the federal government to undermine their popular sovereignty would be met with dire consequences. From the perspective of the Mormons, the massacres in Missouri and Nauvoo were still fresh in the minds of church leadership. They were thus alarmed about the prospect of a military expedition into their new refuge in the Great Basin. Brigham Young was particularly paranoid about non-Mormons coming to Utah for economic or political reasons. To this end, he kept the Mormon militia, the Nauvoo Legion, active and ready to defend his people. A full-scale confrontation between the federal expeditionary forces and the Mormon militia was avoided by mediation. Yet skirmishes in northern Utah and a massacre in southern Utah suggested that the likelihood of the conflict's escalation was a dire possibility. Brigham Young ultimately abandoned his earlier threats toward the federal troops and the Utah War (1857–58) ended without an actual battle. The net result of this standoff was the undermining of Young's theocratic model and his claims to unfettered Mormon popular sovereignty. However, the tensions during this period only added to the existing mistrust between the two sides.

In 1857, at the peak of the dispute between the Mormon settlers and the federal government, an estimated one hundred California-bound settlers were killed by Mormon militia when they stopped to rest at Mountain Meadows in southern Utah. The attackers included some members of the local Paiute Native American tribe, as the Mormon militia leaders aimed to give the attack the appearance of a Native American conspiracy. This massacre was carried out on the basis that the California-bound migrants had links with the past persecution and damages the Mormons had suffered in the Midwest. The facts of the Mountain Meadows incident are fairly clear and Major John D. Lee of the Mormon militia was tried, convicted, and executed in 1877. Others involved in the massacre lived in guilty secrecy. A dramatic deathbed expression of this guilt by one of those involved in the massacre after nearly a century would ultimately motivate a local Mormon teacher and author, Juanita Brooks, to investigate the massacre. In 1950 Brooks published her findings as a book entitled *The Mountain*

Meadows Massacre, which uncovered the conditions of the incident and pushed the church to revisit its policy of silence (Prince and Wright 2005, 55–58). The disagreement among historians concerns the extent to which the LDS leadership in Salt Lake City was complicit in the massacre.[4] The church acknowledged the wrongdoings of some members and the local leadership, but it denied any direct involvement on the part of Brigham Young and other top church leaders. However, for the rest of his life, Brigham Young had a fear of being arrested and perhaps assassinated while in custody for his alleged role. Driven by this fear, Young fled to southern Utah in the early 1870s; he died in 1877. As a sign of good faith, the church later tried to reconcile with the descendants of the victims, who founded a group called the Mountain Meadows Association. The church offered prayers for healing the wounds of the victims' descendants and restored and maintained the monument at the site.[5] The Mountain Meadows Massacre remains one of the darkest moments in Utah's history. It is also emblematic of the tensions between the Mormons and the larger American public during this period.

Overall, during the first two decades of settlement in the Utah Territory, the LDS Church governed the affairs of its followers—and the rest of the Utah Territory—at the expense of the civil government. Mormons and federal appointees were in almost constant conflict until Utah was admitted to the Union in 1896. For example, even the Utah legislature's seemingly progressive law granting suffrage to women was perceived by the federal government as a move on the part of the church to increase its electoral weight. In response, Congress targeted female suffrage in the Utah Territory in the Edmunds-Tucker Act of 1887.

4. For a sample of different accounts, see Brooks 1962; Bagley 2002; and Turley, Walker, and the Church of Jesus Christ of Latter-day Saints 2009.

5. "Mountain Meadows Grave Site Memorial," news release by the Church Public Affairs Department, September 7, 1999, Church History Library Archives, Salt Lake City, Utah.

The Crusade Against Polygamy

The practice of plural marriage in Kirtland and Nauvoo was not widespread and was kept largely secret. By the time the Mormons reached Utah and established settlements, the practice had become more common; the church publicized the practice of polygamy in 1852. The public acknowledgement of the practice further contributed to the sense that Mormons were "others" in the eyes of the American public: Mormons were not just different—they were also very un-American. During the 1856 presidential campaign, the newly established Republican Party, already fighting against slavery, declared polygamy to be the other frontier in the fight against the "twin relics of barbarism" (Van Zile 1882). Once again, Mormons invoked the principle of freedom of religion to practice "celestial marriage" as dictated by their faith. Congress denied Utah admission to the Union until the church renounced polygamy and took concrete steps to stop the practice. Utah joined the Union in 1896. As much as the federal response to polygamy was grounded in moral and legal questions, it was also a symbolic struggle against the theocratic model in Utah that raised questions of loyalty to the nation and the Republic.

Congress enacted a series of antipolygamy legislation between 1862 and 1890. The first was the Morrill Act (1862), which made bigamy punishable by a fine and a prison sentence. The Morrill Act also limited the amount of property the church could hold to $50,000. In 1874, the Poland Act increased the powers of the federal government by giving the US marshal the exclusive right to select jury pools and probate judges. Granting federal authorities this power undermined the juridical independence of the Utah territory and ended the de facto impunity of the church leaders (Gordon 2002). Utah courts became the battleground between the church and the federal government during the next three decades. In order to overcome the Mormon control of the local courts, the Edmunds Act of 1882 amended the earlier antibigamy legislation, criminalized cohabitation outside of legal marriage, disenfranchised polygamists, and deemed polygamists ineligible for jury duty.

The federal courts and the US Marshals began their offensive against plural marriage and received convictions from friendly juries whose members had been selected based on their disbelief in polygamy. After the Supreme Court upheld the antipolygamy sanctions of the federal statute in *Reynolds v. US* (1878), secrecy became the only option for Mormons who engaged polygamy. Church President John Taylor resisted federal pressures to end the practice until his last breath and died in 1887 while underground trying to avoid prosecution due to his polygamous marriage. The 1887 Edmunds-Tucker Act was the culmination of the congressional fight against the power of the LDS Church in Utah. The church was disincorporated, its property seized, and all Mormon women were disenfranchised. When challenged, the Supreme Court upheld the seizure of church property in 1890, ruling once again in favor of the federal government against the Mormon interests.[6]

During this time, Mormons put together a multifaceted strategy of resistance. At the popular level, they used counterarguments against the antipolygamists, claiming that polygamy was more natural than monogamy; that polygamy was more humane than monogamy; and that since polygamy was grounded in the old scripture—revived by the modern revelations, it created a better public order for the Millennium. Many of the pro-polygamy arguments used by Mormons were appropriated from the existing critical literature on monogamous ethic (Hardy 1992, 84). On the political front, Mormon activists sent representatives to Congress and employed the lobbyists used by the powerful railroad industry. If the political strategy of securing statehood for the state of Deseret had worked, Mormons would have found it much easier to enforce their local sovereignty. The exact legal status of US territories was ambiguous, but the federal government clearly exerted a great deal of control. Yet the Mormon practices of bloc voting; boycotting non-Mormon businesses, which increased in

6. *Late Corporation of the Church of Jesus Christ of Latter-Day Saints v. United States*, 136 US 67 (1890).

number as a result of the completion of the transcontinental railroad; and granting suffrage to women were strategies that the Mormons were able to use to maintain political control inside Utah Territory. In the 1870s and 1880s, Mormon political leaders would attempt to appease the federal government and non-Mormon Utahns by introducing various modifications to the state constitution (White 1996). However, by the mid-1880s, the hopes for the church to survive the conflict without discontinuing polygamy was dwindling. The federal government was determined not to accept any solution short of ending polygamy and Mormons believed the practice would continue until the return of the Christ. Nothing short of a miracle could end the conflict on terms favorable to the Mormon side. Many church members in fact anticipated such a miracle through divine intervention, believing the return of Christ was imminent (Hardy 1992, 128).

The Third Era: Normalization and Americanization

The failure of the Mormon political strategies brought a sobering realization that all courses of action in the four-decade struggle had been exhausted. Strategically, the only remaining option for the survival of Mormonism was to surrender. Soon after the decision of the Supreme Court to uphold the Edmund-Tucker Act in 1890, Church President Wilford Woodruff announced the intention of the Saints to follow the federal laws and thus discontinue their practice of plural marriage; this decision was made to ensure the "temporal salvation of the Church" (Clark 1965, 193). During the General Conference of the Church in October 1890, the members affirmed the act of the Church President abolishing polygamy; this act would come to be known as the Manifesto. At first, many Mormons saw this less as a change in doctrine or practice and more of a tactical move to appease the federal government and save the church from extinction. Secret plural marriages continued well into the twentieth century (Hardy 2012). The church, however, did enforce the antipolygamy policy more strictly, thanks to the federal government's scrutiny, and excommunicated the leadership who entered into or authorized plural marriages after 1890.

One event that resulted in such scrutiny was the debate surrounding the seating of Senator Reed Smoot, a Republican Mormon Church leader elected in 1903 to represent Utah in Congress. B. H. Roberts, a Utah Mormon Democrat elected to Congress in 1899 had previously been denied his seat because of his practice of polygamy. However, Smoot had only one wife and the initial move came from non-Mormon Utah business owners who were critical of Mormon economic practices in Utah. After Smoot's credentials were confirmed and he took the oath, his position in the Mormon Church hierarchy attracted more national attention from the press and mobilized the Protestant congregations and women's organizations. The Senate was inundated with incoming petitions against Senator Smoot. As a result of this pressure a committee was formed to investigate the complaints about the LDS Church's complete control over its members' lives, its meddling in Utah politics, economic practices, and violation of the antibigamy laws.[7] The publicity surrounding questions of whether Smoot would be permitted to join Congress served as a public trial of the LDS Church with reports and testimonies on its hierarchical priesthood structure, secret temple rituals and oaths, and, of course, polygamy. After three years of investigations and deliberations, the Senate finally voted against the expulsion of Smoot. During this period, many high-ranking members, including the Church President Joseph F. Smith, would publicly defend the church and promise to respect the civil government's authority and abide by the laws. The result of the Smoot hearings was not an absolute victory for any of the parties involved, but rather a political accommodation to recognize a secure place for Mormons in the American public sphere, while pushing them to the mainstream. After decades of conflict, Senate was able to find a political solution to the nation's "Mormon problem"

7. "The Expulsion Case of Reed Smoot of Utah (1907)," US Senate Historical Office, *United States Senate Election, Expulsion and Censure Cases: 1793–1990* (Washington, DC: Government Printing Office, 1995), 272–74, (https://www.senate.gov/artandhistory/history/common/expulsion_cases/091ReedSmoot_expulsion.htm.

that military and criminal legal approaches could not (Flake 2005). The Smoot hearings also marked a last-ditch effort by the Protestant establishment to deny Mormonism a legitimate place in the American public sphere. The century-long Protestant establishment was slipping as a result of immigration and demographic shifts, with the growing number of Catholic and Jewish populations and the progressive turn in the country's politics. The Progressive Era (1890–1920) would transform the Protestant establishment itself, pushing the mainline denominations in what would become the liberal camp against the conservatives. Ironically, as Mormons moved to the center they would become one of the staunchest defenders of the Christian identity and Christian morality in the American public sphere, much like the Protestant establishment did at their expense in the nineteenth century. The conservative turn in Mormon politics in the 1960s marked the beginning of the fourth historical stage of the Mormon identity in the American body politic, which chapter 7 examines in more detail: the era of globalized church and slick public affairs.

Even though the 1890 Manifesto and the Smoot hearings ended polygamy in doctrine and practice for the LDS Church, some Mormons in rural regions rejected the new policy and created the Fundamentalist Church of Jesus Christ of Latter Day Saints (FLDS). The founding of the FLDS was driven by the belief that polygamy was a necessary practice for salvation and abolishing a practice closely associated with the distinct Mormon identity symbolized admitting defeat and giving in to the demands of the enemies of the faith. In reality, despite its symbolic importance, plural marriage was never practiced by a majority of Mormons. Leonard Arrington and Davis Bitton estimate that only about 5 percent of Mormon men and 12 percent of Mormon women practiced polygamy between 1850 and 1890 (Arrington and Bitton 1982, 199). More recent research indicates that 23 to 30 percent of Mormons practiced plural marriage at the end of the nineteenth century, a number that encompasses a larger share of the leadership who could afford to do so (Alexander 1986, 64; Flake 2004, 65).

The church's disengagement from civil government was a multidimensional process. The most obvious of these was the normalization of politics. The (Mormon) People's Party, which had been formed as a response to the emerging organized opposition from the non-Mormon Liberal Party in Utah, was dissolved in 1891. The Mormons were divided into Democrats and Republicans, sometimes literally split down the middle of a given congregation by church leadership (Bowman 2012, 155). At the beginning a greater share joined the Democratic Party, mostly because the Church President Joseph F. Smith became a Democrat. As a balancing act and to garner the Republican support for Utah's statehood, other church leaders joined the Republican Party and similarly influenced their congregations (Shipps 2016, 74). In the coming decades a more socioeconomic-based party affiliation emerged with well-educated, urban, and middle-class Mormons supporting the Republican Party, and more rural-based farmer Mormons supporting the Democrats. Disestablishment of Mormonism in Utah was complete by the time Congress approved its statehood in 1896 and the church had ended its claims on the state's domain within the public sphere. The church's official withdrawal from party politics, however, was not the end of its political involvement. Using its position as the most influential civil society actor, the church continued to influence politics through its public statements, letters to the congregations, and interest group politics via its public affairs organs. Chapter 7 investigates these dual civil- and political-society roles of the church leadership and organizations.

In considering the separation of church and state in Utah, an analysis of two important steps in this process is in order: the formation of civil courts, and the support for a public education system outside the church structure. The particular forms of disengagement, regulations, and arrangements offer insights regarding the church's response to external political factors.

Secular and Religious Education

When Congress passed the Enabling Act of 1894, one of the key requirements for Utah's statehood was a nonsectarian public school system with a strong assurance of religious freedom. Given the apparent assimilation mission of the common schools, this stipulation was rather unsurprising. In spite of the constant turmoil they experienced during their formative years, the Mormons highly valued education and had managed to establish significant institutions and projects. One such institution was the School of the Prophets in Kirtland, Ohio, founded in 1832. This school was chiefly focused on equipping church leadership with an understanding of the broader society and the world so leaders would be able to provide widely appealing religious messages. The curriculum was devoted to the study of languages, history, politics, and literature, and it directly addressed the needs of missionary functions. The second attempt to create an educational institution was in 1841, with the creation of the University of the City of Nauvoo. This university had a respectable start with a reasonably qualified faculty for a frontier town, but, just like the Kirtland experience, it was short-lived, owing to the social upheaval that characterized the early Mormon experience.

After the westward migration, the idea of a center of learning for religious and secular subjects together was revived with the University of Deseret, established in 1850. The university's chief goal was to educate the teachers who would then become the foundation of the Utah school system. Due to financial problems, there were not enough registrations, which led to insufficient tuition revenue to sustain the school. The University of Desert would last only two years. With respect to primary education, the concerns related to the survival of the community proved to be a great obstacle. Mormons in Utah did not have a widespread functional primary-education system until 1890. There were sporadic schools in huts and tents as early as nine months after the first settlements. These schools solicited students by advertisements, were taught by private parties, and cost few cents per week. They were not very effective. Many children had to work on the farms and few families could afford the cost. Later on, after the community was able to build an economy and provide some basic infrastructure, church meetinghouses were used for education. These church schools followed LDS teachings. Church leadership encouraged students to attend and pay tuition, but the credentials of the teachers were not very impressive (Cranny 1992; Gardner 1992).

The opening of Saint Mark's Episcopal School in 1867 ushered in a new period of competition for Utah's educational system. Representatives from other denominations, including Presbyterians, Catholics, Methodists, Baptists, Lutherans, and Congregationalists, followed suit and opened their own schools. Initially, these schools were established for missionaries from these non-Mormon denominations and for their new converts. However, some Mormons perceived these schools to be of higher quality than their own church schools and thus preferred the schools of the other denominations (Hough 1960).

The educational system of the church took a new turn after the 1890 decision of the non-LDS territorial school officials to remove sectarian education from the curriculum. The LDS Church continued offering education to its members through some secondary academies. However, the cost of sustaining these schools and the new post-Manifesto environment—characterized by the retreat of the church from many public pursuits—pushed the church to abandon its insistence on providing a comprehensive education system. The next step, then, was to find a place for church teachings and instruction in the new public education system. The solution was the Supplemental Church Education System, currently known as the CES.[8] As a consequence, the existing church academies and schools were either converted to seminaries or handed over to the state.

The first seminary was opened in 1912 in Salt Lake City. This followed the closure of church-owned secondary schools. In 2018, there were approximately 350,000 students enrolled in the seminary programs. In places with a large LDS student population, students attend CES during release-time from public school. In places with relatively smaller Mormon populations, students attend CES before or after the school day. If the LDS population is scattered or very small, the third

8. For an analysis of the CES's curriculum and engagement with secular education, see Fowles 1990.

option is homeschooling. Teachers in any of these models can be full-time instructors and volunteers.[9]

The church owns and administers the LDS Business College in Salt Lake City, Utah and Brigham Young University (BYU). BYU has campuses in Provo, Utah; Rexburg, Idaho; and Laie, Hawaii, and a study-abroad program center in Jerusalem. These schools all aim to integrate secular education with religious teachings, values, and a religious lifestyle. Thus, there are required religion courses as well as an honor code. Only a fraction of Mormons (about 45,000 out of 15 million) attend a church-owned college; most members go to other public or private universities. The LDS Church maintains Institutes of Religion in and around college and university campuses with significant populations of Mormon students. In 2017, these Institutes of Religion enrolled nearly 340,000 students in over 2200 programs worldwide. The institutes offer classes in church history, scripture, and doctrine as well as preparing students for other life events, such as missionary work and marriage. They primarily serve single Mormon students, but married Mormons or non-Mormons can also be found taking classes at the institutes. The institutes offer spiritual support in a social environment: in the words of a former president of the church, Mormon students at the institutes "find learning, social experience, and even husbands and wives within the faith."[10]

The change in the educational system and the philosophy of the church is parallel to and reflective of its relationship with the state. During the church's early formative years in the Midwest and in the Utah Territory, there was no separation of church and state or division between religious and (secular) public education. The creation of a public education system independent of the church was an indication of the church's disengagement from the state's domain. However, the church was still dominant in the civil society and influential in

9. The Church of Jesus Christ of Latter-day Saints, "Education," Mormon Newsroom, http://www.mormonnewsroom.org/ldsnewsroom/eng/background-information/education.

10. "This Great Millennial Year," *Liahona*, January 2001, 80.

Utah politics, and it found alternate ways to supplement the secular education curriculum, thereby making public education safe for Mormon values and beliefs. Why did the church create supplementary seminaries instead of private schools, as many other religious groups in America have done? The answer is twofold. First, economic concerns carried significant weight: when the church made this decision in the early 1900s, the cost of maintaining church schools was simply too great for the church coffers. In this era, the church was going through financial troubles following years of tension with the federal government, and the practice of the United (Economic) Order had a communitarian outlook that limited private enterprise. Second, there was considerable outside pressure on the Mormon Church to move closer to the key American institutions, such as separation of church and state, democracy, and capitalism, and integrate with the values of the mainstream (Protestant) American society. The church could not afford to offer the larger society another source of suspicion by creating a separate and independent private school system in a majority-Mormon state. The existence of a separate school system would have likely served to prolong the existing tensions with the non-Mormon population and with the federal and non-Mormon state officials. This decision of the Mormon Church regarding public schooling and the CES did not dilute the social cohesion or bonding of the Mormon community; rather, it made it more acceptable and hard to oppose.

From Church Courts to Disciplinary Councils

Another area of importance in disestablishing Mormonism in Utah was the judicial system. During much of the nineteenth century, the church court system adjudicated all types of disputes in Mormon communities. With the exception of the city of Nauvoo, where Mormons controlled politics, the Saints never trusted the civil courts because of the social and political tensions that marked their relationships with the communities in which they resided. In territorial Utah, the church courts adjudicated criminal and civil disputes as well as intrachurch disciplinary issues such as excommunication and disfellowshipment (membership with major restrictions). The 1874 Poland Act created civil courts that were administered by the federal territorial government, but the church discouraged its members from using these civil courts: church members who sued other church members in civil courts were subject to disciplinary measures by the church, including excommunication. These civil courts were extensively used by the federal government during the campaign against polygamy.

The church court system was the only justice system available for husbands, wives, and children in plural marriage arrangements. During this period, there were also county probate judges who were appointed by the LDS-dominated territorial legislature. Many county judges were Mormon bishops or local stake presidents who oversaw several congregations; Mormons often turned to these judges when they had a dispute against a non-Mormon. This dual court system in which church courts conducted business parallel to secular courts ended after Utah's admission to the Union in 1896. As had happened with the separation of church education from public education, the church retreated from the role the state had assumed: the LDS ecclesiastical courts conceded their authority to the civil courts in matters of private disputes (Backman 1992).

The modified church court system was called the Church Disciplinary Council, and it assumed jurisdiction over members' spiritual affairs (Hafen 1992). The functioning of these disciplinary councils and their treatment of dissenting Mormon intellectuals have at times drawn strong public attention in the last three decades and became a public image concern for the church leadership. The church defines the purpose of church discipline as threefold: "to save the soul of transgressors," "to protect the innocent," and "to safeguard the purity, integrity and good name of the Church."[11] A church disciplinary council is mandatory for murder, incest, child abuse, apostasy, and various transgressions, including by those who hold prominent positions in the priesthood. Likewise, those deemed to be predators are subject to a mandatory church disciplinary council. A disciplinary

11. https://www.lds.org/topics/church-disciplinary-councils?lang=eng.

council is also necessary when an individual has an abortion or a transsexual operation.[12] Last, disciplinary councils are part of the procedure to request name removal for members who initiate termination of their membership. Church members can be tried in absentia if they refuse to appear before the council.

The church disciplinary councils do not deal with civil or financial disputes between members, or instances in which a great deal of time has passed since the transgression, or occasional failures to comply with some less serious church standards, such as dietary code (Word of Wisdom) violations, failures to tithe or to engage fully in the church, or inattention to church-assigned duties. Potential disciplinary measures include private counsel with the bishop resulting in a warning, formal or informal probation to temple rites, disfellowshipment, and, ultimately, excommunication (Church of Jesus Christ of Latter-day Saints 1998).

The highest-ranking priest in a ward (congregation) or stake (group of congregations) and the high-council members all attend disciplinary council meetings. The proceedings fall short of the legal standards expected in a civil court: there are no lawyers, no established procedures for establishing a case, no set standards for proving guilt, and no defense is provided. The Mormon watchdog group the Mormon Alliance has argued that the church trials do not provide defendants with clear charges or with the means for an adequate defense.[13] Additionally, the practice of combining the roles of prosecutor, judge, and juror, has led the Mormon Alliance to call the Church Disciplinary Councils "confusing, arbitrary, and unfair" (Ostling and Ostling

12. M. Russell Ballard, "A Chance to Start Over: Church Disciplinary Councils and the Restoration of Blessings," *Ensign*, September 1990.

13. The Mormon Alliance was founded in 1992 to purportedly deal with abuses of power in the LDS Church. The group's purpose is, in its own words, "to identify and document ecclesiastical/spiritual abuse, to promote healing and closure for its survivors, to build more sensitive leadership, to empower LDS members to participate with more authenticity in Mormonism, and to foster a healthier religious community" (http://mormon-alliance.org).

1999, 359). It should be noted that it is possible to appeal the decision of a disciplinary council. The priests are also advised on how to ensure fairness in trials. However, these efforts fall short of professional standards and formal training expected from other civil associations, such as a bar association, to take disciplinary actions against their members.

Other than the "moral failures" of the members, church disciplinary councils also address "intellectual failure," classified under apostasy: deliberate public opposition to the teachings of the church or its leaders; persistent teaching of a church doctrine other than the official version; or practicing teachings, such as plural marriage, that are associated with the "apostate sects."

In the early 1990s, the existence of a committee called "Strengthening the Members Committee" inside the general headquarters of the LDS Church caused a public uproar in Utah. An internal memo was leaked to the public and a group of liberal Mormon intellectuals held public discussions at the Sunstone Symposium about the church general authorities' attempts to intimidate and silence critical voices inside the church. A church statement confirmed the existence of the committee and justified it with reference to scriptures and asked members not to publicly debate church doctrine, policy, or procedures.[14] Strong disciplinary measures were taken against six outspoken liberal Mormon intellectuals.[15] They were charged with apostasy based on their publications and speeches; their work addressed the historical origins

14. "Church Defends Keeping Files on Members," *Sunstone*, August 1992, 63.

15. *Paul Toscano*: Lawyer and author, and the founder of the Mormon Alliance, had criticized the church for misconduct and (spiritual) abuse. He was excommunicated.

Maxine Hanks: Wrote on Mormon Feminism, the Heavenly Mother, women and the priesthood in the LDS Church. She was excommunicated.

Michael D. Quinn: Mormon historian, his account of early church history included the existence of a female priesthood, the influence of magic on the origins of the Book of Mormon, and church-sanctioned plural marriages after the 1890 manifesto. He was excommunicated.

Lavina Fielding Anderson: Wrote critically about the church's treatment of scholars and also served as a trustee of Mormon Alliance. She was excommunicated.

of the Book of Mormon and its teachings, the male-only priesthood, the doctrine regarding the female deity "Heavenly Mother," and the abuses of church authority. Charges of apostasy became the mechanism for punishing dissent and critics within the church.

The Church Disciplinary Councils were announced in quick succession, suggesting that they were orchestrated from LDS headquarters.[16] Speaking to a Mormon audience in May 1993, apostle Boyd K. Packer warned the audience about feminists, homosexuals, and "so-called scholars and intellectuals" as the three largest dangers to the church. He urged local leaders to deal with these individuals with "ever increasing urgency."[17] Considering the hierarchical nature of the church, these words, as well as similar critiques from the general authorities, sent a very strong message to local leaders with respect to initiating disciplinary actions. Despite admitting that reports were sent to the local LDS priests regarding certain members whose activities had violated church standards, the leadership rejected claims of direct involvement. The church argued that the actions were all taken at the discretion of the local priests.[18] Michael D. Quinn, who was one of the excommunicated, pointed out that handing such information to a local priest would carry enormous weight, tantamount to an instruction from church leadership.[19] President Hinckley defended the disciplinary actions as a necessary course of action when a member

---

Lynne Kanave Whitesides: Then-president of the feminist Mormon Women's Forum. She was disfellowshipped.

Avraham Gileadi: Conservative theologian and biblical scholar whose writings on the Apocalypse and the Second Coming attracted attention from the church. He was excommunicated (but was rebaptized in 1996).

16. "More Stories Point to LDS Leaders as Source of Dissident Crackdown: Elders Influenced Crackdown," *Salt Lake Tribune*, October 16, 1993.

17. "As the Mormon Church Grows, So Does Dissent from Feminists and Scholars," *New York Times*, October 2, 1993.

18. "The Church Isn't Conducting a 'Purge,' LDS Apostle Says," *Deseret News*, October 2, 1993.

19. "The Church Isn't Conducting a 'Purge,'" *New York Times*.

"speaks openly and actively and takes measures to enlist others in opposition to the church and its programs and doctrines."[20]

Some of the members who were subject to disciplinary measures spoke publicly about their cases. The church was not happy about the increased publicity, arguing that the disciplinary councils and verdicts were private and confidential. The church refused to discuss any details. The church's stance was also very convenient from a public relations perspective, because the church could stress both its ongoing desire to show wayward members the true path and its official theological positions. Church authorities have maintained that disciplinary actions are sanctions that aim to "bring the transgressors back to the fold," thereby expressing the willingness of the church to work with the excommunicated. One of the reasons for the church's strong reaction to its critics was the fear that more nuanced and critical perspectives would undermine the principal objective of the church: to spread a simple and uniform message as a "mainstream American religion" across the world and to expand its global reach and membership. This goal required minimizing discussions about the unorthodox aspects of Mormon theology, including the feminine divine and the perfection of man into godhood.

The works of the Church Strengthening Members Committee became a source of public outcry on the part of liberal Mormons. The committee was created during President Benson's tenure (1985–1994), to monitor "critical" activities of church members, including their writings and academic presentations. This daunting task led to the creation of classified files with information on many church members; these files were stored at the LDS Church headquarters, to be shared with local leaders if needed (Quinn 1997). The leadership did not deny the existence of the files—it defended the committee's work.[21]

20. "The LDS Church Has Great Tolerance, Pres. Hinckley Says," *Deseret News*, July 9, 1994.

21. "Scriptural Mandate Cited for LDS Committee," *Deseret News*, August 14, 1992.

Conclusion

The revelation received by Joseph Smith in 1830 stated: "Verily, I say unto you, that all things unto me are spiritual, and not at any time have I given unto you a law which was temporal."[22] Brigham Young later reiterated the essential idea of this revelation by explaining that there was no division of spiritual and temporal in the mind of God, nor should there be such a division in the practice of the Saints.[23] However, current LDS leaders go to great lengths to stress the loyalty of the Mormons to the American political institutions and being part of the mainstream public culture. Church leaders often reference Mormons' belief in the separation of church and state and their commitment to political liberalism, including the two-party system and the official neutrality policy of the church in elections. The church hierarchy has embraced the necessity of using existing political channels, such as lobbying and building coalitions with other interest groups, to influence public policy.

As the history and doctrine of the LDS Church show, early Mormonism offered a plan for the creation of the Kingdom of God, in both the temporal and the spiritual senses. Many of its provisions were later modified, reformulated, or postponed after facing strong challenges from outside forces. Some of these challenges were existential: danger to lives and property in the Midwest; migration, settlement, and survival in the Great Basin; and the overwhelming set of sanctions from the federal government faced by Mormons in the Utah Territory. The other set of challenges were more cultural than economic or political. In particular, these challenges concerned the integration of Mormons into mainstream American society. By the beginning of the twentieth century, the first set of existential challenges had been overcome largely as a result of the adjustments made by the Mormons

22. The Church of Jesus Christ of Latter-day Saints, *Doctrine and Covenants*, D&C 29:34, http://lds.org/scriptures/dc-testament?lang=eng, August 15, 2018.

23. The Church of Jesus Christ of Latter-day Saints, *Journal of Discourses*, J&D 11:18; 10:329, http://www.journalofdiscourses.org/volume-11/, August 15, 2018.

to their claims to autonomy and to some of their lifestyle choices. The question of cultural fit with respect to mainstream American society remains the single most important factor influencing the behavior and attitude of the church in public. Chapter 7 examines the way in which the church manages its public relations in such a context.

PART THREE

Religion and Civil Society

6

From Islamic Counterpublics to Organizing Civil Society

The Gülen Movement as a Civil Society Actor

As a global social movement with roots in the Turkish-Islamic context, the Gülen movement experienced a transformation from faith-based community building into a movement of volunteers as it expanded its areas of activities toward a series of larger social service projects—hence the original name of the movement preferred by the participants, *Hizmet* (service). As the community evolved from its early restorationist identity on the Turkish periphery, it has gradually widened its appeal, incorporated an increasingly universal-humanist language, and achieved a considerable global reach within the last three decades. This transformation also marked the transition from a passive resistance strategy of establishing Islamic counterpublic spaces against the state-dominated Kemalist secular public to active presence in the larger public sphere and leading sites of social opposition by organizing the civil society. The movement's public presence and civil society activism have been cultivated around clusters of nongovernmental institutions, including schools, tutoring centers, universities, business associations, community organizations, humanitarian aid, health care, and media outlets. The movement found a niche in the fragmented Turkish public sphere and developed a brand around its signature outreach efforts toward other religious, ethnic, and national groups.

As an attempt to overcome the fragmentation and polarization along ethnic, religious, sectarian, and ideological lines in 1990s

Turkey, Fethullah Gülen initiated the interfaith/intercultural dialogue activities by meeting with leaders from Greek Orthodox, Armenian Orthodox, Jewish, and Alevi communities. Gülen also met with Jewish leaders from Israel and the Catholic Pope John Paul II and ushered his movement into the global arena of interfaith activism. The movement acted as an organizer of the civil society and allied itself with other civil society actors to ostensibly promote a more pluralist, inclusive, and dynamic public sphere. This vision was subsequently expanded to include many parts of the world, including central Asia, the Balkans, Asia-Pacific, sub-Saharan Africa, and the Western Hemisphere. Movement activists and volunteers have engaged in interfaith/intercultural work, transformative education projects, and community building through a network of loosely connected local organizations.

This chapter first reviews the religious and cultural roots of the Gülen movement's public activism in Turkey. Next it turns to its most visible public organization, Journalists and Writers Foundation (JWF) and its Abant Platform. The study of JWF and the Abant Platform sheds light on how the broader structure of Turkey's republican public sphere shaped the strategies of Turkey's civil society organizations and intelligentsia to balance the power of the state. One particular strategy was coalition building to surpass the immediate agendas, objectives, and interests of civil society organizations. The Abant meetings aimed to soften the ideological tension and polarization in the society. This "outreach" attempted to weaken the justification for authoritarian reflexes of the Turkish state, which were manifested through the domination of politics by the military and judicial bureaucracy. The Abant platform represented the search for what can be described as a problem-solving civil society in Turkey. Moreover, the platform indirectly contributed to a reevaluation of the boundaries between the three domains of the public sphere—the state, political society, and civil society—by offering a much-needed vertical dialogue and contact on concrete issues between politicians, the media, and civil society groups. The combination of these two effects granted the political society a context prone to confidently tackling some of the country's chronic problems, such as civilian-military relations, Alevi and Kurdish issues, and relations with neighboring countries.

Civil Society Activism: Ideational and Cultural Background

The Gülen movement comprises a network of transnational institutions and linkages that aim to cultivate a modern Muslim identity by actively engaging with social issues and offering a series of social services in the public arena. The origins of the movement's religiously inspired civic activism is rooted in the faith-based renewalism of the Nur community, the Sufi worldview, and the politics of modernization from the late Ottoman empire to Republican Turkey.

The intellectual and organizational progenitor of the Gülen movement lies with Turkey's faith-based renewalist teachings of Said Nursi (1878–1960) and his text-based Nur community (Sahin 2011; Vahide and Abu Rabi 2005). Nursi had revolutionized and democratized Islamic commentary literature by offering a novel form of Quranic interpretation. His writings were comprised of short lessons directed to the average Muslim rather than the traditional *tafsir* discipline's comprehensive commentary on the entire Quran, accessible primarily to the learned scholarly (ulema) community. The contents of his writings were based on practical themes for the average Muslim who was increasingly challenged by the questions of modernization: how to understand Islam in relation to the advances in scientific knowledge, technological developments, and secular nationalist politics. Nursi went through stages of personal transformation as he witnessed the colonial penetration into Muslim societies, the collapse of the last Muslim empire, the Ottomans, and the subsequent turmoil many Muslim communities experienced as they experimented with various forms of secular nation-state building. During his early life, he engaged with reformist Islamic and liberal circles to challenge the absolutism of the Ottoman sultan. He recognized the changing context of Muslim politics and advocated for an inclusive merit-based system to embrace the multiethnic, multireligious nature of the society. He later became disillusioned with politics as he witnessed the rising nationalism and authoritarianism of the Young Turks, which proved quite disastrous for the Ottomans. Even though Nursi supported Mustafa Kamal in his leadership of the Turkish War of Independence, he became a critic of the top-down secular nation-building process that attempted to create a homogenous nation, discriminating against non-Muslims and denying any central role to Islamic and Kurdish identities in public life. Nursi developed a passive resistance to the secular revolution by contesting its legitimacy, and he dearly paid for his opposition by spending the rest of his life in courts, prisons, and exile.

Fethullah Gülen was born in this environment of antagonistic state-society relations, in 1938, in the eastern Turkish province of Erzurum. Having taken the paternalistic last name of Ataturk ("father of Turks") Mustafa Kemal had drastically changed the ideological references of the state from the guardians of the Sunni-Islamic tradition to the enforcers of Turkish-secular nationalism. Ataturk's secular revolution was continued under his successor, İsmet İnönü. The community in which Gülen spent his early childhood was marked by fear of state repression under President İnönü for teaching and practicing religion, as well as the anxiety and hardship surrounding World War II. Gülen was introduced to Nursi's ideas and movement in the 1950s. Even though they never personally met, Nursi's blueprint for developing a modern Muslim identity resonated with Gülen's vision of an Islamic revival. They both understood revival first as a form of individual spiritual awakening, with social spillover effects. Nursi talked about the stages of renewal starting from faith and moving onto social and political life; however, he never elaborated on how the following stages would come about. For Gülen, Nursi's grand ideas had to be put in practice by building a community of devotees and volunteers in all aspects of everyday life. Even though Gülen respected the elders of the Nur movement, his ambition and vision of popularizing Nursi's ideas through mass media and other institutional means gradually drove him apart from the rest, since his methods were seen as a deviation from Nursi's text-based, individualist approach to renewal.

A Presence Movement

Gülen adopted Nursi's Islamic lexicon to carve counterpublics and popularized his description of one's duty to be in the service of God and his religion, *hizmet*, gradually expanding it into what can be described as a presence movement. Gülen's philosophy departed from a belief that Muslims should be present in all facets of the public sphere and everyday life, hold positions of influence, and contribute to the well-being of their communities. The community can be the local neighborhood, the city, the country, or the globe. Gülen approached the world from a civilizational perspective and encouraged his followers to be the best scientists, doctors, writers, businesspeople, workers, farmers, musicians, media producers, and to bring their best to their professions by emphasizing Sufi concepts of *ihsan* (integrity) and *itkan* (excellence). He maintained that excellence in one's conduct comes out of internal peace, personal integrity, and spirituality.[1] As he encouraged Muslims to cultivate internal peace, to aim for excellence, and to engage in a new civilization-building mission, he agonized about the decline of the Muslim civilization and dreamt about a brighter future. Gülen (1998) did not hide his disappointment with violence, despotism, ignorance, and corruption in Muslim societies, yet he believed renewal was possible if Muslims were to adopt the spirit of Islamic teachings in light of modernity to embrace knowledge, hard work, and dedication. Gülen (1997) saw service activities and the movement as the proper form of jihad: striving for peace, justice, and excellence.

Gülen's *hizmet* philosophy differed from its Islamist counterparts by its strong emphasis on the primacy of the individual rather than the sociopolitical system, and its proactive engagement with the modern world rather than keeping a reactionary distance. Even though Gülen criticized colonialism and postcolonial meddling in Muslim countries, he did not shy away from admiring Western advancements in science, technology, human rights, democracy, and freedoms. He believed

1. "İçte ihsan olmali ki dışta ihsan olsun." Fethullah Gülen, "İtkan ve İhsan Ufku," May 13, 2006, http://tr.fgulen.com/content/view/11424/3/.

many Western democracies provided better opportunities to freely practice Islam, compared to Muslim majority countries.[2] Gülen also believed that to transform society one must first transform the individual. Hence, Gülen's ideal golden generation (*altın nesil*) must balance the body, the mind, and the heart, and by going through a training like that of the discipline of the army, the science of the school, and the spirituality of the Sufi lodge.[3] This three-pronged strategy to revive and empower the Muslim individual became the blueprint for transforming contemporary Muslim communities.

The idea behind the presence movement has roots in the Sufi philosophy of recognizing divine presence while busy with everyday services ("*halk içinde Hak'la beraber*"). Instead of fully withdrawing from social life to find and experience the divine, one must serve the community as part of one's service to God. This also connects with Nursi's philosophy of abandoning the world inside one's heart, instead of in one's conduct ("*dünyayi kesben değil kalben terketmek*"; Nursi 2013, 229). In other words, one can make money, do business, and interact with others as long as one's actions seek to please God and one does not get attached to the material world by turning worldly pursuits into their "idols."

With its goal of societal presence, the small core group of Gülen's religious circle gradually evolved into an outreach movement (Pandya and Gallagher 2012). The movement's beginnings in 1960s Turkey's most secular province, İzmir, is particularly noteworthy. In Kestanepazarı seminary, Gülen was the lead teacher, and he found a core group of disciples who would become the "first elders" (*ilk abiler*)

2. Jamie Tarabay, "A Rare Meeting With Reclusive Turkish Spiritual Leader Fethullah Gülen," *Atlantic*, August 14, 2013, http://www.theatlantic.com/international/archive/2013/08/a-rare-meeting-with-reclusive-turkish-spiritual-leader-fethullah-gulen/278662/.

3. Fethullah Gülen, "Kendi Kaynaklarımızdan Azamî Derecede İstifade," May 28, 2012, http://www.herkul.org/kirik-testi/kendi-kaynaklarimizdan-azami-derecede-istifade/.

to lead the subsequent outreach and institutional growth of the movement. With the help of the first cohort of the seminary graduates, Gülen initiated a series of youth activities, such as summer camps and conferences. His ideal was raising a "golden generation" of Muslims who are at ease with modernity and their religious identity. Unlike the top-down project of the Islamists, Gülen believed that a bottom-up, grassroots approach to raise well-educated, patriotic, and idealistic youth would help the ills of Muslim societies. He also reappropriated the Islamic tradition of fund-raising events, calling them *himmet*, to help with subsidizing dorms, student apartments, and stipends for students. In addition to pledges from wealthy businesspeople, movement participants at all levels began donating 10 to 15 percent of their annual income, as a norm (Ebaugh 2009). Along with time commitments in volunteer activities, donating to movement projects forged stronger bonds between the movement participants and its projects.

The Movement's Civil Society Organization and Activities

Since his adolescence, Gülen had imagined a renaissance of Islamic civilization. Even though he was from the more traditional eastern Turkish province of Erzurum, he knew that he needed to go to the more modern, western parts of the country in order to realize his dreams of cultivating a modern Muslim public enlightenment (Yavuz 2013). His ideas had a better chance of realization in the secular and modern Turkey than the conservative and traditional parts. In western Turkey, Gülen quickly emerged as an enigmatic *hoca*, a pious leader who combined a strong personal charisma with an effective sentimental and intellectual message. His sermons attracted massive audience outpouring from the mosques to the streets, and he led this growing number of dedicated followers—college students, small business owners, and workers—to establish student apartments, dorms, tutoring centers, and, later, private schools as the locus of movement's inception.

Gülen's ideas struck a chord among the urban dwellers who faced the challenges of adapting their traditional Islamic identity to modernization. In contrast to many other Islamic movements of his time,

Gülen was not asking his followers to build traditional Islamic centers of learning, such as *madrasa*s or even the state-owned Imam Hatip seminaries, but modern schools that would teach modern subjects. Gülen's Islam was not fundamentalist, yet it was not necessarily liberal or individualist, either. Its conservatism carried elements of modernist charismatic movements with a missionary ethos (Tittensor 2014, 133).

Despite its moderate message and pro-systemic politics, the state closely monitored Gülen's activities and saw his movement as a potential threat to the secular order. Gülen and his close associates had to spend time before the state security courts and in prison during military interventions of 1971 and 1980. In face of opposition and enmity from secularist media and state security institutions, Gülen devised strategies to protect the movement and its assets by gradually building influential allies in the state and the intelligentsia circles. The early decades of state suppression of religion under Republican Turkey and the continued control under the secular state establishment made Gülen quite prudent in his approach. Even during times of flourishing, the movement continued its cautionary organizational and discursive strategies (Agai 2003), thus opting for a "circumspect activism" (Balci and Miller 2012) rather than more assertive forms of human rights advocacy and political agitation.

Building on its growing human capital, the movement ventured into new projects, which in turn became opportunities to reach out to business owners. Most projects became self-sustaining after initial investments. Over time, participation in movement-led social projects created entrepreneurial opportunities for businesses in a form of network capitalism. The movement encouraged the creation of local business associations and umbrella federations to aggregate and represent business interests at local, national, and global levels. Institutionalization drove the movement's transnationalism; local business associations started supporting social projects in other countries. For example, business owners and investors from the Kirsehir province of Turkey, organized under a local business association (KAHIAD), would go to Niger and Burkino Faso in order to support movement schools as well as search for business opportunities.[4] Such organizations created vertical and horizontal ties with other societal groups and political institutions, leading to various levels of social capital formation.

The movement sent pioneers to other parts of the world and created linkages between Turkish cities and countries where they supported activities in. At first, these linkages were informal, but later volunteers and supporters of the movements founded their local, regional, and global business associations and federations. TUSKON (Confederation of Businessmen and Industrialists of Turkey), AKSIAD (African Countries Cultural, Social, and Economic Development Association), and PASIAD (Association for Social and Economic Cooperation between in Pacific Asian Countries) are some examples of organizations that created transnational linkages for movement participants and donors.

Islamic identity plays the role of connective tissue between different facets of social activism and services in the movement. Through this "activist pietism" (Özdalga 2003) the movement has been quite successful in promoting collaboration among various socioeconomic groups, helping with the creation of social capital at three levels. At the first level, horizontal bonding occurs among people of similar backgrounds and social positions, such as associations among students, businesses, workers, and academics. At the second level, the movement promotes vertical bridging across socioeconomic groups, societal identities, and ideologies; students, teachers, business owners, and workers with varying degrees of traditional and modern identities establish mutually reinforcing identities of service providers and receivers. At the third level, the movement facilitates linkages between the state and the society and the elite and the masses by forming institutions of horizontal and vertical representation, such as associations

4. "Kahiad Üyeleri Nijer ve Burkina Faso'yu Gezdi," Haberler, January 29, 2014, http://www.haberler.com/kahiad-uyeleri-nijer-ve-burkina-faso-yu-gezdi-5603538-haberi.

of private schools, federations of business associations, labor unions, and dialogue platforms.

In the last three decades, the movement widened its areas of activity to include private high schools, tutoring centers, universities, intercultural and interfaith platforms, humanitarian relief, and hospitals. Following student housing and dorms, private colleges and tutoring centers operated by movement volunteers became the most prestigious educational chains across Turkey. Even though they primarily relied on tuition, they also offered sliding scales based on income, as well as merit-based scholarships. One of the key reasons for the schools' success was their emphasis on recruiting promising students from rural areas by offering them scholarships in the cities. As a result, many movement schools offered upward mobility and combined students from upper-middle-class and lower socioeconomic backgrounds under one roof.

The movement's sophisticated use of intellectual, mystical, experimental, and affectional methods for recruitment and its emphasis on renunciation of the self kept it primarily a charismatic movement with considerable control over participants' lives (Tittensor 2014, 127–32). The movement provided continued support and socialization for the graduates of its high schools and tutoring centers and sustained its networks in professional organizations after students graduated from college. As the movement's activities and supporters grew, so did its influence. The growing number and influence of its media network, business associations, schools, hospitals, and worldwide connections gave the movement great stakes in policy. Throughout its five decades of social activism, the movement negotiated its autonomy with the state (Turam 2007) and selectively engaged in politics to protect its organizational interests and build access to power. In order to maintain its growth, the movement promoted economic and political stability, rule of law, democracy, and a realist balance of power politics and liberal internationalist foreign policy.

Calling it a movement of volunteers, Gülen believed that barriers to enter the movement should be minimal and even nonpious people should be able to participate and contribute to movement projects and activities. Such an open door policy created a very amorphous structure with varying degrees of dedication and involvement, and also broadened its message and language. In his dozens of interviews to scholars and journalists since the 1990s, Gülen increasingly tokenized human rights, liberties, democracy, religious freedoms, and peace through dialogue and engagement.[5]

Growth and Transformation of Movement's Civil Society Activism

In order to understand the movement's strategies in public affairs, one must understand its growth stages and the political and cultural context in which it operates. As chapter 4 demonstrated, there are clear parallels between the interests/vision of the movement and its political preferences. Gülen does not sacralize the state; yet, in general he sees the need for a strong state to provide security, order, and prosperity. He also believes that the state should reflect the values of the society and maintain an environment to help the fulfillment of its citizens' needs. This thinking became a major driving force behind and a source of justification for encouraging people from the movement's network to enter civil service (Mercan 2013, 240–46).

Gülen's engagement with politics has been influenced by how he identified the root cause of societal problems. At the height of the Cold War in the 1960s and 1970s, he identified communism and anarchism as the main problems and adopted a pro-security and pro-public order stance on the increasing ideological polarization and political violence. His pro-state stance, however, did not save him from the periodical wrath of the state after the 1971 and 1980 military interventions in politics.

Against the backdrop of violent left-right confrontations of the 1970s, the military junta leading the 1980 coup aimed to depoliticize the Turkish society and promoted Islam as an antidote to communism and as a source of public order and morality. 1980s witnessed

5. See Mercan 2016 for a topical compilation of Gülen's comments.

flourishing of the movement not only because the movement's teachings were in line with the new Turkish-Islamic synthesis, but also because Prime Minister Turgut Özal's neoliberal reforms during this period created opportunities for growth. Privatization and deregulation reforms gradually opened more space for private education, mass media, small businesses, and export-oriented industrial sectors. The beneficiaries of privatization and free-market reforms from Anatolia became a key supporter for the movement's activities in education and community organization.[6]

The collapse of the USSR and the emergence of newly independent Turkic republics in central Asia created opportunities for the movement's expansion abroad. Gülen sent a group of dedicated youth and businessmen to meet the state elite in the newly independent nations and to start schools. The premise of the movement's schools was their combination of modern subjects with character education. The language of instruction was primarily in English and the national languages of the country in which the schools operated, with Turkish being offered often as an extracurricular and elective course. Following the early model of the private high schools in Turkey, the schools abroad also invested in science, math, and technology. Thanks to dedicated teachers, many of whom came from top Turkish universities, the schools were very successful and quickly achieved recognition in national and international competitions. Most of the schools did not teach religion directly, yet systematically displayed model lives by the examples of the teachers, dorm advisors, and tutors. The schools were inspired by Gülen's teachings about the importance of providing moral education along with academics and building productive relations between teachers and parents (Gage 2013). In conflict-prone parts of the world, such as Bosnia, the Philippines, and Iraq, the movement schools aimed to educate children of different ethnic and

6. "Islamic Calvinists: Change and Conservatism in Central Anatolia," European Stability Initiative, September 19, 2005, http://www.esiweb.org/pdf/esi_document_id_69.pdf.

religious groups under one roof and sought to provide a model of peace-building and coexistence (Michel 2014). Education became the most influential activity of the movement worldwide. The opening of schools also created business opportunities, paving the way for its students to become either self-sufficient or locally supported.

Besides its worldwide private schools, some movement volunteers also opened charter schools in the US. These schools were publicly funded yet privately administered. In line with the movement's educational philosophy and experience, most charter schools emphasized science and technology education, college preparation, after-school tutoring, extracurricular activities, intercultural trips, and close teacher-parent relations. Many of the schools received recognition for their success and contribution to underserved urban communities in metropolitan areas. Harmony Schools in Texas, Magnolia Schools in California, and Horizon Schools in Illinois received substantial publicity not only due to their academic achievements, but also to questions about their financial management practices, and their ties to the movement. The charter schools whose numbers approach 120 in the continental US have been a challenge for the movement.[7] On the one hand, they are not Gülen schools, since they are publicly funded, yet they are also run by many administrators and teachers who subscribe to Gülen's ideas of education as a form of service and come from the movement's network.

Abant Platform and Organizing Civil Society

Despite its quick success in private education and the ensuing fame and prestige, the movement remained relatively obscure at the beginning of the 1990s. To dispel the suspicions and to raise public visibility, the movement started to more deliberately invest in its public relations in the mid-1990s. The key component of its public relations strategy

7. "120 American Charter Schools and One Secretive Turkish Cleric," *Atlantic*, August 12, 2014, http://www.theatlantic.com/education/archive/2014/08/120-american-charter-schools-and-one-secretive-turkish-cleric/375923/.

was civic engagement. Among its most popular civil society initiatives was the Abant platform. The platform was part of a sustained effort to organize the civil society to balance and challenge the dominance of the state in Turkey's republican public sphere. Gülen openly met with prominent figures of government and politics and gave interviews to some popular newspapers and magazines. He underscored the significance of tolerance and dialogue between Turkey's various ideological, religious, ethnic, and political camps. Rather than denying differences, tensions, and problems, he proposed opening a new page in relations. The Abant Platform was one of the biggest steps in this process to institutionalize Gülen's ideals and outlook.

One may see a contradiction in the ostensible pluralism of the JWF initiatives and how chapter 4 described Gülen's core worldview about the primacy of the state for public order. In the movement's practice, the Abant initiatives did not necessarily position civil society actors in opposition to the state; rather, Gülen and the JWF departed from a reimagined Ottoman past where the paternal state extended tolerance toward non-Muslim minorities under its multiethnic, multireligious *millet* system (Tittensor 2014, 76). In a way, the movement was taking it upon itself to fill in the void that it saw was the result of the republican Turkish state failing to play its role vis-à-vis the citizens.

The motives behind the platform informed its format and practices, resulting in a series of workshops that brought academics, politicians, and intellectuals together to discuss some of the thorniest issues of, first, Turkey, such as secularism and pluralism, and then the Muslim World, such as war, globalization, and modernization.

Background and Emergence of the Abant Platform

In June 1994, the movement introduced the JWF to the media in a much-publicized reception. Gülen, as the honorary president, made his first media appearance and gave warm messages to the public, emphasizing dialogue, tolerance, pluralism and democracy. In subsequent years, the foundation organized annual *iftar* (fast-breaking) dinners with participants from different walks of life and gave "tolerance awards" to people who were seen as key contributors to social peace in

Turkey. Later, the JWF formed three platforms, each with a particular mission and focus: the Abant Platform, which organized annual and semiannual workshops on social issues in Turkey, Europe, Africa, the US, and the Middle East; the Intercultural Dialogue Platform, which focused on increasing understanding between different religious, ethnic and cultural groups; and the Dialogue Eurasia Platform, which worked with mostly former Soviet Republics to forge close cultural ties, and published the DA Magazine in Turkish and Russian (with contributions from Russia, the Turkic Republics of Central Asia, and Turkey).[8] As the pioneer of dialogue activities and the first public face of the movement, the JWF inspired a growing number of similar civil society organizations in various parts of the world where the movement became active.

The platform chose Abant, a remote recreational area in northern Turkey, as the venue for the first six meetings. Hence, the notions of "Abant Platform" and "Abant spirit" have been used to refer to the initiative. The participants can be divided into two categories. The first group is the "core" group of participants, which includes the platform's executive committee, most members of the JWF's board of trustees, and academics who share the vision of the platform. The second group consists of academics and intellectuals, who were invited based on their expertise and the theme of the workshop; politicians and statesmen, depending on the political climate; and media representatives. The academics were primarily from the social and behavioral sciences. The politicians who participated were primarily from conservative parties and movements with the exception of some figures from

8. This platform organized interfaith trips and meetings in Harran, Urfa (Turkey), where Prophet Abraham was believed to have spent the earlier years of his life. The concept of "Abrahamic Religions" and the commonalities between them were emphasized with Muslim, Jewish, and Christian participants. The platform also raised awareness about the tragedy of Bosnian Muslims, organized interfaith prayer services for peace, and held a celebration of the seven hundredth anniversary of the asylum granted by the Ottoman Empire to the Sephardic Jews, who escaped from the Spanish Inquisition and the Reconquista.

the social democratic left. The participants naturally varied based on location and the topics, but there was also an identifiable change in the participation of politicians in relation to the movement's relationship with the state and the political authority.[9] The early meetings between 1998 and 2007 drew on leftist, liberal, and Islamist intelligentsia who promoted democratic pluralism against the Kemalist authoritarian state control over the public sphere. The participation of conservative politicians and retired or active bureaucrats increased in parallel to the movement's growth in popularity and political influence. There was a decline in participation of leftist and liberal politicians and intellectuals after the movement's thinly disguised alliance with the AKP during 2007–13. The platform attracted some opposition politicians and civil society activists from the social democratic left and the Kurdish left after 2013. However, this last round failed to correct the movement's partisan image, likely due its earlier entanglement with the government, nor did it help the movement escape the wrath of the post-Kemalist state during its power struggle with the AKP government.

The Abant Platform was a self-governing entity supported by the JWF. Its executive committee included some key members of the foundation's board of trustees, as well as some independent academics and public intellectuals. The executive committee addressed the themes of annual meetings, the participants to be invited, and other organizational issues.[10] The mission statement of the platform mentioned dialogue and reconciliation in light of knowledge and expertise as the key principle. The platform aimed to create a collective consciousness

9. See a professional breakdown of the participants in the platform's thirty-four meetings in appendix A.

10. The theology professor Mehmet S. Aydin, who served as the minister of the state in charge of religious affairs in the AKP cabinet (2002–10), chaired the committee for eight years. Another academic, Professor of History Mete Tunçay of Istanbul University, replaced Aydin in 2006. Mete Tunçay defines himself as agnostic and his support for the Abant Platform gave it credit as an inclusive and nonconfessional organization. Levent Köker, a professor of constitutional law and a prominent liberal intellectual, replaced Mete Tuncay in 2010.

that could define social problems, break them down into manageable bits, and brainstorm in a collective manner to inform the public and propose policies and solutions. The challenge was finding a common ground without necessarily giving up particular beliefs and values,[11] and tackling difficult conversations by engaging in a constructive dialogue: what some organizers called "the Abant spirit."[12]

Meeting Format and Topics

The starting point for the Abant meetings was the possibility and necessity of dialogue across people of different beliefs, values, and identities. The organizers, sponsors, participants, and supporters of Abant frequently stressed the need for open debate, consensus building, and conflict resolution. Almost every meeting declaration referred to these convictions. The fourth meeting was in essence an embodiment of this position, with philosophical and analytical underpinnings. The main purpose of pluralism was described as the recognition of difference and the achievement of a societal consensus. The consensus was not defined as the transformation of differences—rather, as finding a social compromise (similar to the concept of "social contract"), so as

11. Harun Tokak, "Abant and the Feeling of Responsibility," Opening Speech for the First Abant Meeting (1998).

12. The early philosophical guru of the platform, Mehmet S. Aydin, explained the notable success of the platform by stressing five traits of Abant:

> 1. Disengaging the so-called controversial issues in deadlock from ideological and fanatical realm and bringing them into the world of knowledge and rationality
>
> 2. Formation of an "Abant spirit" that is intellectually brave and tolerant of opposing ideas
>
> 3. A democratic attitude by which a free debate and deliberation is possible
>
> 4. A dialogic logic with three steps: accumulation of knowledge, critical and analytical mind, and the existential step in touch with reality
>
> 5. The possibility of meeting on the common denominator in spite of seemingly irreconcilable philosophical and ideological positions

Mehmet S. Aydin, Opening Remarks for the Second Abant Meetings, *Abant Platformu: Din, Devlet ve Toplum*, 10–11.

to be able to live together in spite of differences. Obviously, the virtue is for the constituents of the society to live among one another in peace, with a meaningful dialogue. The document celebrated diversity and openly called for a new constitution based on a manifestation of the new social contract. Later on, the fifteenth meeting specifically addressed the necessity of a new constitution that would meet the standards of the EU accords. The twenty-sixth meeting made some bold substantive recommendations for the new constitution on questions of citizenship, national identity, minority rights, and religious freedoms. In earlier meetings, the Kemalist ideology was openly criticized for attempting to homogenize the society in the prolonged period of nation-state building and blamed for "social engineering" in the name of modernization to attain the desired ideological and political outcomes. The meetings between 2007 and 2013 were more pragmatic in terms of offering practical solutions and policy proposals rather than criticizing the state ideology to build consensus among different social actors. This change in tone was likely due to the movement's close relationship with the AKP government and its desire to shape post-Kemalist politics. However, this access to power was short-lived and the platform became more critical of the AKP government when the two former allies turned against each other in 2013.

The thematic changes in the platform's meetings hint at the changing strategies of the movement, which in turn hint at the changing power dynamics in the Turkish public sphere.[13] Between 1998 and 2007 the Kemalist military-bureaucratic establishment was dominant in Turkey's republican public sphere. During this period, the Abant Platform emerged as an attempt to build a broad coalition and organize the civil society to balance the power of the state. The civil society led a soft opposition to the authoritarian turn in Turkish politics after the 1997 soft military intervention. Following the surprising electoral victory of the AKP in 2002, elements from the civil society and the political society formed an alliance against the Kemalist establishment.

13. See appendix B for a complete list of meeting themes in chronological order.

As argued in chapter 4, 2007 was a turning point, when this alliance shifted into an offensive strategy against the establishment by using the EU accession criteria to empower the civilian politicians against the military bureaucracy, passing constitutional amendments and purging the Kemalist bureaucrats through a series of legal trials. The Gülen movement became relatively more assertive during this struggle and the Abant Platform reflects this change of strategy. The movement and the AKP, however, never fully trusted each other and their alliance was based on uniting forces against a common foe. Once Kemalist state control was dismantled, the political society was empowered and didn't need the civil society to govern. As is common in other democratic transitions, civil society and political society found themselves in confrontation after their success in weakening the authoritarian state (Linz and Stepan 1998). After passing the 2010 constitutional amendments, up until the end of 2013, the two Islamic actors formally continued their alliance, but prepared for the eventual face-off. After 2013, the Gülen movement tried to use the same strategy of coalition building against the AKP government, much like in the first period, but they had lost a significant portion of their political capital due to their involvement with the AKP during the 2007–13 purges, which alienated other leftist and liberal civil society groups. Despite the movement's attempts to reclaim the moral ground against AKP after 2013 by drawing parallels to the authoritarianism of the Kemalist state, the movement's image was tarnished as a result of its involvement in the purges and many of its influential allies were disillusioned about the sincerity of the Abant platforms in promoting public good as opposed to shielding the Gülen movement in the public sphere.

The workshops started with an opening session, where the executive committee introduced the topic, the participants, and operational aspects of the meeting. Usually, politicians and a select number of community leaders delivered speeches on the importance of the meeting and their reflections on that year's theme. After the opening, the workshops proceeded either with some specialized committee meetings or thematic panels. The earlier meetings were more in the form of workshops where different aspects of issues were debated to come up with some consensus conclusions—for the news release and concluding declaration. This format was criticized for functioning as a mechanism to force consensus. In response to the critiques, starting with the sixth workshop, the meetings were reorganized to be more like academic conferences, with presentations and panels. This format change is also evident in the concluding documents. The first five meetings declarations contain more specific points and the later meetings were summarized with broader concluding remarks and conference proceedings.

The positive references to religion in general in the statements hints at a tacit belief that Islam can be a positive factor in social, political, and economic life. The first Abant meeting undertook the challenging question of the relationship between Islam and secularism. Being the first of its kind in Turkey and organized by a religiously based civil society group, this meeting not only attracted a lot of attention at the beginning, but also provoked some interesting public debate afterward. The meeting ended with casting some doubts on some clichés and taboos in Turkey regarding the position of Islam on secularism and democracy.[14] The participants agreed on positions such as:

- There is no contradiction between revelation and reason according to the prevalent position in the Islamic scholarship.
- No person or group has a monopoly or divine authority over the understanding and interpretation of Islam.
- Muslims in the earlier periods of Islam engaged in more independent judgment (*ijtihad*) to solve problems in accordance with the general principles of the religion and necessities of the time. (This was a direct challenge to the "orthodox" position in Sunni Islam about the closing of the gates of *ijtihad* since the 12th century AD).

14. Although the movement never claimed they agreed or disagreed with the resulting declarations, one can argue that they were in line with the "middle-way" philosophy of the movement. For more on this, see Kuru 2003.

- There is not necessarily a contradiction between the sovereignty of God in religious cosmos and sovereignty of people in politics.
- State is a human construct, rather than a metaphysically and politically sacred entity (in response to the question of the existence and nature of an "Islamic state")
- Other than the universal and basic democratic rights and the rule of law principles, Islam leaves the specifics of the regime type to societies. (Islam and democracy are compatible)
- Turkey should develop a more freedom based form of secularism (Anglo-Saxon version of secularism investigated in depth during the workshop)[15]

The reactions to these bold statements were mixed. Some Islamist intellectuals, such as Ahmet Taşgetiren, declined the invitation to participate and criticized the concluding document for being limited by the conditions of 1997 indirect military intervention in politics.[16] On the other hand, most liberals and some conservative intellectuals praised the meeting organizers and participants for their courage and sincerity.[17]

The topics discussed in the meetings underscore two important points. Firstly, the specific topics were chosen based on the context (time and space). After the indirect military intervention in politics against the Islamist RP-led coalition government, Turkey struggled toward the normalization of civil-military relations between 1997 and 2002. The first four meetings in this context searched for consensus building on some of the intractable issues polarizing the country along the lines of Islamist vs. Secularist and the state vs. the society. After 2002, the themes reflect more global issues. For example, the

15. The first meeting (the comments in the parentheses are author's).

16. Tasgetiren later participated in the fourth workshop and served in the board of trustees of the JWF.

17. See the JWF website for reactions after each meeting: http://www.gyv.org.tr.

2003 meeting tackled the issue of bringing democracy by force in the face of the escalating threat of US intervention in Iraq. The platform discussed the question of Islam and democracy in 2004 right after the beginning of the Operation Iraqi Freedom. It seems, by having this meeting at the very birth place of the Greater Middle East Initiative, the platform aimed to speak to a Western audience. The two Turkey-France conversations (2004 and 2007) were more focused on Turkey's EU membership, with a broad multiculturalism outlook.[18] France was symbolic in being one of the most vocal opponents of Turkey's full membership and its historical influence over Turkish intelligentsia in issues of secularism, republicanism, and citizenship. In 2006, the platform, which had been criticized for not paying enough attention to the Muslim World as much as they emphasized dialogue with non-Muslims, invited Arab, Jewish, and Turkish intellectuals, to discuss the future of the Middle East. And, later in February 2007, the platform co-organized a meeting in Egypt with the prominent Al-Ahram Institute, to discuss the Turkish and Egyptian experience with democracy, modernization, and secularism. Another key meeting in February 2009 took place in Iraqi Kurdistan, to discuss the very question of the future of the Kurds in the region. A meeting in the Turkish city of Gaziantep on the Syrian border debated the implications of the Arab Spring and its aftermath. The meetings after 2010 responded to the widely shared expectation to draft a new constitution for the post-Kemalist "new" Turkey. As the AKP drifted away from its reformist platform and adopted a strategy of hegemonic control over what the "new" Turkey should look like, the platform featured opposing perspectives from the secular, social democratic, Kurdish, and Alevi communities' representatives.

Along with the platform's close consideration of the sociopolitical setting, the second striking fact is the increased frequency of the meetings in time. As a result, the participants and the target audience also grew. The first set of meetings probed the problems that were

18. For more on the Greater Middle East Initiative, see note 39 in chapter 4.

most chronic and the source of significant tension in Turkey. Secularism, the Kurdish problem, and Alevi-Sunni relations were just a few of the issues that remained at the center of public debate. Later, the platform looked into issues that were more global in nature but with clear implications for Turkey, such as democratization, peace, stability, and globalization. The meetings in the US, Europe, and the Middle East were more attuned to bringing in a Turkish perspective and Turkey's experiences with democracy and secularism to the forefront of discussion. This also aimed to put up bridges between Turkish, Middle Eastern, and Western intellectual and policy circles.

Proceedings and Declarations

The initial Abant workshops that had concluding declarations resulted in reports. These documents were then shared with the public in a news release and were either sent or presented to statesmen and members of the political society. The JWF also published transcripts and proceedings of some of the earlier workshops. Mehtap TV, a channel that specialized in cultural and educational programs and was known for its ties with the Gülen movement, also aired some of the Abant meetings live. This was a concerted effort to make these meetings more accessible to the general population. The public declarations demonstrate three key perspectives:

1. Belief in the possibility of cooperation despite differences and tensions
2. Commitment to a liberal-democratic framework at large
3. Appreciation of the crucial link between local, national, and global issues

The question of Islam and modernity assumed another pivotal position in the seventh Abant meeting at Johns Hopkins University, in the US. American and Turkish intellectuals scrutinized the Turkish experience with Islam, modernization, secularism, and democracy. Unlike the first meeting, the seventh meeting did not produce a consensus public declaration, and the general tone was more about the unique historical and contemporary dynamics in Turkey's experience with Islam.

Another characteristic of the declarations is their liberal democratic tone, which challenged the republican characteristics of the public sphere. Freedom of religion and conscience along with the right of individuals to practice their beliefs was the central thesis of the first and second meetings, which examined secularism and the social role of religion. There was also a clear liberal bias in regard to state-society relations. By questioning the effective sacralization of the state, participants portrayed the state in service to its citizens, contrary to the traditional state-dominant Turkish political culture. In that sense, the state was urged to liberate itself from totalitarian, authoritarian, and top-down ideological-doctrinal tendencies. The concept of raison d'état justifying exceptional immunity for state actors was rejected in favor of a full-fledged rule of law and a neutral referee state.[19] This speaks to the danger of creating a police state with human rights violations in the name of national security and war on terror. The strongest critique of *laïcité* also comes from this avenue: Turkish secularism under the Kemalist order was not simply a separation of religious and political authorities, but a subjugation of religion to state control, which raises serious questions about the freedom of religious practice (e.g., the headscarf ban in public schools; regulations and restrictions on minority religious community rights and status). Finally, the platform strongly rejected the state's pleadings for exceptionalism in human rights, democracy, and civil liberties, due to Turkey's "special circumstances," and maintained that Turkey needed more democracy to solve its ethnic, religious and social problems.[20]

Although it is hard to measure the exact role of the Abant initiative in the liberal turn in Turkish politics during the 2000s, it would be safe to argue that the platform was more than an ad hoc meeting for the sake of publicity for the movement. It attracted participants from a wide array of ideological positions and identities. The platform attempted to institutionalize its vision with additional lecture series

19. The third meeting's concluding declaration, www.gyv.gov.tr.
20. The third meeting's concluding declaration, www.gyv.gov.tr.

and seminars. The relatively open dialogue and reconciliation that took place in the Abant meetings initially played the role of demystifying social problems that were seen as intractable. This in turn contributed to the deescalation of political conflict over social problems. And, paradoxically, depoliticization opened more space for the political society to overcome the resistance of the state bureaucracy toward reform. A civil society mindful of its interest in balancing the coercive power of the state and a political society that can transmit the societal preferences into policy and legislation are two indispensable elements of a functioning democracy.

A critical promise of the Abant Platform was the empowerment of the civil society vis-à-vis the state. Many civil society organizations in Turkey failed to retain their independence from the state, jeopardizing the autonomy of the civil society as a whole. This was the case for some Kemalist organizations, which were orchestrated by some retired army generals. A series of public demonstrations against the AKP in 2007 underscored that the boundaries between the military and the "civil" society organizations were blurred.[21] Many of the civil society organizations in the post-Kemalist "new" Turkey after 2013 were also co-opted, controlled, and repressed by the AKP government and lacked autonomy.[22] The Abant Platform adopted a broad civil society position as opposed to a particular interest group approach to challenge the limits of Turkey's strong republican tradition. Moving toward more liberal, pluralist form of democracy requires a strong attitudinal basis from the civil society, as well as a legal-institutional framework. In a way, the Abant Platform not only consumed the existing social capital by bonding (within the Gülen movement fellowship) but also created more social capital by bridging (across different groups). There

21. See, for example, "'Vatanseverlik' yarışındaki örgütler emekli asker dolu; Al sana 'sivil' toplum!" (Organizations Competing for "Patriotism" Are Full of Retired Army Generals, a "Civil" Society!), *Radikal*, February 17, 2007.

22. Jessica Doyle, "Between Control and Co-option: The Future of Civil Society in Erdoğan's Turkey," NGO Advisor, June 14, 2016, https://www.ngoadvisor.net/csos-erdogan-turkey-doyle/.

was also a linking social capital effect, which is similar to the bonding but involves more vertical relationships between unequal powers and uneven institutional access—in a way, linking the state to the civil society (Woolcock 1998).

The strategy of combining all three forms of social capital is related to the prevalent model of the public sphere. The republican Turkish public sphere has emphasized the general will and public order, as opposed to a liberal pluralistic public sphere that legitimizes inclusion of particular moral, philosophical, and ideological values. Operating within such a context, societal actors like the Gülen movement used collective-interest rhetoric and consensus-building, to boost their claims to legitimacy in the Turkish public sphere.

The Gülen movement's coalition building and ambiguity in the public sphere is a stark contrast to the LDS Church's assertive public affairs strategy in the US. As chapter 7 demonstrates, the LDS Church's public engagement in general conforms to the interest-group politics in the pluralist liberal American context. The church's participation and endorsement of a broadly inclusive immigration policy platform called Utah Compact comes closest to the civil-society-organizing role of the Gülen movement in the Abant Platforms. However, while endorsing and participating in the initiative, the church retained its independent position and referred to its own principles of Christian neighborliness and commitment to strengthening the traditional family.[23] The Gülen movement, in contrast, referred to broader civic and political values of pluralism, reconciliation, democracy, public order, national unity, and national interest as the basis of its public positions. These discursive strategies are in line with the logic of liberal and republican public spheres in which the two religious actors operate.

23. The news release expressing the Church support of Utah Compact also mentions importance of border security and law enforcement, but the sequence of the principles unmistakably prioritizes the particular Christian and conservative values: "Church Supports Principles of Utah Compact on Immigration," Mormon Newsroom, November 11, 2010, https://www.mormonnewsroom.org/article/church-supports-principles-of-utah-compact-on-immigration.

While the substance of policy debates, initiatives, and moral questions assume priority in the pluralist American liberal public sphere, the procedures and civic norms assume priority in the state-dominant Turkish republican public sphere. In the latter case, strengthening the civil society and ensuring its autonomy precedes pushing for specific reforms and political change. According to this position, in absence of genuine democratic rule, specific democratic rights would be hard to achieve and retain even if there were short-term gains.

Conclusion: The Future of the Movement's Civil Society Functions

Despite some short-term effects, the long-term success of the Abant Platform in achieving its stated objectives failed to materialize due to two factors. First, the ostensible efforts of movement loyalists inside the state bureaucracy to use their judicial and law enforcement positions against movement opponents during the Ergenekon and Balyoz trials overshadowed the movement's claims to being a benign civil society actor. Second, the movement's power struggle with the AKP after 2013 undermined the nonpartisan claims of its organizers. The botched coup attempt in July 2016 ultimately shut down all movement initiatives, including the JWF, and ended the Abant Platform in Turkey. As the movement struggles to survive the state crackdown in Turkey, it remains to be seen if the platform will continue to convene abroad and how it will evolve in its public identity and messages.

The intellectual, institutional, and activity profile of the Gülen movement underscores its vibrancy, fluidity, pragmatism, and adaptability. It is a civil society movement with everyday activism and engagement with the state; it is a nonpartisan social movement that devises political strategies to survive and flourish. It is also a transnational movement with a very strong Turkish accent. Its fluidity may be a double-edged sword: it helps with its broader appeal and ability to crisscross socio-economic, ideological, and identity boundaries, but it may lose its effectiveness and lead to internal rivalries.

The Gülen movement at its core retains its charismatic nature despite the expansion of its activities worldwide. Achievements in community-building and civil-society organization during the movement's first three decades carved a common space for potentially conflictual Turkish-Kurdish identities, conservative-liberal values, modernist-traditional Islamic interpretations, local-global cultures, and various socioeconomic interests. This common space proved to be quite effective for the growth of the movement and its ability to reach out to many communities. However, after five decades of building these ties and developing projects, the movement faces the challenges of substantiating its organizational accomplishments with intellectual depth, educational content, economic sustainability, and cultural vibrancy. The Turkish government's crackdown on movement participants and institutions since 2013 has brought such challenges to the surface and, in many respects, the movement is at a crossroads. Thanks to continued ostracization by the pro-government media, the movement lost much of its popularity in Turkey, except for a small core group of underground supporters. Its ability to raise funding and provide services has also been significantly circumscribed. Due to government pressure, the movement could not even rent hallways for its annual conferences or cultural events, such as the Turkish Olympiads. Many of the movement activists and leadership left Turkey to escape from the witch hunt. This increasing pressure to dissolve the movement pushed the participants to start soul-searching and negotiating their identities with local, national, and global forces. One immediate result has been to make the movement more transnational and its activities visibly less centered around Turkish culture. For example, the Turkish Olympiads were renamed as International Festival of Language and Culture in 2015, and they were held in several places outside of Turkey. Many movement-affiliated institutions that relied on donations and full-time movement associates are looking for more sustainable institutional arrangements. Since times of crisis are also times of opportunity and renewal, the movement is likely to channel its dynamism and grassroots energy toward more locally connected and sustained projects and to move away from its previous Turkey-centric stage of development.

7

Between Political Neutrality and Moral Politics

The Public Affairs of the LDS Church

During the early years of their church, Mormons saw politics as an instrument to promote their survival and defend their interests. They voted as a bloc to support candidates who promised protection and autonomy, they appealed to national leaders and parties for help with hostile local authorities, and they ambitiously ran for office. After concluding that living under the same political structure with non-Mormons was practically impossible, the leadership moved to create independent political institutions based on Mormon teachings and Mormon millennial beliefs. Nauvoo and the State of Deseret are two failed examples of this search for political autonomy.

The creation of the Utah Territory and the admission of the state of Utah to the Union were both turning points in the federal and national efforts to tame the role of the church in politics. The church has gradually withdrawn from politics in the wake of these events. During the transition period between Utah's admission to the Union in 1896 and the change of the church's top leadership in 1918, politics remained under the control of the church's powerful General Authorities, led by President Joseph F. Smith and Apostle and Republican Senator Reed Smoot (Croft 1985). From the 1920s until the 1960s, church leaders still endorsed candidates and openly tried to influence referenda and votes in Utah. Some of these attempts backfired; the church then began using more subtle ways to influence politics and public policy (Sharkansky 1997). Since the 1960s the church has consistently conveyed its commitment to the political neutrality principle, but in practice supported conservative causes against communism, the Equal Rights Amendment, and same-sex marriage. Some prominent General Authorities, such as Ezra Taft Benson, served in Republican administrations and established close ties with far-right anticommunist groups, such as the John Birch Society. Church members in Utah voted overwhelmingly for Republican candidates. The need for public relations management become more pronounced for the church to distinguish between its officially neutral position in politics and its support for conservative platforms and the Republican Party in practice. Moreover, during the second half of the twentieth century the church also became more global, making significant inroads in Latin America, East Asia, and sub-Saharan Africa. The conservative politics of the Utah-based church increasingly became at odds with the needs of its globalizing missionary work, especially in the exclusion of blacks from priesthood. To reconcile these conflicting imperatives and realities, the politics of Mormon religious identity in the American public sphere often played out through backdoor coalitions, unpublicized letters from the General Authorities to congregations, as well as through internal memos and official public statements.

One needs to decipher church public relations to uncover the politics of Mormon representation in the American public sphere. This chapter seeks to account for the church's changing public-relations profile in terms of the separation of church and state, political activities, and relationships with other groups within the civil society. The chapter offers an explanation based on the mutually constitutive relationship between church doctrine and its political context. More specifically, an investigation of the operations of the Church Public Affairs Department through its organization, news releases, and other communication strategies will explicate the nature of this relationship between the church and the political context. The chapter also examines how the concept of "moral issues" has been used as a source of legitimacy for the church's orientation with respect to political issues, as a mobilization strategy for church members, and as an effective tool of engagement with the rest of the American public.

Political Relations in Theory and Practice

The LDS Church officially adheres to a directly articulated policy of political neutrality. The church as an institution does not endorse candidates or political parties; it advises its lay priesthood to follow this principle as well.[1] However, when it comes to what the church defines as "moral issues," it does express its opinion and takes positions on such matters in referenda, initiatives, and ballot measures. There are two main factors that the church seems to take into account regarding these moral issues: the legal framework for the involvement of religious organizations in politics and the public image of the church.

US federal law provides tax benefits to nonprofit organizations. Under section 501(c)(3) of the Internal Revenue Code, public charities are exempt from federal tax, provided that they comply with the law to maintain their status as a charity. Such organizations must ensure that they serve the public interest without offering private benefits to individuals associated with the organization; they must also avoid involvement in (partisan) political campaigns and substantial legislative activity, such as extensive lobbying. However, these provisions are not meant to restrict the constitutional right to freedom of expression for individuals within tax-exempt organizations. The LDS Church sees the First Amendment as being applicable to organizations, thereby giving the church the right to take positions on political matters concerning what it deems to be moral issues.[2] The church is very careful in such situations, chastened by a warning issued from the local Internal Revenue Service (IRS) office in Utah for the church's

1. "Political Neutrality," Mormon Newsroom, n.d., http://www.mormonnewsroom.org/official-statement/political-neutrality.

2. See, for example, "Transcript of Elder Dallin H. Oaks Speech on Religious Freedom," given at Brigham Young University-Idaho on October 13, 2009, Mormon Newsroom, https://www.mormonnewsroom.org/article/oaks-religious-freedom.

heavy involvement in an election in 1954.[3] The church does not make direct contributions; rather, it mobilizes its members to become politically active. It does have registered lobbyists,[4] but their involvement in legislative matters is limited, and the church aims to keep clear of running into problems with the "substantial part" test of the IRS in lobbying by expenditure or activity criteria.[5] In general, the church is very selective, strategic, and circumspect about its direct involvement in the legislative process—what may be described in many cases as "advocacy avoidance" (Magleby 2006).

The other factor that influences the church's involvement in politics is its consideration of its public image. When it comes to public affairs, the church has put forward three main interests: the rights and welfare of the church and its members, missionary work, and moral values.[6] Promoting these interests requires flexibility, pragmatism, and diplomacy. Maintaining its image as a mainstream but unique faith is very important for the success of its missionary work.[7] That is a key reason why the church does not use a strong political or moral language even when it does take clear positions on issues.

3. The church leadership openly supported the Legislative Apportionment Act that would have given each county one senator, regardless of population. This act would have had the effect of boosting the political power of the less populous—but predominantly Mormon—rural counties (Williams 1997, 239).

4. The number of active registered lobbyists working for the LDS Church varied from three to seven between 2006 and 2018, a higher number than any other organization or business (https://lobbyist.utah.gov/Search/LobbyistByPrincipal).

5. "Charities, Churches, and Politics," IRS Revenue Ruling 2007–41; 2006 Political Activity Compliance Initiative, https://www.irs.gov/uac/charities-churches-and-politics, updated on July 30, 2018.

6. These are the three main rationales cited in First Presidency statements (accessed at the Church History Library, microfilms covering 1991–99) and in news releases by the Church Public Affairs Department (accessed online at http://newsroom.lds.org, dated between January 2002 and December 2009).

7. For an analysis of how this is reflected in the attitudes of church members, see Brinkerhoff, Jacob, and Mackine 1987, 90–96.

If and when the church enters into coalitions with conservative groups, these cooperative arrangements are often indirect and the church is often guarded about such arrangements. However, this strategy is not immune from image problems, either. In some cases where the church has been less than fully transparent regarding its financial support and the mobilization of its members, church involvement has drawn quite bitter responses from the opposition. In turn, this revives or reinforces the stereotype of the LDS Church as a secretive organization with ulterior motives of political control.

As an example, one need look no further than the 2008 California Marriage Protection Act (Proposition 8), which defined marriage as a union between only a man and a woman, effectively banning marriage between partners of the same sex. Compared to most other moral issues, the LDS Church was deeply involved in this struggle in terms of grassroots mobilization and financial contributions. One of the reasons for the sharp critique Mormons received after the passage of Proposition 8 was the decisive stealth role played by the church during the campaign.[8] After the election, the church was fined by the State of California for not reporting a significant portion of its contribution in a timely manner.[9] The basis of this fine was a technicality, but the sanction served as a symbolic reproach of LDS Church for not fully disclosing its involvement.

The role of the LDS Church in California's Proposition 8 campaign gained the praise of the social conservatives and infuriated gay-rights activists. Despite some tactical victories like Proposition 8, the conservatives lost the bigger culture war by 2015 when the US Supreme Court guaranteed same-sex marriage as a nationwide right.[10] As same-sex marriage became the law of the land, conserva-

8. "Prop 8 Involvement a P.R. Fiasco for LDS Church," *Salt Lake Tribune*, November 22, 2008.

9. "LDS Church Fined for Tardy Financial Reports during Prop 8," *Salt Lake Tribune*, September 17, 2010.

10. *Obergefell v. Hodges*, 576 US (2015).

tives turned toward their state legislatures to pass laws that granted businesses and county clerks the right to refuse to serve same-sex couples. The LDS Church distanced itself from the latter conservative movement and worked with LGBT activists in support of a 2015 antidiscrimination law in Utah.[11] In an unusually strong way, the church also warned against changes to the enacted antidiscrimination laws a year later.[12] The change in the church position was surprising, given its deep involvement against same-sex marriage, and put it at odds with other social conservatives, who were not ready to throw in the towel. The church heavily lobbied for the passage of the 2015 antidiscrimination laws and encountered a backlash from some conservative Mormon legislators.[13]

The three main interests that the church is supposed to promote through its public relations may not always be in harmony: the rights and welfare of the church and its members, missionary work, and moral values. In order to maintain a balance between these sometimes conflicting goals, the church has moved to increase the level of institutional control over its official policies and its interactions with other political and social groups. It has become rare for even the powerful church General Authorities to speak without institutional clearance. This helps the church have more control over its official doctrine, policies, and positions.

Reasonable Religion in Public: The Mormon Politics of Moral Issues

The most politically important—and, hence, the most contentious—aspect of the Mormon involvement in the public sphere are the positions taken by the church on moral issues. A letter from the highest

11. "Utah—Yes, Utah—Passes Landmark LGBT Rights Bill," *Washington Post*, March 12, 2015.

12. "Mormon Church Warns against Upsetting 'Careful Balance' of LGBT Anti-discrimination Law," *Salt Lake Tribune*, February 17, 2016.

13. "Mormon Church Lobbying in Utah's Capitol—Hardball or Light Touch?" *Salt Lake Tribune*, March 29, 2015.

authoritative body of the church General Authorities, the First Presidency, states that the First Presidency and Twelve Apostles reserve the right to "declare a particular issue to be a moral issue and worthy of full institutional involvement" (Bergera 2007, 321). Elsewhere, the church refers to the public interest (public health, safety, and welfare) and the welfare of the church and its members as grounds for involvement in political issues. A church testimony before the Utah Alcoholic Beverage Control Commission further calls this involvement a "constitutional[14] and moral obligation" within the "democratic process" in a "pluralistic society."[15] Church members are asked to use their influence to introduce "proper legislation" that will combat evils of "drinking, gambling, immorality and other vices."[16] These efforts are meant to create environments "conducive to spirituality" and "eternity."[17] In Utah, the liquor laws have constituted the chief issue on which the church has openly taken positions, hired registered lobbyists, and offered testimony in legislative hearings.

The church has taken broadly conservative positions on a number of other public policy issues, yet it has generally stayed away from supporting specific legislations or electoral endorsements on them. In the case of abortion, the church is clearly pro-life and does not endorse abortion other than in a limited number of situations,[18] but the church has not favored any legislative proposals or participated in any public

14. The document in the next footnote cites the Supreme Court ruling on *Walz v. Tax Commission of City of New York (1970)* as the legal basis of the constitutional right of churches to make their position known on social and moral issues.

15. "Church Submits Additional Testimony on Alcohol Advertising Policy in Utah," news release, October 10, 2001, Salt Lake City, Utah, LDS Church History Library Archives.

16. First Presidency letter, US and Canada, January 27, 1969, Salt Lake City, Utah, LDS Church History Library Archives.

17. "President Kimball Limits Political Role of Church," *Deseret News*, March 31, 1978.

18. Special exceptions are situations involving the health of the mother, the health of the baby, and rape.

demonstrations on abortion.[19] Similarly, the church opposes euthanasia, but does not take a strong position on continuing artificial life support. The church also has a pragmatic stance toward evolution, one of the most salient issues for the Christian Right, and has not issued any official statements that might invite controversy on the topic. One can find only occasional discussions of the issue in the First Presidency statements or press releases, which generally treat evolution as a theory rather than the final verdict on the origin of humankind.[20] There are other issues on the conservative agenda on which the LDS Church takes no positions whatsoever, such as embryonic stem cell research and capital punishment.

The selective approach of the church on moral issues achieves two things: it locates the church on the conservative end of the political spectrum, but it also draws a line between the church and the Evangelical conservative bloc known as the Christian Right. The LDS Church thus appears more flexible and reasonable and contributes to the image of its members as law-abiding mainstream American citizens. This strategy is due to the doctrinal differences identified above, but is also related to an enduring legacy from when the church was under scrutiny to prove its commitment to American cultural and political values. Mormons have diligently participated in America's wars, avoided radical movements, and supported the government's foreign policy positions. Many mainstream or left-leaning Christian

19. For more than a decade, several conservative Christians have protested the semiannual LDS General Conference sessions, arguing that, among other things, Mormons are "baby-killers" because of the church's stance on abortion. The LDS Church doesn't call abortion "murder," largely because it apparently has no specific doctrine on when life begins. This may also explain why the church has not taken a position in the debates regarding the use of stem cells (Stack 2007).

20. Some examples of memos and letters from the Church History Library archives in Salt Lake City, Utah: Clare Middlemiss, secretary to David O. McKay, letter dated May 8, 1964; Joseph Anderson, secretary to the First Presidency, to Harold J. Bissell, May 3, 1960; Joseph Anderson, secretary to the First Presidency, to Armin J. Hill, February 25, 1959; David O. McKay to A. Kent Christensen, February 3, 1959.

denominations, such as Catholics, Episcopalians, and Unitarians, have seen those issues that the LDS Church eschewed as moral matters and offered commentary drawn from their faith traditions or engaged in direct political involvement. The Mormon drive to demonstrate patriotism and a mainstream identity is largely why the LDS Church does not take a stance against war, nuclear weapons, or any foreign policy issue involving these matters. The most visible exception to this was the church's vocal opposition to communism, a position which was in line with American foreign policy during the Cold War.[21]

As scholar of religion and politics Jeffrey Haynes (1998) rightly observes, religion influences politics through what it says and what it does, yet the opposite is also true. What religion does not—or prefers not to—do or say is also very influential. In the case of the LDS Church, its almost blind support for the 2003 War in Iraq was a serious concern for many liberal-leaning Utahns. These individuals wanted the church to assume the role of prophetic critique, in which it speaks the truth as a moral authority to those in positions of political power.[22] There are some indications that the church leadership may have had other reasons for not being critical, such as an expectation that the war would open Iraq for missionary work.[23]

Preferences, Cues, and Political Neutrality

The church adheres to the principle of political neutrality in elections and states that "principles compatible with the gospel may be found in the platforms of all major political parties."[24] Therefore, it does not

21. Clare Middlemiss, secretary to David O. McKay, letter dated December 8, 1965; *Deseret News*, October 23, 1964; First Presidency to Presidents of Stakes, US, September 25, 1962.

22. My conversation with various church members during 2007 and 2008 Sunstone annual meetings.

23. "Leaked Videos Pull Back Curtain on Mormon Leadership," *New York Times*, October 16, 2016.

24. "Letter by LDS Leaders Cheers Utah Democrats: Missive's New Language Underscores Neutrality," *Deseret News, March 15, 2006.*

endorse any political candidates, platforms, or political parties.[25] The church has long maintained that there is no member occupying any official position in the church that is authorized to speak on behalf of the whole institution on political issues.[26] The candidates who are Mormon are commanded by the church not to imply that their candidacy is endorsed by the church and to avoid any statements to that effect.[27] Local church leaders are instructed not to allow meeting spaces in stakes or wards to be used for political purposes and to maintain an impartial position.[28] In spite of these cautionary words, the church also encourages members to fulfill their civic duties and to be involved members of the society, asking them to "be actively engaged in supporting and defending the principles of truth, righteousness, and freedom."[29] The church identifies the desirable qualities of political leaders to be integrity, wisdom, goodness, and honesty.[30]

Despite this official policy of political neutrality, some church leaders and prominent members have been very open supporters of political parties, especially the socially conservative wing of the Republican Party. For example, Ezra Taft Benson, the thirteenth president of the church and the secretary of agriculture for both Eisenhower administrations, was closely involved with the ultraconservative, anticommunist John Birch Society and was an active supporter of the anti–Equal Rights Amendment (ERA) legislation movement.[31] However, such

25. "Church Reemphasizes Political Neutrality," news release, December 6, 2007, http://newsroom.lds.org/article/church-reemphasizes-political-neutrality.

26. "Political Neutrality," news release, October 19, 2006.

27. Church News, October 28, 2000, LDS Church History Library Archives.

28. First Presidency to "Dear President," May 23, 1960, LDS Church History Library Archives.

29. "Civil Government and Law," *True to the Faith*, 2004, 38–39.

30. "Political Participation, Voting, and the Political Neutrality of the Church," LDS First Presidency letter, September 22, 2008, http://newsroom.lds.org/article/first-presidency-issues-letter-on-political-participation.

31. At the semiannual General Conference in 1961, Benson reportedly said that "no true Latter-day Saint, and no true American, can be a socialist or a communist, or support programs leading in that direction" (Fox 2006, 1–2).

Table 2. The LDS Church and a sample of ballot results on moral issues

Issue	Year	Specific Vote/Initiative	Church Doctrine	Official Church Position	Result
Liquor Laws, National	1933	Repeal of Prohibition	Against	Against	61% For
Political Representation, UT	1954	Legislative Apportionment Act	NA	For	63% Against
Liquor Laws, UT	1968	Liberalization of UT Liquor Laws	Against	Against	65% Against
Pornography, UT	1984	Cable Decency Act	For	For	61% Against
Gambling, UT	1992	County Option on Parimutuel Wagering	Against	Against	60% Against
Same-sex Marriage, CA	2000	*Proposition 22* Ban on same-sex marriage	For	For	61% For
Same-sex Marriage, UT	2004	*Amendment 3* Defines marriage as between a man and a woman; no domestic union or partnership can be given equivalent legal effect	For	For	66% For
Same-sex Marriage, CA	2008	*CA Proposition 8* Defines marriage as between a man and a woman	For	For	52% For

potentially divisive figures and opinions have been carefully contained by the church hierarchy.[32] During Benson's tenure as president of the church (1985–94), he softened his rhetoric. This was likely due to the conclusion of the Cold War and institutional constraints imposed by the General Authorities (Fox 2006).

32. For the intraelite conflict over this political activism, see Quinn 1993.

Public Policy, Ballot Propositions, and the Church

Looking at its positions on public issues (summarized in table 2), the church's public strategy is conditioned by an interaction between its doctrine and the political context in which it operates. Religious doctrine is crucial to understanding why the church takes the positions it does and why it wants to influence ballot results on moral issues, such as liquor laws, same-sex marriage, gambling, and pornography. The political context shapes the particular approach adopted by the church in response to such issues. The choice of church leadership to take a clear public position, give cues to church members, encourage them to act independently, or join in coalition with other likeminded groups is the result of calculations based on the political context.

The 1954 Legislative Apportionment Act is a good example of the church's strategy to maximize its leverage in politics based on demographics. The act called for one senator from each Utah county, irrespective of its population density. This would have effectively diluted the power of the more populous and diverse counties, like Salt Lake County, while benefiting more rural and heavily Mormon counties. Despite strong support from church leaders, who lobbied the legislators to enact the measure and mobilized church resources to pass it in the referendum, the measure was defeated with a large margin. Looking at the effectiveness of the church taking such positions, it is also crucial to consider possible internal disagreements among its leadership. In fact, a close examination shows that such disagreements, especially when they are publicized or leaked, adversely affect the success of political cues. In the defeat of the 1954 Reapportionment Act, a critical development was publication of a First Presidency letter distancing the church institutionally from the campaign in the face of public scrutiny and a warning from the Salt Lake IRS office during the campaign (Williams 1967, 239). The indication of internal disagreements among the leadership, perhaps with an intent to save the church from liability, was sufficient to sway the electorate against the measure (Croft 1985, 8–9).

There are usually two lines of justification for church positions. One is a public reasoning based on a rational assessment of the pros and cons for the church members and the larger society. With respect to liquor regulations, the church refers to public health concerns and the prevention of underage drinking. The second rationale preferred by the church is a reference to a broadly conservative worldview with clear roots in religious doctrine. This discourse is significantly shaped by the pillars of the US liberal public sphere: the separation of church and state, pluralism, religious freedoms, and freedom of expression and speech. Church leadership has not been shy about invoking the interests or welfare of the church and its members when it takes positions. However, there have been times when the church's perceived interest was trumped by its own ideology. For example, it did not seek federal funding under President George W. Bush's Faith-Based Initiatives for fear of the "government interfering to the internal working of the church and its affairs."[33]

The church has learned that taking open positions on votes and issues can sometimes backfire, as in the 1933 Prohibition Repeal, the 1954 legislative Apportionment Act, and the 1984 Cable TV Decency Act. Having seen this, the church now takes a more subtle approach and uses its institutional network and influence to indirectly affect outcomes, as in the case of Proposition 8 in California.[34] However, there are also instances in which church-endorsed positions have won decisively, such as the 1992 antigambling measure and the 1968 liquor referendum in Utah. Even with such successful efforts, church leadership is very cautious and does not want to be seen as controlling Utah

33 Larry King's interview with Church President Gordon B. Hinkley, CNN, September 14, 2001.

34. A First Presidency letter on "preserving marriage and strengthening traditional marriage" was read on June 27 in the California congregations, urging church members to get involved in campaigning for a new ballot initiative defining marriage as only between one man and one woman (http://newsroom.lds.org/ldsnewsroom/eng/commentary/california-and-same-sex-marriage).

politics. Some community activists in Utah argue that the Catholic Church and the Episcopalian Church are more vocal in articulating the positions on social justice issues.[35] One plausible interpretation is that the LDS Church does not feel the need to speak up, because a majority of lawmakers and the population know its positions on many issues and share its culture and values.[36]

Other than actual votes, the church watches public debates closely and takes carefully considered positions as it sees fit. On controversial and divisive issues, such as immigration, the church has claimed the mantle of the higher moral ground, calling for compassion, civility, and tolerance.[37] Additionally, the church-owned *Deseret News* published editorials against a proposed strong anti-immigration bill in Utah similar to Arizona's, whose chief sponsor, Senator Russell Pearce, also happened to be a Mormon. The fact that a Mormon member of the Arizona legislature sponsored a bill that most members of the immigrant communities saw anti-immigration had negatively affected the view of the church among Hispanics.[38] Some analysts thus argued that the *Deseret News* was trying to appease that constituency.[39] From a public relations point of view, it would be unwise for the church to turn against Hispanics, the second largest ethnic group in the US and a group from which the church hopes to see many potential converts.

35. Based on my interviews in March 2007 with members of the Salt Lake Interfaith Roundtable who were active in congressional advocacy.

36. The fear of institutional liability sometimes leads to an overstated caution. My experience in "Bridging the Religious Divide" initiative was instructive. Almost all Mormons repeatedly stated that they were expressing their personal opinions, not speaking for the church.

37. "LDS Church Repeats Call for 'Civil Discourse' on Immigration," *Deseret News*, July 18, 2010.

38. "Arizona Immigration Law Fallout Harms LDS Church Outreach," *Arizona Republic*, May 18, 2010.

39. "The Mormon-owned Newspaper Stands with Immigrants," *New York Times*, September 19, 2010.

In a rare example of compromise between business, religious, law enforcement, political, and community leaders, the Utah Compact was signed as a declaration of guiding principles on immigration legislation.[40] The LDS Church also put its weight behind the platform.[41] In fact, many credited the LDS Church for the much weaker immigration enforcement law that was passed by Utah legislature in 2011 along with a surprisingly accommodating guest worker program.[42] In response to critiques of the church abandoning its political neutrality principle, the church defended its open support for the bills based on its determination to take positions on issues with "significant community or moral consequences."[43]

In addition to its proactive role in passing comprehensive immigration reform in Utah, the LDS Church also distanced itself from the anti-immigration and Islamophobic wing of the conservatives. In an implicit response to Donald Trump's proposed Muslim ban during the 2016 presidential primaries, the church released a statement on religious freedoms and pluralism with quotes from Joseph Smith that defended the rights of non-Mormons, including Muslims.[44] Prominent Mormon politicians criticized Donald Trump more openly. Mitt

40. The compact highlighted the federal nature of the ultimate solution to immigration reform, the priority of local over federal law enforcement, the importance of not separating families, the economic contribution of immigrants to Utah's economy, and a welcoming cultural environment in Utah (https://the-utah-compact.com).

41. "Church Supports Principles of Utah Compact on Immigration," Mormon Newsroom, November 11, 2010, http://www.mormonnewsroom.org/article/church-supports-principles-of-utah-compact-on-immigration.

42. "LDS Church Takes Public Stance on Immigration Legislation," *Salt Lake Tribune*, March 17, 2011.

43. "A Principle-Based Approach to Immigration," Mormon Newsroom, March 17, 2011, http://www.mormonnewsroom.org/article/a-principle-based-approach-to-immigration.

44. "Church Points to Joseph Smith's Statements on Religious Freedom, Pluralism," Mormon Newsroom, December 8, 2015, https://www.mormonnewsroom.org/article/church-statement-religious-freedom-pluralism.

Romney came out quite strongly against Trump, sought to block him up until the party's national convention.[45] Even after failing to block Trump, a group of Mormons fielded an independent candidate, argued for voting their conscience, and supported a Mormon as an independent candidate against him.[46] Another prominent Mormon politician, the three-time Republican Utah Senator Bob Bennett's touching remarks from his deathbed—acknowledging the contribution of American Muslims and apologizing for his party's candidate, Donald Trump—also reflects the more sensitive and compassionate position of Mormons in immigration and minority rights.[47]

The LDS Church leadership is composed of highly motivated and ambitious individuals. Most church leaders have strong opinions and they like to see their opinions influence public debates. However, sometimes there is confusion on the part of church members regarding whether statements by leaders reflect official church positions or are merely personal opinions. Candidate endorsements and public statements can thus become problematic. Until the 1950s, it was quite common to hear conflicting opinions and cues from the church leadership based on the personal political positions of the leaders. The conflicting views among the leadership undermined the church's ability to influence electoral outcomes. The 1933 vote to repeal the Prohibition was a case in point, where the clear message of the General Authorities during the 1933 Annual Conference against consumption

45. Ryan Lizza, "How Mitt Romney and the Mormons Saved the 'Never Trump' Movement," *New Yorker*, March 23, 2016, https://www.newyorker.com/news/daily-comment/how-mitt-romney-and-the-mormons-saved-the-never-trump-movement.

46. Michael Worley, "My View: Vote Utah's Conscience: Evan McMullin, Not Donald Trump, Is the Candidate Worth Rallying Around," *Deseret News*, September 8, 2016, https://www.deseretnews.com/article/865661919/My-view-Vote-Utah7s-conscience-Evan-McMullin-not-Donald-Trump-is-the-candidate-worth-rallying.html.

47. "Dying GOP Senator Bob Bennett Apologized to Muslims for Donald Trump," Daily Beast, May 18, 2016, https://www.newyorker.com/news/daily-comment/how-mitt-romney-and-the-mormons-saved-the-never-trump-movement.

and sale of alcohol was undermined by politicians who were General Authorities also (Campbell and Monson 2003, 607). For his part, Church President David O. McKay understood the importance of a unified and disciplined voice for a centralized organization: during his leadership (1951–70), he exercised institutional control over the public image and messages of the church.[48] He was instrumental in reversing its lead role in the 1954 Referendum on the Legislative Apportionment Act by issuing a letter that distanced the institution from the campaign. McKay's efforts to control the official message later found a home within the church when the Special Affairs Committee and the Public Affairs Department were created. These bodies sought to bring a more disciplined approach to the church's handling of public issues and to its dealings with politicians. Now, it is rare to hear church leaders making public political comments as individuals. Rather, the church communicates with the public through these official organs, although leaders are occasionally selected to represent the church and explain its positions. Among the Public Affairs officials, there are registered lobbyists who are authorized to officially represent the church and speak on its behalf when necessary.

Mainstreaming the Mormon Image: The Public Relations of the LDS Church

Owing to the church's growth and diverse membership, its public relations gained more importance in the eyes of the Mormon leadership during the second half of the twentieth century. The church administration was able to transform the earlier popular perception of Mormons as bearded outcast polygamists into a new image of clean-shaven, mainstream American patriots. Even before the advent of modern-day professional image management, under Church President David O. McKay the LDS Church came up with guidelines for

48. For an excellent biography of David O. McKay and a detailed analysis of his handling of internal divisions among the church authorities and management of public affairs, see Prince and Wright 2005.

leadership and temple workers on how to dress, believing white clothing and the good grooming image were key to promoting the modern mainstream image to contemporary Mormons.[49] The information booths installed in the Temple Square in Salt Lake City exemplified the church's renewed efforts to presenting a curated view of Mormonism to the outside world. The first Public Relations Committee was organized in 1972 under the Department of Public Communications; the Public Affairs Department was founded in the 1980s. In the 1990s, the church hired a New York–based public relations firm to conduct its affairs in a more professional manner.[50]

The Office of Public Affairs is in charge of the relationship of the church with the media and the larger society. It is a point of contact and a source of information for journalists and academics. The press releases issued by this office illustrate how it functions. The church publishes its most recent press releases on its website; a more extensive collection of news releases and select internal memos are accessible at the LDS Church History Library archives. The website also features a newsroom area, where one can find links to media articles and news about the church. These resources shed light on the objective and priorities of the public affairs mission over time, which in turn explain how the church has positioned itself with the American polity.[51]

According to the church sources, the public affairs department seeks to build relationships with key "opinion leaders" to help the church accomplish its missions and develop a positive image in the larger

49. Peggy Fletcher Stack, "How Beards Became Barred among Top Mormon Leaders," *Salt Lake Tribune*, April 5, 2013.

50. For a public relations perspective from within the Church, see "Marketing the Mormon Image: An Interview with Wendell J. Ashton," *Dialogue: A Journal of Mormon Thought* (Spring 1977: 15–20). For a comparative historical perspective, see Lythgoe 1968, 45–58.

51. Robert F. Bennett, a public relations professional and a Mormon, cogently argues that the church leadership has been cognizant of public relations since the time of Joseph Smith and that its longstanding goal has been "positioning" rather than image management (Bennett 1977, 120–22).

society.[52] The church's public affairs work is broadly secular; the purpose is not baptism or conversion. However, one key goal—even with this more secular work—is to help the church's missionary programs.

This missionary work is, arguably, the church's most important priority.[53] There are full-time missionary staff at church headquarters in Salt Lake City. There are also local missionary branches under the stakes. These local affiliates are mostly staffed based on a calling received by the church authorities in which members render service in the designated areas; this is, essentially, a form of lay priesthood. Some members are asked to travel and serve the church in other US states and foreign countries. In addition to the widely known young Mormon missionaries whose primary goal is to convert and baptize non-Mormons, there are other missions in which called members act as ambassadors of the church. The latter are usually retired couples, and they are typically sent to locations where they may have previous contacts or know the language and culture.

There is a clear hierarchy and command structure in the Public Affairs Department. First, everybody who works for the department is a member of the church. These individuals see themselves as the representatives of the senior church leaders.[54] There is also the Public Affairs Committee, which is a platform for discussing issues with the senior church leaders. It is not clear if this committee is separate from the Special Affairs Committee of the Church.[55]

The church's public affairs work in the American pluralist liberal context is focused on building strategic relationships that are not

52. Philip M. Volmar, "Public Affairs: Linking Church and Community," *Ensign*, July 2012.

53. Bennett argued that the church would not be in need of public relations management if they were "like the Jews, who are not seeking converts" (1977, 120).

54. Author's interview, December 2008.

55. During my interview, the public affairs staff corrected me that it was the "public affairs committee," not "special affairs," as the latter phrase feeds into the negative public perception of the secrecy and behind-the-scenes involvement of the church in politics.

necessarily based on shared ideology, but on the desire to see similar outcomes. This requires a functional level of pragmatism and engagement with other social and political groups. The challenge for the church is to make sure that it builds political capital and uses this to promote its interests and vision. Coalitions are part of this strategy, yet they may also undermine the church's independent image. The church must balance the desire to be part of mainstream American society with the devotion to its own doctrines and the desire to be seen as a unique—but not strange—faith. The Office of Public Affairs walks this fine line on a regular basis.

The specific implementation of these public relations goals depends on the context. For example, the priority for the church in the US and in Western democracies is interfaith relations and the media, whereas in postcommunist countries or authoritarian regimes, the church places a much stronger emphasis on building trust and good relations with the governments and bureaucracies. Public Affairs representatives reference the words of the former Church President Gordon B. Hinckley, in stating that the church will not enter any country under false pretenses and will always seek to be in good standing with the laws of the land.[56] This strongly supports the main thesis of this study: that the political context largely shapes the strategy of religious groups and accounts for the cross-national variation in the public activism strategies of similar religious groups.

Both the Gülen movement and the LDS Church have similar doctrines on public activism: they largely remain outside of contentious politics and do not engage in civil disobedience. These groups are very concerned about the well-being of their members and the longevity of their programs throughout the world. For the Mormons, this concern is driven by their desire to access countries for proselytizing and to receive assurances of their right to practice their religion and own property. For the Gülen movement, this concern is driven by their desire to secure the right for movement-affiliated schools and

56. Author's interview, December 2008.

other social service organizations to operate. In order to secure those rights and to maintain their presence, the Gülen movement is willing to work with authorities, even under authoritarian regimes. In fact, a close analysis of the organization and activities of both movements in Washington, DC, demonstrates that they rarely get involved in policy-related lobbying; rather, they use Washington as a base for their networking efforts and outreach.[57] The Office of Public Affairs of the LDS Church has a Washington office. Individuals in this office use their access to American bureaucrats and politicians as well as their access to representatives of other countries' foreign missions primarily to advance the missionary work of the church rather than for congressional advocacy on its behalf (Fowler 2010). Similarly, the Turkic American Alliance and the Rumi Forum, both affiliated with the Gülen movement, work diligently to build friendships and courteous relations with foreign and national representatives in Washington, DC.

In speaking with public affairs representatives of the church, they offer very broad, cautionary answers, some of which can seem very thin and unsatisfactory. These official spokespeople know that they are representing an organizational interest and are reluctant to admit anything that may remotely resemble a wrongdoing, a mistake, or a lack of transparency on the part of the church. These individuals are very hesitant to share any primary sources, even if the items in question have been previously published.[58] This approach does not

57. For example, see Levine 2009 for an overview of the Church's lobbying activities in Washington, DC, in pursuit of legal rights in Italy.

58. I experienced this twice. First, when I was reviewing the "circular letters" or the letters from the First Presidency to be read before the LDS congregations. I was given the titles of the letters. I then asked to view some of the letters that dealt with political issues. However, the library supervisors got suspicious, began to question my intentions and the nature of my research, and ultimately collected the letters that the clerks had already started to share with me. No clear rationale as to why they withdrew the materials was provided to me, although I did observe a conversation between the front desk clerk and his supervisor. The supervisor did not want to speak to me. The clerk told me there was a policy of restricted access; I was never able to

advance the organizational interests of a group that is perceived with suspicion and skepticism among Utah's non-Mormons because of its purported secretive behavior. When I asked the Public Affairs representatives about this perception, the representatives simply suggested that I should pursue this line of questioning with individuals who held those perceptions.[59] These examples are also reflective of the present well-grounded confidence of the LDS Church within the pluralist liberal American public sphere. The church officials know their legal rights to freedom of expression and to privacy.

The church is otherwise quite aware of the negative perceptions that individuals in the larger society may hold about Mormons. The church sometimes addresses these beliefs in a form of "teaching by example." Church members seek opportunities to demonstrate that they have nothing to hide in those practices that are at the core of their religion but that also give rise to the persistent stereotypes of

---

learn more about this policy. Of course, the attitude of these individuals is never a strong, upright rejection, but rather a denial wrapped in the smile and niceness of a typical customer-service approach. The second instance occurred when I asked for copies of the news releases issued by the Public Affairs Department. I was told that even the supervisors have problems locating news releases! It was a little hard for me to believe given what I know about the excellent record-keeping habits of the church. The reluctance on the part of these individuals to provide the documents may stem from a desire to be wary of giving away any official document that may later be used against the church.

59. I even tried to pose the question as a self-reflection opportunity, by asking if some actions of church members or some church policies may have had a part in the persistent suspicious attitude of at least some Americans toward the LDS Church. Church representatives provided a broad answer, saying that there are thirteen million members and they are not infallible. When I asked about some specific examples where the church public affairs representatives had needed to correct a mistake of a General Authority or church policy, they explained to me how the church leadership is guided by revelation and nobody drives limousines or Ferraris. They argued that this reality made their job much easier because they have perfect confidence in the leadership of their institution. They cited this as a hard thing to understand with "secular reasoning."

Mormons as a strange and secretive cult. The temple open houses are a good example of this kind of transparency. The temples and temple rituals had created popular perceptions that likened them to Masonic temples and of the rituals as cult-like. Before every temple is dedicated, the church now holds well-organized open houses, turning these events into a public relations opportunity.

As work in the public affairs department is considered a secular calling by the church members, the job of these individuals is to make sure that the official version of church policies and positions is communicated clearly and that the interests of the church are protected. In pursuit of these goals, church representatives must also appeal to the public to gain support for general provisions that ensure the rights of religious groups are protected and to gain support for specific provisions, such as liquor laws, that the church supports. In order to persuade the public to adopt such restrictions, the church often resorts to secular rational arguments, referencing health care, traffic safety, and social order claims. The public affairs officials give examples from all over the US and the world, arguing that the particular issue under question is not necessarily a religious issue. Rather, the representatives assert, it is because of the religious profile of Utah that the church's position is perceived as religious by the public. Mormons elsewhere have taken similar positions to those they took in Utah or have lobbied politicians in support of similar issues, but, owing to their smaller numbers outside of Utah, these efforts usually occur as part of a larger coalition.

Although there is a great deal of institutional discipline, church officials are not always consistent in their approaches to public debates. For example, contrary to their rational-secular reasoning on liquor laws, there is some hesitation on the part of church officials to address the issue of same-sex marriage with rational language alone. The responses I received during my interviews defended the right of a social group to take positions on public policy matters while also mentioning that the church reserves the right to take positions on moral issues. Church officials were quick to turn to the First Presidency as the source of church authority and decision-making.[60] This reflects both a pragmatic and selective use of rational-legal reasoning alongside a self-assured reference to religious doctrine.

The level of religious diversity and majority-minority relations are important in understanding how social groups operate within the parameters of the liberal public sphere. The argument made by church representatives—that the structure of the public sphere in Utah influences how positions on public issues are perceived by the broader public—has some merit. There is hardly another state in America where a religious group enjoys such an unrivaled majority position.[61] Mormon dominance is more than mere demographics and is reflected in Mormons' language, ways of doing things, social ideology, and insider-outsider dynamics. In what can be called "Mormon culture region" (Yorgason 2003), the LDS Church is deeply established in the affairs of the community, with great resources and organizational capabilities, and has a strong position relative to any other social group. Given this organizational advantage and strong fellowship ties among members, other social groups in the state struggle to balance the dominant position of the LDS Church in local politics. The basic premise of the liberal public sphere is limited government ruling over the competing interests of a pluralistic society. Utah has an almost identical institutional design to other states with respect to the rule of law, the separation of church and state, and the protection of civil liberties. However, the actual distribution of power in the state creates a very unique environment regarding issues on which Mormons and non-Mormons have divergent preferences. Liquor laws have historically reflected this division. On most other issues, though, Utah follows national trends. A conservative-liberal continuum is usually more meaningful than the Mormon versus non-Mormon axis on issues such as immigration,

60. Author's interview, December 2008.

61. One can argue that evangelicals have a similar cultural dominance in the South; however, there are multiple big and small denominations that collectively make up evangelical Christians. Also, the diversity among evangelicals is much greater than diversity among Mormons in Utah.

same-sex marriage, and other ballot initiatives; underlying this is the obvious pattern of Utah's Mormons favoring predominantly conservative positions. Utah may be unique in some key aspects, but the role of the church in politics can still be best understood with reference to the broader liberal public sphere of the US.

Constructing and Negotiating the Mormon Identity through Official Channels

An in-depth analysis of LDS Church press releases shows that the church engages in very effective public relations efforts through the Public Affairs Department. There were on average ten releases per month between 1997 and 2007, and this increased to about fifteen in the following decade.[62] These church communications target both members and nonmembers, and topics can be classified under seven main categories:

1. *Church news*: Reports of new callings; appointments; dedications; missionary news; events and worship service information; and birthdays, deaths, commemorations, and memorial services for prominent LDS figures

2. *Holiday messages*: Greetings (primarily) for Christmas and Easter

3. *Media corrections*: Statements raising awareness or offering clarifications and critiques of publications and audiovisual media concerning the church, its members, history, or doctrine and practices

4. *Moral issues*: Statements on select public policy matters, such as alcohol consumption and advertising, gambling, abortion, same-sex relations and marriage, adoption, pornography, education, or domestic violence and abuse

5. *Political neutrality*: Reminders related to activities of the church and the political activities of its members

62. The 2008 CA Proposition 8 and marriage equality campaign along with the national and state level immigration debate were the major reasons for the increased frequency of news releases by the church. Also, with a modernized and dedicated online newsroom, the Public Affairs Department's engagement with public issues maintained higher levels compared to the pre-2008 period.

6. *Corporate interests of the church*: Items related to copyright protection, nonprofit organization benefits, property rights, economic activities, or legal issues

7. *Community relations*: News of interfaith relations and topics concerning community and social issues

The press releases aim at promoting an accurate, positive, mainstream image for the church. This messaging starts with the church's persistent emphasis on the correct use of its name. The media is asked to mention the church's full official name, the Church of Jesus Christ of Latter-day Saints, first and then the acronym (LDS Church or the Church) is recommended for subsequent references in the same piece. When speaking about church members, the term "Latter-day Saints" is preferred. The name Mormon is acceptable to refer to church members but not to the church itself, which does not wish to be known as the "Mormon Church." According to the church, the term "Mormonism" should be used in reference to the "combination of doctrine, culture and lifestyle unique to the Church of Jesus Christ of Latter-day Saints."[63] The First Presidency letters offer reminders of the authentic (revealed) name of the church to its members and stress the importance of "proclaiming the name of the savior throughout the world."[64]

As opposed to the Gülen movement's efforts to emphasize its activities more than its name, the LDS Church is very keen on requesting members and nonmembers alike to use its lengthy official name, and there are a few reasons why the LDS Church ardently highlights it. First, this serves as a response to stereotypes that paint the LDS Church as a non-Christian church. The name Jesus Christ is written in a larger font than all other words in the official church logo that has been in use since 1995. Additionally, this emphasis on the church's full name aims to distance the LDS Church and its members from other groups or denominations who also claim to be Mormons, such as the

63. First Presidency letter, February 23, 2001; press release, March 5, 2001, Church History Library Archives, Salt Lake City, Utah.

64. First Presidency letter, February 23, 2001.

Fundamentalist Church of Jesus Christ of Latter Day Saints (FLDS), the Reorganized Church of Jesus Christ of Latter Day Saints (RLDS or the Community of Christ), and the Church of Jesus Christ of Latter Day Saints (Strangite). For example, the church's official name was adamantly emphasized to the international media during the 2002 Winter Olympics in Salt Lake City. Likewise, in the early 1980s, the church added the subtitle "Another Testament of Jesus Christ" to the title of the Book of Mormon, the church's sacred scripture, as part of a public relations campaign to be recognized as a Christian church.

There are certain themes that elicit a near-certain reaction from the church whenever the media covers a story on Mormonism that addresses one of these points: polygamy, the priesthood of blacks, the Mountain Meadows Massacre, Mormons vs. other Christians, Utah politics, and Mormon politicians.

Polygamy became much more topical after the leader of the FLDS Church, Warren Jeffs, was jailed for charges of arranging an under age marriage.[65] The HBO series *Big Love*, which premiered in the US in March 2006, was another form of undesired publicity for the LDS Church. The television series is about a fundamentalist Mormon family who live a polygamous lifestyle in a suburb of Salt Lake City; the plot concerns the challenges they face in the society and within their household. The LDS Church criticized the series on three main points. First, the church took issue with making polygamy a source of entertainment, which, according to the church, "minimizes the seriousness of that problem and adds to the suffering of the abuse victims."[66] In particular, the church referenced the emotional and

65. For a sample reaction of the LDS leadership to splinter groups, see the news releases "Polygamous Sects are not Mormons, the Church Says," October 25, 2006, http://newsroom.lds.org/article/polygamist-sects-are-not--mormons,--church-says; and "Use of the Word Mormon in News Reports," November 21, 2006, http://newsroom.lds.org/article/use-of-the-word-mormon-in-news-reports.

66. "Church Responds to Questions on TV Series," Mormon Newsroom, March 6, 2006, http://www.mormonnewsroom.org/article/church-responds-to-questions-on-hbos-big-love.

physical abuse suffered by the women and children in the series. Second, the church strongly opposes the concept of "fundamentalist Mormon" and goes to great lengths to distance the practice of polygamy with modern-day Mormonism.[67] In that sense, the church may fear that the series will reinforce popular stereotypes about Latter-day Saints. Last, the church's critique of the television show was embedded in a larger critique of American popular culture from a moral point of view. The church takes a disapproving attitude toward the larger society's "unhealthy preoccupation with sex," coarse humor, and foul language.[68]

The ability of African Americans to serve as priests in the LDS Church has been an issue, especially in the wake of the civil rights movement. The previous inferior status of blacks in church doctrine and practice was ended by official declaration in 1978, when the church's leaders proclaimed that "all worthy members of the Church may be ordained to priesthood without regard for race or color."[69] However, this was not enough to appease some African American groups, who felt that the church's newly articulated policy was insufficient—they asked for a formal apology.[70] Some black LDS Church members who learned of the church's history of racial relations demanded the General Authorities publicly disown these past practices as well as remove the residue of racist teachings in LDS doctrine and Mormon culture. The First Presidency and the Quorum of the Twelve Apostles reportedly held discussions in response to these pressures, but after the existence of such discussions was disclosed to the

67. See, for example, President Gordon B. Hinckley's October 1998 general conference statement, cited in the press release "Mormon Fundamentalists," Mormon Newsroom, March 6, 2006, https://www.mormonnewsroom.org/article/mormon-fundamentalists.

68. "Church Responds to Questions on TV Series," March 6, 2006, http://newsroom.lds.org/article/church-responds-to-questions-on-tv-series.

69. First Presidency statement, September 30, 1978.

70. "Black Mormons Resist Apology Talk," *Los Angeles Times*, May 18, 1998.

media, the church denied their existence. This killed the potential for any further declarations on the race issue (Ostling and Ostling 1999). Ultimately, the church argued that the 1978 official declaration was sufficient and that it "speaks for itself."[71]

It is very common for the church to comment on national news stories, publications, and TV programs about Mormons. The September 10, 2001, *Newsweek* story "Mormons" and the 2007 PBS Documentary *The Mormons* are two examples of how the national media prominently covers the LDS Church and its members. In a didactic treatise, the Public Affairs Office took the *Newsweek* story as a case study with which to address the religion writers and editors in the national media in order to clarify some points on which the church "takes issue." In response to the below phrases in the *Newsweek* story, the church offered a rebuttal that reveals the institutional concerns, expectations, and agenda of the Church Public Affairs:

- *". . . zero tolerance for homosexuality . . ."*
- *"Business in Salt Lake is done the Mormon way or not at all?"*
- *". . . readiness to press their temperance code on non-Mormon citizens"*
- *". . . the church hopes to emphasize what Mormons share with historic Christianity, not what makes them different."*
- *"Mormon rhetoric is becoming more overtly evangelical . . . the stress on grace and forgiveness of sins and on Jesus as atoning savior of the world sounds almost Methodist or even Southern Baptist."*
- *"Mormons consider theirs the only church of Jesus Christ: all others are apostate."*
- *Mormons have the only church structured like a corporation . . . almost every member of the Salt Lake hierarchy is a successful, politically conservative businessman"*
- *". . . when young Americans began experimenting with drugs and dropping out, Mormons began advertising their abstemious purity code . . ."*

71. "Black Mormons Resist Apology Talk."

- *". . . there'll be reporters wondering what lies behind the church's many veils."*[72]

The Public Affairs Department took the opportunity to reiterate that the official position of the church is based on church doctrine. With respect to homosexuality, the church indicated that it does not hate people of a particular sexual orientation, yet, just like everyone else, gay people should be subject to a "God-given rule of conduct." In a similar rebuttal with nuance, the church sees the description of all non-Mormons as apostates in the story as an overstatement: the church believes there may be good and truth in other religions, but that the LDS Church is the only true church of Christ. In general, the church does not welcome comparisons to Evangelical churches—the distinctiveness of the LDS doctrine is always emphasized.

The second group of concerns are related to social issues. The influence of the church on liquor laws, economic life, and Mormon youth are favorite themes for journalists because of their controversial nature. Yet the church must also expect that few journalists will write stories that wholly reflect the church's perceptions. However, to protect its public image, representatives of the church challenge anything that may contribute to the view that the church is intolerant, has peculiar practices, dominates the social life of its members, or is secretive in its functioning. Some elements of church doctrine and in the church's organization provoke suspicion in the minds of nonmembers. For the most part, the church's corrections do not concern the substance of the media coverage; rather, they are an attempt to soften the media's rhetoric, which tends toward sharp contrasts and thus emphasizes the particular attributes of the LDS Church. The church is also very diligent in presenting its own version of a story whenever there is a window of opportunity, using its own PR efforts to educate the larger society—a practice I call "continuing education through public relations."

72. "Clarifications to Religious Writers and Editors Regarding *Newsweek* Report," news release, September 7, 2001.

The perspective of church members regarding the church's public relations is also important. During one of my presentations on this topic, I was struck by the uneasiness of church members in response to my discussion of the different way in which the church conducts issues-based outreach to members and nonmembers.[73] Many of these individuals had experience with the behind-the-scenes involvement of the church in political matters. They were familiar with the church's denial of said involvement until faced with irrefutable evidence presented by the media. Some liberal Mormons are also uneasy about what they described as the church pushing for doctrinal orthodoxy through the Public Affairs Department, even suggesting that the department alters doctrinal issues.[74] The Book of Mormon, the Covenant and Doctrines, the Pearl of Great Price, and the Bible together are the basic sources of LDS doctrine. Because of continued revelations in LDS doctrine, this is a dynamic structure. There is a significant level of confusion in terms of when and under what conditions an existing revelation is replaced by a new one. Some scholars of Mormonism have argued that this uncertainty has especially characterized the last twenty-five years with respect to eternal progression, polygamy, and the infallibility of the General Authorities.[75] These issues have been discussed by the General Authorities, but no final position has emerged. Yet the Public Affairs Department has been in a position to frame these issues in a way that is acceptable to the average American. The department's role as the representative organ of the

73. August 2007, at the Annual Sunstone Symposium in Salt Lake City, organized by independent and liberal leaning Mormons, catering to a largely Mormon audience.

74. Some feminist Mormon women, such as Janice Allred and Margaret Toscano, were excommunicated for their ideas about female Mormon deity. Mormon scripture has references to Heavenly Mother, but it has been downplayed by the contemporary Church authorities, motivated by promoting a mainstream Christian image ("A Mormon Mystery Returns: Who Is Heavenly Mother?" *Salt Lake Tribune*, May 16, 2013, http://archive.sltrib.com/article.php?id=56282764&itype=CMSID).

75. Author's interview with Becky Jones of Weber State University at Sunstone Symposium, August, 2007.

church means that the way it presents issues necessarily impacts the way Mormons themselves understand their faith. This thus gives rise to questions regarding the role played by the Public Affairs Office in redefining doctrinal issues.

Relations with Other Communities and Social Programs

A second recurring theme in the news releases is the church's involvement in humanitarian aid, disaster relief, and social programs. This also promotes the image of the LDS Church as a faith community that does good works not only for its own members but also for the larger society and the world. The work of the Church Relief Agency during the 1989 San Francisco earthquake and 2005 Hurricane Katrina in New Orleans garnered the Mormons much media attention and provided many Americans a firsthand introduction to the LDS Church. Many residents of Mississippi remember Mormons from the "Mormon Helping Hands" t-shirts worn by church volunteers and the "Joining Hands as Neighbors and Now Friends" campaign motto during their relief efforts.[76] Similarly, the number and geographic range of the countries mentioned in church news releases—Kosovo, East Timor, Indonesia, Iraq, Peru, Zimbabwe, Mozambique, Russia, North Korea, and many others—portray a church that is a global actor with an increasing international presence and vision.[77]

Dating to the early years of the church, the Mormon Tabernacle Choir[78] and the General Conferences are two other significant chan-

76. Mormon Helping Hands have been renamed Just Serve (JustServe.org).

77. "Church Formally Recognized in Russia" (May 15, 1998); "Church Relief Agency Sends Aid to Famine Threatened North Korea" (July 11, 1997); "Church Sending Aid to Kosovo Refugees" (April 3, 1999), "Aid to Flood-Stricken Zimbabwe and Mozambique" (March 7, 2000); "Plight of Timorese Refugees Eased by Church Aid" (May 3, 2000).

78. Formed in 1847, the choir has released more than 130 musical compilations and several films and videotapes, and has received "platinum status," "gold status," Emmy, and Grammy awards. The choir has sung in important national ceremonies, including the inauguration of President Ronald Reagan, and represented America

nels by which the church presents the public face of Mormonism.[79] The Tabernacle Choir still sings the old Mormon hymns, but has added an emphasis on biblical Christian themes. Consistent with the stress on larger Christian themes is the image of the Mormons as good people. In a July 22, 2001, statement President Hinckley reminded church members of the experiences of the early Mormon pioneers and advised them to be neighborly, including mingling with Utah residents of other faiths and acknowledging the diversity of the Salt Lake Valley.

The call for neighborliness can be better understood within the context of the 2002 Salt Lake City Winter Olympics and the ensuing controversy surrounding planning and land-use regulations for a proposed plaza adjacent to the temple square in downtown Salt Lake City, known as the Main Street Plaza Controversy. Both of these events prompted concern on the part of church leadership for the church's public image. The challenge for the church during the Olympics was to ensure accurate and positive media coverage of Mormonism. With the help from civic leaders and residents, the church was quite successful in countering stereotypes about Mormonism. Due to these efforts and the church's media outreach strategy, prominent scholar of Mormonism Jan Shipps has argued, the church's image was transformed. In particular, the image of the church as a "provincial out-of-the-way" faith tradition in the Mountain West was replaced with an image in which the church is a "forward and outward looking" worldwide body whose members are polite and gracious hosts rather than clean-cut zealots with a mission to make converts (Shipps 2004).

---

in different parts of the world, and it is sometimes called the American Choir. For more information, visit its website: http://www.mormontabernaclechoir.org/.

79. The LDS Church has convened general conferences since its very foundation. The first conference was organized by Joseph Smith in 1830 with twenty-seven members participating, and 2017 will be the 187th Annual (April) and 177th semi-annual (October) general conference. Members still attend from all over the world in the 20,000-capacity Conference Center in Salt Lake City.

As the preparations for the Olympics were underway, Salt Lake City residents faced another challenge regarding the role and place of religion in their public space. The Main Street Plaza Controversy concerned the proposed sale of a section of Main Street in downtown Salt Lake City. Main Street is adjacent to the main LDS temple complex; the church sought to build a plaza that would connect two blocks to the existing Salt Lake Temple complex. The issue divided the public almost exclusively along the lines of Mormon supporters of the church's efforts versus non-church-member opponents of the plan. The proposal for the plaza provided for public access to the plaza even after it was to become private church property, but it also recognized the right of the church to restrict certain conduct that may be offensive to it, such as smoking, obscenity, and protests. Secular groups, such as the American Civil Liberties Union of Utah, and minority religious groups, such as the First Unitarian Church, argued that the deal violated constitutional principles of freedom of speech. The litigation and the ensuing legal battle did not result in a clear victory for either side. The US Court of Appeals for the Tenth Circuit ruled that the plaza was a public forum and behavioral restrictions were unconstitutional. The court suggested that either the city terminate its easement on the property—hence the plaza would no longer be a public place—or the city could enforce "reasonable time, place, and manner restrictions."[80] The initial reaction from both sides escalated the scale of the conflict. Finally, after some unpleasant scenes in the plaza, a compromise was reached. The church engaged in a considerable public relations campaign to find a compromise in line with the court's suggestions and to proceed with the sale. Some civic groups, such as the Unification Alliance, and prominent community leaders came together to find a solution. Ultimately, a compromise was reached in which the city's easement on the plaza was terminated in exchange for cash and a church-held land transferred to the city, on the west side.

80. *First Unitarian Church v. Salt Lake City Corp.*, 308 F. 3d 1114 (10th Circuit, 2002).

The plaza was turned into a religious park where the LDS Church retains the right to regulate conduct and limit protest.[81] In effect, the LDS Church had lost the initial legal battle, but won the public relations battle by mobilizing its base and utilizing well-connected power brokers (Monson and Norman 2007).

If we extend the idea of neighborliness to national and global levels, relations among different faiths and cultures is crucial for peace and harmony. One of the intellectual debates about the future of the world is based on Samuel Huntington's much-debated clash of civilizations thesis, which predicts that the prevalent source of conflict in the world will be cultural, not economic or ideological differences. According to the Gülen movement, the antidote to this grim view is interfaith-intercultural dialogue and tolerance. Unlike the Gülen movement, for whom interfaith dialogue is one of the pillars and legitimizing factors of their public relations, the LDS Church does not usually organize exclusive interfaith programs. Rather, the church maintains a mutually respectful and cordial relationship with other faiths and supports the efforts of other groups in their dialogue activities. Along with the First Presidency message to Utah Mormons about the historic tensions between the Mormon majority and other non-Mormon minorities, the church encouraged respect for the Islamic faith following the events of 9/11.[82] The church later worked with local Islamic groups in Indonesia and Iraq to provide humanitarian aid.[83] On April 2, 2005, the First Presidency issued a sympathy message in response to the death of Pope John Paul II and on April 19, 2005, the church issued a message of congratulations to the new Pope, Benedict XVI. The church also expressed condolences for the death

81. "SLC, LDS Win Fight over Plaza," *Salt Lake Tribune*, October 4, 2005.

82. A September, 21, 2001, press release pointed to the mutually respectful relations long enjoyed between Mormons and Muslims, advised caution against generalizing the terrorist ideology as representative of all Muslims, and condemned acts of retribution to innocent Muslims in America.

83. For example, "Muslims and Mormons Join in Iraqi Relief Efforts" (May 10, 2003).

of Mother Teresa upon her death in 1997.[84] The presence and growth of the LDS Church, especially in Latin America, makes such moves an important gesture—if not a public relations necessity. Additionally, the church has also hosted an all-Spanish Christmas celebration in a church building.[85]

Conclusion

Based on the press releases and the statements of the First Presidency, this chapter demonstrated that the LDS Church endeavors to promote a public image for itself as distinct yet mainstream (not "strange"), conservative yet moderate, politically engaged but not partisan, and supporters of the democratic process, the Constitution, and basic freedoms and human rights, not blind followers of religious hierarchy. Mormons are presented as law-abiding, community-minded, family-oriented, neighborly, patriotic, and striving middle-class Americans. This kind of strategy indicates that the Mormons are in a later phase of normalization. The church officially reinforces that message of a mainstream American faith doing good work. The church's strategy of focusing on primarily substantive issues also differs from the Gülen movement's preoccupation with procedural issues and its emphasis on basic liberal democratic norms and institutions at the expense of concrete policy questions.

Despite the church's assertiveness in managing its public image and message, it also maintained a defensive posture against journalists, academics, and even critical church members. The defensiveness may become more acute during times of high negative publicity as was the case with the church's behind-the-scenes involvement in California's Proposition 8 campaign on behalf of the conservative coalition. The church was also concerned about Mitt Romney's Mormon faith being politicized by his opponents when running for president in 2008. The

84. "First Presidency Issues Statement on Mother Teresa" (September 1997).

85. "Church Opens Doors of Marriott Center to Hispanic Community for All-Spanish Christmas Celebration," press release, November 25, 2003.

church initiated a publicity campaign shortly after, featuring ordinary Mormons from different walks of life. Judging by the coverage during Romney's 2012 campaign, one can argue the church's efforts were successful and the church's engagement may be expected to become less defensive. However, slick and professional public affairs management does not guarantee a long-term improvement in public perception. Aggressive public affairs management to the extent of alienating one's own members is often symptomatic of lack of transparency and trust in an organization. The cases of polygamy, black priesthood, and same-sex marriage suggest Mormonism adapts to the changing cultural and political context, but the adaptation comes after a long period of resistance and with a cost to its public image. The liberal public sphere offers protection for groups who may be outside of what is considered mainstream in the society. The incentive for attitudinal shift on moral-political issues comes from the societal change. In contrast, in the republican public sphere, the state plays the decisive role rather than the society, as the Gülen movement's dramatic story of rise and fall in power and popularity in Turkey demonstrates.

Conclusion

This study started with the broad question of understanding strategies of religious movements in the public sphere. The research design was based on the selection of two religious groups that are similar enough in their goals in the public sphere and doctrine concerning political involvement, engagement, and representation. The variation in the means to achieve those basic goals was explained with a reference to the political context in which they formulate their preferences. More specifically, the liberal public sphere in the US and the republican public sphere in Turkey have shaped their organizational and discursive strategies.

Both groups have had to deal with the issue of exclusion, albeit in different forms. The Mormons experienced exclusion and persecution at the hands of the majority Protestant establishment, facing existential threats to their lives and faith traditions. The Gülen movement faced existential threats of their own, first from the secularist Kemalist state until the early 2000s, and, more recently, an even graver crackdown after falling out of coalition with the popular AKP government in late 2013 and especially after the July 2016 coup attempt. Chapter 4 discussed the Gülen movement's relations with the Turkish state and underscored that "infiltration" and "taking over" were commonly used against the Gülen movement sympathizers who were recruited by the national bureaucracy. As chapters 5 and 7 explained, comparable allegations were made against Mormons, in terms of their loyalty to the political system, their patriotism, and their ulterior motives. The main difference between the two treatments was that Mormonism has remained a minority religion with lower levels of popularity in the US,[1] and the Gülen movement enjoyed considerably higher levels of popularity in Turkey during most of the period under study in this book, up until 2014.[2] Even with a largely supportive public attitude, the state-dominant republican public sphere continued to enforce limitations on the Gülen movement's integration with the polity. After the movement fell out of its alliance with the popular AKP government, which consolidated its power and replaced the Kemalist state establishment, the movement became the enemy of the state and lost its popularity.[3] In spite of the persisting negative view of the Mormons for almost two centuries, the LDS Church survived social and political adversity and is now much better integrated into the American polity, thanks to its ability to transform its message, public identity, and public perception from one of an outcast, bearded polygamist sect into a mainstream, striving middle-class American

1. Despite some improvements in the last decade, Mormons continue to rank close to the bottom of the list of religions that Americans feel most warmly about. A 2017 Pew survey found that Americans have colder feelings toward Mormons compared to any other religious group, except for Muslims and atheists ("Americans Express Increasingly Warm Feelings toward Religious Groups," February 15, 2017, http://www.pewforum.org/2017/02/15/americans-express-increasingly-warm-feelings-toward-religious-groups/).

2. A GENAR Poll, published in *Yeni Safak*, July 18, 2008. 65.4 percent of the respondents said they endorsed the Gülen movement functions, compared to 32.8 percent who believed that the movement tries to "capture" and control the state.

3. A 2014 GENAR poll found that 73 percent of the public blamed the Gülen movement for establishing an illegal "parallel state" to overthrow the government.(http://www.ensonhaber.com/17-aralik-operasyonu-sonrasi-en-kapsamli-anket-2014-01-13.html). A 2016 Andy-AR survey found 64 percent of the Turkish public believed the movement was behind the July 15, 2016, military coup attempt ("Andy-AR araştırması: Seçmen siyasetteki ılımlı havanın devamını istiyor" BBC Türkçe, 26 July, 2016, http://www.bbc.com/turkce/haberler-turkiye-36896251). These survey results can be questioned because of the political climate under which they were conducted, but it would be safe to argue that the support for the movement significantly declined. As a reflection of the political climate, the Freedom House downgraded Turkey to "not-free" status from "partly free" in 2018 (https://freedomhouse.org/report/freedom-world/2018/turkey).

religion. As the Mormons transformed themselves, so did the American public sphere, which became more diverse in social demographics and identity, and more pluralist in its politics and law, throughout the twentieth century. The changing perception of religious groups can be expected, but the main source of the changes can give clues about the form of public sphere that exists in a polity. In the American liberal public sphere, the major cleavages emerged between Mormon and non-Mormon communities in the society, and the relative economic and political power of each side was decisive in government policies. In the Turkish republican public sphere, the state's definition of threat from religious communities not only affected public opinion, but the bureaucratic establishment frequently pressured and at times forced civilian governments to conform to their threat perceptions.

There was a key difference in the discussion of the two cases in terms of substantive (and more particular) and procedural (and broader) issues. The chapters on the LDS Church were more about the church's acts, declarations, and beliefs. This was in line with the approach of the Church Public Affairs to public issues. The chapters on the Gülen movement revolved around the collective picture of the public sphere as the movement tried to reach out to different societal groups and build coalitions to balance the power of the state. For the Gülen movement, reaching across the aisle, dialogue, democratization, and deliberation were more important than promoting a particular conservative view on social or moral issues. In the American case, there was less need for discussions of metapolitics, as the basic liberties and the institutionalized checks and balances in the political system made particular social issues more central in the public sphere. The sociopolitical actors in the Turkish public sphere had to address the "rules of the game" and the structural problems, as the political context remained very restrictive of their rights to participate in the public sphere. Another reason for this seeming disparity is the fact that the public sphere in the US is more society-centric (civil and political) and the Turkish counterpart is more state-centric. This led to more emphasis on state policies in the Turkish case and more emphasis on the social groups themselves in the American case.

Chapter 1 offered a theoretical framework for a public-sphere perspective of the politics of religious representation and developed the liberal and republican models of public sphere. Along the liberal-republican continuum, acting within the political society as an interest group is easier and more likely in a liberal public sphere than in a republican public sphere. The liberal public sphere in the US enabled the LDS Church to:

1. Exist as a religious institution with legal recognition under the protection of the First Amendment
2. Benefit from tax exemption as a non-profit organization
3. Freely express opinion on public and political issues.

In terms of the political involvement of groups like the LDS Church, there is a gray area: nonprofit organizations registered with the IRS for tax exemption cannot get involved in partisan political campaigns or direct their tax-exempt income for substantial legislative activity, such as extensive lobbying. However, these provisions are not meant to restrict the constitutional right to freedom of expression for the individuals within tax-exempt organizations. The LDS Church has been very careful about avoiding legal trouble for their involvement in ballot initiatives, but it has also been assertive enough in promoting grassroots mobilization, raising money, and getting their points across concerning moral issues, such as liquor laws, same-sex marriage, and gambling. The church did receive a few warnings and fines from the IRS, as in the case of its involvement in 1954 Legislative Apportionment Act in Utah and the Proposition 8 campaign in California, both discussed in detail in chapter 7.

The liberal framework provides basic protections, liberty, and equality of opportunity. Legally speaking, the playing field is relatively even for the competing social groups. Differentiation is largely based on the available resources and their effective management. Unlike bureaucratic hurdles common in republican countries such as France and Turkey, there are minimum government regulations in terms of property ownership, registration requirements, or restrictions on proselytizing. Such limitations change the calculus for religious groups in terms of their public profiles, and their strategies take those structural factors into account. The LDS Church since the admission of Utah into the Union in 1896 enjoyed such basic rights, and their strategies in the public sphere were concerned with institutional interests and considerations of public image more than the fear of getting in trouble with the established system.

The republican public sphere in Turkey, on the other hand, has had five critical influences over the Gülen movement's public profile:

1. The semicorporatist policy of the state on religious organizations made it practically impossible for the movement to claim an independent legal status. Consequently, it remained as an amalgam of various service organizations with certain contractual ties among its institutions, but mostly informal ties among the followers.

2. The lack of official status and membership rolls gave the movement flexibility in its public affairs. In absence of binding spokespeople and official representatives, there were only editorials of movement affiliated newspapers, TV stations, and civil society organizations, but no definitive movement positions on most controversial issues.

3. The state's policies of selective cooptation and coercion gave often conflicting incentives to the movement. For example, during the early 1990s, the movement was seen by the secularist state establishment as a potential antidote and a balance to the rising popularity of political Islam. The Turkish state also saw the movement's educational and cultural activities beneficial for promoting Turkish culture abroad, much like the French state supported French Catholic missionary schools despite its anti-clericalism. This strategic accommodationism paved the way for the Gülen movement's access to some members of the state elite and politicians, who proved to be quite useful allies for the movement during the following decade. In return for the state's accommodationist incentives, the movement openly criticized the Islamists and almost sided with the military against them during the 1996–97 confrontation between the two. This made it possible for the movement to cautiously go public, as the process with the Journalists and Writers Foundation and the Abant Platform suggest. However, in the late 1990s, the movement also witnessed the

coercive face of the state, leading to Fethullah Gülen's settlement in the US and more exposure to the liberal public sphere.

4. The lack of proper protections for religious freedoms, communal property rights, and civil liberties under the Turkish Kemalist secularist regime made the movement wary of open advocacy or even formal organizational identity, giving incentives for its cautious public activism strategy with an amorphous organizational arrangement. The liberal shift in Turkish politics during 2003–13 provided more opportunities for the movement's access to power and made it relatively more assertive in the public sphere. However, this opening was short-lived, and the next round of state crackdown since 2014 has been much more severe than the earlier round in 1990s.

5. The state control over religion and restrictions in the public sphere ironically made the movement more aware of other social groups in similar positions in the society, incentivizing alliance and coalition building rather than an interest-group approach. The movement's increasing access to power between 2003 and 2013 alienated some of its former allies in the civil society and this proved to be a major weakness in the movement's attempts to create a broad coalition after 2013.

As a result of the incentives and disincentives offered by the republican public sphere, the Gülen movement developed organizational and discursive strategies. Although it had already passed its infancy by the mid-2000s, it still remained a "movement" rather than a properly institutionalized and established organization with headquarters and spokespeople. Part of this set-up is related to the lack of clergy in Islam, but it is possible to have certain administrative posts and clear lines of organizational authority for religious scholars and imams as the official Turkish bureaucracy—Diyanet—demonstrates. As a result of the structure of the public sphere in Turkey, the Gülen movement had to take into account its survival and protection, adopting symbolic and broadly inclusive language.

Explaining the coalition building and dialogue promotion by the Gülen movement as a pure strategy based on the external factors would be overdeterministic, and an underestimation of the importance of ideology and the role of agency. The movement's intellectual roots in Sufism and the Nur tradition are significant. However, even specific ideologies are shaped with external factors, and the need to engage or isolate are responses to incentives from the political system. The findings in this study demonstrate the mutually constitutive role between the agency and the structure. As discussed in chapters 4 and 6, the Gülen movement emerged as a restorationist Islamic movement from the Turkish periphery in response to the contemporary experiences of Turkish modernization and offered a modernist form of Turkish Islamic conservativism.

Looking at the discourse of the two groups, one can conclude that both are influenced by the concepts and ideas that are prioritized in their respective public spheres for legitimacy. Despite some increase in utilizing religion as an oppositional language against the AKP government since 2013, the Gülen movement primarily refers to concepts of national interest, public good, consensus, harmony, and order. The state is seen as a necessary organization, whose absence would bring anarchy. The movement has emphasized the importance of its educational activities, business links, and associations for an orderly society, its benefit for the Turkish language, and its contribution to Turkey's diplomatic relations with other countries. The prominent figures in the movement also repeatedly attempted to ensure that they would never do anything against the interests of the public or the government. Since the public sphere in Turkey lacks comparable pluralist liberal notions of interest articulation and aggregation of its counterpart in the US, concepts like partisanship, lobbying, and interest groups have delegitimizing effects and the Gülen movement has so far preferred not to describe its activities by using these concepts.

At one level, the LDS Church also demonstrates elements of American patriotism and had put emphasis on the participation of its members in America's wars, helping in disaster areas, and representing American values abroad. However, as Mormonism became more integrated, even assimilated, into American society, there was less need to emphasize these sources of legitimacy. The dominant paradigm in the church's current public discourse is the welfare of the church and its members, as well as quick references to the liberties that are ensured by the Constitution, such as freedom of religion, expression, and assembly. Congressional advocacy does not comprise a large part of Mormon public activism, yet the LDS Church has not avoided having registered lobbyists and public relations professionals. There is also an adaptation to the rational discourse along the lines of the Rawlsian idea of public reasoning, rather than mere reference to religious dogma, in justifying most positions on moral issues.

One premise of the historical comparison in this study was to understand how the change in the contours of the public sphere over time would influence strategies of religious groups. In the Turkish case, the drastic change in the form of a rupture after the end of the Ottoman Empire made the popular religious groups go underground and disappear from the public sphere, which was very much monopolized by the state. When the political context in Turkey gradually became more pluralist and inclusive, the Islamic movements including the Gülen movement also became more visible. Chapter 4 discussed how the EU-led political, legal, and economic reforms during the first decade of the twenty-first century in Turkey changed the distribution of power and led to the Gülen movement's more direct involvement in political processes.

In parallel to the discussion of the evolution of the Turkish public sphere, chapters 3 and 5 discussed the historical stages of the Mormon identity in the American public sphere. At the local level, Mormons employed strategies of self-governance and survival in face of the enmity and tensions in Missouri, Illinois, and Utah. At the national level, their struggle for statehood was influenced by the dominant Protestant discourse and moral values, as reflected in issues of polygamy, hierarchical clergy, and loyalty to the nation. When Protestant nondenominationalism gave way to a more inclusive monotheistic civil religion, Mormons moved closer to the American mainstream of Judeo-Christian identity along with Jews and Catholics. Since the 1960s Mormons have joined the conservative countermobilization and struggle in securing more space to religion in the public sphere and morality. Ironically, after the Supreme Court rulings granted more exemptions to the nonaffiliated, including secularists, agnostics, atheists, and non-Judeo-Christians, the formerly excluded Mormons moved closer to the conservative bloc, with much in common with their opponents from the nineteenth-century Protestant establishment.

Comparing different political strategies used by the same religious group across different political contexts can be instructive. This involves comparing the Gülen movement's public activism in the US vs. Turkey and the LDS Church in Turkey vs. the US. The foregoing chapters used this as a secondary means to understand the relationship between the dependent and the independent variables. It can be argued that the Gülen movement has been more self-assertive in the US, whereas the Mormons have been less direct in their missionary activities in Turkey, which is subject to strict state regulations and control. In the Gülen case, the movement has had a relatively short history in the US and it is still in a process of adaptation, learning, and seeking access to the political system. The movement simultaneously tries to keep the Turkish culture alive and also to integrate the community into the American mainstream. Although it is not a systemic analysis, initial observations suggest that the movement is more open about its identity in the US than Turkey. The cultural and community groups are less likely to hide their affiliation with Fethullah Gülen than they would be in Turkey. The movement has even organized at the national level to have representative umbrella organizations, like the Turkic American Alliance in Washington, DC. Thanks to a combination of their doctrine and earlier political socialization in Turkey, they still remain disinclined to call their efforts lobbying. The movement's political operators have come to understand the importance of money in American politics very well, and made campaign contributions. Yet they were usually made as private individuals.[4] When

4. For a journalist's account of the Gülen movement's activities and activism in the US, see Aslı Aydıntaşbaş, "Gülen Cemaatinin Washington Ayagi" (The Washington Extension of the Gülen movement), *Aksam Daily*, September 7, 2009.

movement-affiliated organizations and activities faced investigations in the US, they were in more concrete terms, compared to broad allegations in Turkey for crimes against national security and principles of the constitution, such as secularism.[5] In its fight against the Gülen movement in the US, the Turkish government's approach remained limited in its success and the evidence presented to request Gülen's extradition to Turkey on charges of being behind the July 2016 coup attempt so far faced skepticism[6] from the American government and Gülen remained a legal US resident as of early 2019.

The Gülen movement participants in the US come to appreciate their rights as residents or citizens, the importance of diversity in the public arena, and strong foundations for liberty and the rule of law. Their adaptation to the American political system is likely to accelerate after many of them had to flee Turkey and seek asylum. After operating at times as an informal foreign lobby group on behalf of the Turkish government for more than a decade, the movement's public identity is likely to become more Americanized and shaped by minority politics. Engagement in issues concerning Muslim Americans is likely to gradually replace its earlier Turkish diaspora activism. With their ties severed to Turkey, the new generation is much less likely to

5. Some charter schools founded and administered by Turkish Americans with ties to the Gülen movement were investigated for their financial practices by state boards of education in states where the schools have widely grown in number, such as Texas ("Charter Schools Tied to Turkey Grow in Texas," *New York Times*, June 6, 2011). The movement-affiliated business associations, civic organizations, and federations of these local branches sponsored trips to Turkey for politicians, businessmen, academics, journalists, and other civil-society groups. Their financial practices have been scrutinized for ethics violations and forced some politicians to return donations or distance themselves from Gülen associates ("US Lawmakers Got Suspect Turkish Campaign Cash," *USA Today*, November 23, 2015, http://www.usatoday.com/story/news/nation/2015/11/20/lawmakers-got-suspect-turkish-campaign-cash/75982732/).

6. "US Unlikely to 'Speed Up' Gulen's Extradition to Turkey," *Voice of America News*, September 13, 2016, http://www.voanews.com/a/us-unlikely-to-speed-up-gulens-extradition-to-turkey/3505529.html.

see value in doing the Turkish state's bid in issues like the recognition of the Armenian genocide.

Such a cross-comparison for the LDS Church is practically more difficult because of the limited presence of the church members and limitations on church activities under Turkey's strictly secular system. Mormon missionaries came to today's Turkey under Ottoman rule as early as the 1850s and some British Mormons established a congregation while fighting the Crimean War (1853–56). The church opened its Turkish mission in 1884 and converted very few Christians living in the Ottoman territories, and, thus, had very limited success in expanding its membership. As many Christian missionaries came to the Ottoman land now penetrated by colonialism and the European economy, they faced suspicion and hostility, and were often treated as a fifth column. The adverse conditions continued, if not intensified, after the breakup of the Ottoman Empire and establishment of new nation-states, as the newly independent states were quite anti-Western. Mormon missionaries from the very beginning found less direct ways of missionary work, such as teaching English, French, and, later, computer courses. Members gathered at private apartments for worship and met at hotels for fellowship. In addition to the generally hostile and skeptical public attitude, bureaucratic hurdles to purchasing property, holding worship places, and proselytizing under the secularist Turkish republic limited opportunities for a Mormon presence and representation in Turkey. Republican public spheres exert more control over religious organizations, as opposed to liberal public spheres' freer and more decentralized approach to the religious market. In the last two decades, reforms for minority rights in line with EU membership criteria and the LDS Church's increased emphasis and visibility in disaster relief and helping refugees provided another avenue for church presence in Turkey. As of 2018 the church listed 513 members in seven congregations under one mission.[7]

7. "Facts and Statistics," The Church of Jesus Christ of Latter-day Saints, http://www.mormonnewsroom.org/facts-and-statistics/country/turkey.

Chapter 7 briefly discussed the management of LDS public affairs in different contexts. The profile and political preferences of the Mormons are quite diverse in western European countries, for example. As the public affairs officials very well knew, there are probably as many social democrats as conservatives in countries like Germany and Norway. The standard operating procedures of public relations would also depend on the country in which they are operating. Church officials and representatives are more likely to cultivate relationships with bureaucracies and government representatives under nondemocratic and/or more bureaucratic states.

One possible implication of the findings in this study would be the desirability of a liberal public sphere over a republican one, as the former appears to offer more favorable conditions for the participation of social groups in the public arena. There are two important points that should be taken into account before discussing the merits of this proposition. One is the fact that the specific conditions created in the Turkish political system have a lot to do with the challenges of institutionalizing democratic rule, not just with republicanism as a dominant paradigm in state-society relations. The other important factor is the fact that these are ideal types that are meant to create a useful framework of analysis rather than a perfect fit with the complex reality.

With the above caveats in mind, it is possible to argue that liberal public spheres are more likely to emerge in settings where the state is historically less autonomous. In such contexts, there may be an inclination for majority groups to resort to republicanism as a way to promote a unified public culture, largely defined by their own values. Such was the case even in many American states during much of the nineteenth century vis à vis the Mormons, Catholics, and the Jews. It would be only after the federal government's gradual empowerment that a minority protection regime was reinforced through the rule of law. The Turkish case, on the other hand, would point to a starkly different dynamic. Since the state was too powerful, the social groups from the periphery tried to push for a more liberal public sphere to balance the exclusionary state policies toward them.

The analysis in this book regarding religion and politics was informed by insights from social movement theory. By treating religiously based activism as part of the broader family of contentious politics and politically relevant collective behavior, explaining religious group behavior in the public sphere through *motives, means,* and *opportunity* results in a more coherent and parsimonious research program. The findings in this study support McAdam, Tarrow, and Tilly's (2002) cyclical approach to understanding the birth, growth and maturation of social movements, as discussed in chapter 1.

The study of social movements also offers great insights into political change, such as regime transitions. One of the key insights in the democratization literature is that transitions do not automatically result in consolidated democracies (Linz and Stepan 1998). Alfred Stepan (1989; 2001) aptly argues that a more nuanced and systematic study of the three domains of the polity would be necessary to explain the success or failure of the institutionalization of democratic rule in the long run. This study has used *the state*, *political society*, and *civil society* as analytically distinct domains to understand the dynamics of the political context. The boundaries of these domains are not fixed, yet a long-term imbalance of power among these domains may significantly undermine the likelihood of democratization and its chances of consolidation. The Kemalist hegemony in the Turkish political system was primarily concentrated in the state bureaucracy, but allied itself with the Kemalist intelligentsia and the media against the popularly elected governments. Despite the conservative political parties being in power for much of Turkey's multiparty era after 1950, the civilian governments operated under bureaucratic tutelage. With the partial liberalization of Turkish economic and political system between 1983 and 2013, the political society and civil society's cooperation played a significant role in weakening the Kemalist hegemony. Unfortunately for Turkey, post-Kemalist politics failed to preserve the emerging balance of power between the three domains of the polity and the ensuing power struggle in the last five years quickly resulted in reversal of the gains made in almost three decades. The emergence of the Gülen movement as an influential societal actor with effective resource mobilization, capacity to induce social capital, and strategic acumen to bypass the Kemalist firewall to penetrate into the bureaucracy was critical for tipping the balance of power in favor of the civil society and the political society. However, rather than ushering in a liberal polity with checks and balances, these newly empowered actors engaged in a costly power struggle, marked by Machiavellian alliances and Byzantine politics.

Religion will continue to get involved in politics through what it says and what it does. It will continue to divide and unite. The LDS Church and the Gülen movement will continue their struggles to strike a balance between preserving their traditional-conservative beliefs and engaging with the modernity. And they will continue to negotiate and renegotiate their representation in response to the incentives and disincentives provided by models of the public sphere along the liberal-republican axis.

Appendixes

References

Index

Appendix A

Breakdown of meeting participants according to affiliation and professional background[1] between 1998 and 2016[2]

	Academic	Media	Politician	Bureaucracy	Civil Society
1st Meeting, 1998	71%	6%	2%	1%	10%
2nd Meeting, 1999	67%	24%	5%	0%	4%
3rd Meeting, 2000	61%	16%	8%	3%	12%
4th Meeting, 2001	55%	13%	16%	0%	16%
5th Meeting, 2002	69%	17%	5%	0%	9%
6th Meeting, 2003	63%	21%	0%	8%	8%
7th Meeting, 2004	64%	8%	8%	0%	20%
8th Meeting, 2004	68%	4%	10%	8%	10%
9th Meeting, 2005	85%	10%	0%	0%	5%
10th Meeting, 2006	36%	20%	0%	9%	35%
11th Meeting, 2006	51%	19%	7%	13%	10%
12th Meeting, 2007	55%	27%	0%	6%	12%
13th Meeting, 2007	47%	18%	7%	4%	24%
14th Meeting, 2007	36%	19%	1%	4%	41%
15th Meeting, 2007	65%	6%	18%	0%	12%
16th Meeting, 2007	77%	10%	3%	3%	7%
17th Meeting, 2008	38%	29%	10%	0%	24%
18th Meeting, 2009	28%	28%	7%	7%	31%
19th Meeting, 2009	42%	4%	42%	8%	4%
20th Meeting, 2010	58%	15%	9%	6%	12%
21st Meeting, 2010	76%	12%	0%	0%	12%

	Academic	Media	Politician	Bureaucracy	Civil Society
22nd Meeting, 2010	48%	23%	6%	2%	21%
23rd Meeting, 2011	85%	10%	5%	0%	0%
24th Meeting, 2011	45%	46%	6%	0%	3%
25th Meeting, 2011	66%	28%	3%	3%	3%
26th Meeting, 2012	21%	32%	26%	3%	18%
27th Meeting, 2012	24%	35%	24%	3%	14%
28th Meeting, 2013	32%	26%	8%	15%	20%
29th Meeting, 2013	23%	8%	15%	29%	25%
20th Meeting, 2013	42%	12%	6%	6%	34%
31st Meeting, 2014	62%	12%	4%	18%	4%
32nd Meeting, 2014	32%	4%	36%	12%	16%
33rd Meeting, 2014	71%	21%	0%	0%	8%
34th Meeting, 2016[a]	44%	44%	7%	0%	5%
Average	53.15%	18.44%	8.94%	5.03%	14.38%

Note: Based on the participant lists and meeting programs on the JWF website and press releases and media coverage. Academics are defined as full-time or part-time faculty members affiliated with a higher education institution. Media representatives include journalists, columnists, and TV and radio program producers. Politicians include representatives of political parties, mayors, and former members of the parliament. The bureaucracy includes ambassadors and other foreign service staff, civil servants, and others affiliated with a state institution. Civil society consists of think tanks, human right organizations, business associations, ethnic-cultural group representatives, religious authorities and clergy, and other independent authors, researchers, and intellectuals. All categories include Turkish and non-Turkish nationalities. Participants who have dual roles (e.g., academics who write newspaper columns) are included in both categories.

[a] The thirty-fourth meeting in 2016 is likely to be the final one, due to the closure and criminalization of the JWF and its activities in Turkey in the aftermath of the July 2016 military coup attempt.

Appendix B

Themes of Abant platform meetings in chronological order

1. *Islam and Secularism*—Abant, Turkey (1998)
2. *Religion, State and Society*—Abant, Turkey (1999)
3. *Democratic State and the Rule of Law*—Abant, Turkey (2000)
4. *Pluralism and Social Reconciliation*—Abant, Turkey (2001)
5. *Globalization*—Abant, Turkey (2002)
6. *War and Democracy*—Abant, Turkey (2003)
7. *Islam, Secularism and Democracy: The Turkish Experience*—Washington DC, US (2004)
8. *Culture, Identity and Religion in the Process of Turkey's EU Membership*—Brussels, Belgium (2004)
9. *New Pursuits in Education*—Erzurum, Turkey (2005)
10. *Republic, Multiculturalism, and Europe*—Paris, France (2006)
11. *Global Politics and the Future of the Middle East*—Abant, Turkey (2006)
12. *Turkey-Egypt Colloquium: Islam, West and Modernization*—Cairo, Egypt (2007)
13. *Historic, Cultural, Folkloric and Contemporary Dimensions of Aleviism*—Abant, Turkey (2007)
14. *Turkey-French Conversations II*—Istanbul, Turkey (2007)
15. *A New Constitution* [for Turkey]—Izmit, Turkey (2007)
16. *Turkey: A Bridge between Civilizations in the EU Process*—Istanbul, Turkey (2007)
17. *Kurdish Problem: Searching for Peace and a Future Together*—Abant, Turkey (2008)
18. *Kurdish Problem: Searching for Peace and a Future Together*—Arbil, Iraq (2009)
19. *Democratization: Political Parties from September 12 [1980] to the EU*—Abant, Turkey (2009)
20. *Democratization for a new Social Contract*—Ankara, Turkey (2010)

21. *Egypt, Turkey and Stability in the Middle East*—Cairo, Egypt (2010)
22. *Democracy and Tutelage*—Abant, Turkey (2010)
23. *New Era, New Constitution*—Abant, Turkey (2011)
24. *Assessment of June 12 Parliamentary Election Results*—Istanbul, Turkey (2011)
25. *The Future of the Middle East after the Arab Spring and Turkey*—Gaziantep, Turkey (2011)
26. *The Framework of the New Constitution*—Abant, Turkey (2012)
27. *Different Perspectives on Turkey*—Abant, Turkey (2012)
28. *Diverse Perspectives on Turkey*—Abant, Turkey (2013)
29. *Africa: Between Experience and Inspiration*—Abant, Turkey (2013)
30. *Alevis and Sunnis: Searching for Peace and a Future Together*—Abant, Turkey (2013)
31. *Turkey's Educational Challenges: Educational Policy and the Search for Solutions*—Istanbul, Turkey (2014)
32. *Freedom of Speech and Respect for the Sacred*—Addis Ababa, Ethiopia (2014)
33. *Turkey's Direction*—Akcakoca, Turkey (2014)
34. *Democracy's Turkey Problem*—Abant, Turkey (2016)

References

Abrams, Paula. 2009. *Cross Purposes: Pierce v. Society of Sisters and the Struggle over Compulsory Public Education.* Ann Arbor: Univ. of Michigan Press.

Agai, Bekim. 2003. "Discursive and Organizational Strategies of the Gülen Movement." In *Turkish Islam and the Secular State*, edited by Hakan Yavuz and John Esposito, 48–68. Syracuse, NY: Syracuse Univ. Press.

———. 2005. "The Gülen Movement: Discursive and Organizational Strategies." Presented at "Islam in the Contemporary World: The Fethullah Gülen Movement in Thought and Practice" Conference, Houston, TX.

Ahmad, Feroz. 2008. "Politics and Political Parties in Republican Turkey." In *The Cambridge History of Turkey: Turkey in the Modern World*, edited by Resat Kasaba, 226–65. Cambridge: Cambridge Univ. Press.

Akçura, Yusuf. 1976. *Üç Tarz-ı Siyaset.* Ankara: Türk Tarih Kurumu Basımevi.

Akyol, Mustafa. 2010. "The Protocols of the Learned Elders of Fethullah Gülen." *Hurriyet Daily News*, March 16, 2010.

Alexander, Thomas G. 1986. *Mormonism in Transition: A History of the Latter-Day Saints, 1890–1930.* Urbana: Univ. of Illinois Press.

Arendt, Hannah. 1958. *The Human Condition.* Chicago: Univ. of Chicago Press.

Arrington, Leonard J. 1992. "Economic History of the Church." In *Encyclopedia of Mormonism*, edited by Daniel Ludlow, 435–41. New York: Macmillan.

Arrington, Leonard J., and Davis Bitton. 1980. *The Mormon Experience: A History of the Latter-day Saints.* New York: Vintage Books.

Austin, Michael. 2012. "As Much as Any Novelist Could Ask": Mormons in American Popular Fiction." In *Mormons and Popular Culture: The Global Influence of an American Phenomenon*, edited by J. Michael Hunter, 1–22. Santa Barbara, CA: Praeger.

Avcı, Hanefi. 2010. *Haliç'te Yaşayan Simonlar / Dün Devlet Bugün Cemaat.* Ankara: Angora Kitaplığı.

Baban, Feyzi. 1999. "National Identity and Globalization: Reflections on Turkey's Uneasy Modernization." PhD diss., Carleton Univ.

Backman, James. 1992. "Courts." In *Encyclopedia of Mormonism*, edited by Daniel Ludlow, 329–30. New York: Macmillan.

Bagley, Will. 2002. *Blood of the Prophets: Brigham Young and the Massacre at Mountain Meadows.* Norman: Univ. of Oklahoma Press.

Balcı, Ali. 2010. "A Trajectory of Competing Narratives: The Turkish Media Debate Ergenekon." *Mediterranean Quarterly* 21, no. 1:76–100.

Balcı, Tamer, and Christopher L. Miller, eds. 2012. *Gülen Hizmet Movement: Circumspect Activism in Faith-Based Reform.* Newcastle: Cambridge Scholars, 2012.

Bellah, Robert Neelly. 1975. *The Broken Covenant: American Civil Religion in a Time of Trial.* New York: Seabury.

Benhabib, Seyla. 1992. "Models of Public Space: Hannah Arendt, the Liberal Tradition, and Jürgen Habermas." In *Habermas and the Public Sphere*, edited by Craig Calhoun, 73–98. Cambridge, MA: MIT Press.

———. 1996. *The Reluctant Modernism of Hannah Arendt.* Thousand Oaks, CA: Sage.

Bennett, Robert F. 1977. "Some Thoughts on Public Relations." *Dialogue: A Journal of Mormon Thought* 10, no. 3:120–22.

Bergera, Gary James. 2007. *Statements of the LDS First Presidency: A Topical Compendium.* Salt Lake City, UT: Signature Books.

Berlin, Isaiah. 1958. *Two Concepts of Liberty.* Oxford: Clarendon.

Berrett, William E. 1985. *The Latter-day Saints: A Contemporary History of the Church of Jesus Christ.* Salt Lake City, UT: Deseret Book.

Bringhurst, Newell G. 2008. *The Mormon Quest for the Presidency.* Independence, MO: John Whitmer Books.

Brinkerhoff, Merlin B., Jeffrey C. Jacob, and Marlene A. Mackine. 1987. "Religious Tolerance: Mormons in the American Mainstream." *Dialogue: A Journal of Mormon Thought* 20, no. 3:90–95.

Bowman, Matthew. 2012. *The Mormon People: The Making of an American Faith.* New York: Random House.

Brooks, Juanita. 1962. *The Mountain Meadows Massacre.* Norman: Univ. of Oklahoma Press.

Bushman, Claudia L., and Richard L. Bushman. 2001. *Building the Kingdom: A History of Mormons in America*. New York: Oxford Univ. Press.

Bushman, Richard L. 2016. "Joseph Smith's Presidential Ambitions." In *Mormonism and American Politics*, edited by Randall Balmer and Jana Riess, 3–13. New York: Columbia Univ. Press.

Cagaptay, Soner. 2009. "Behind Turkey's Witch Hunt." *Newsweek*, May 16, 2009.

Calhoun, Craig J. 1992. *Habermas and the Public Sphere*. Cambridge, MA: MIT Press.

Campbell, David, and Quin Monson. 2003. "Following the Leader? Mormon Voting on Ballot Propositions." *Journal for the Scientific Study of Religion* 42, no. 4:605–19.

———. 2007. "Dry Kindling: A Political Profile of American Mormons." In *From Pews to Polling Places: Faith and Politics in the American Religious Mosaic*, edited by Matthew Wilson, 105–30. Washington, DC: Georgetown Univ. Press.

Can, Eyüp. 1996. *Fethullah Gülen Hocaefendi ile Ufuk Turu*. Istanbul: AD Yayıncılık.

Carroll, B. Jill. 2007. *A Dialogue of Civilizations: Gülen's Islamic Ideals and Humanistic Discourse*. Somerset, NJ: Light.

Casanova, José. 1994. *Public Religions in the Modern World*. Chicago: Univ. of Chicago Press.

Charney, Evan. 1998. "Political Liberalism, Deliberative Democracy, and the Public Sphere." *American Political Science Review* 92, no. 1:97–110.

Chua, Amy, and Jed Rubenfeld. 2015. *The Triple Package: How Three Unlikely Traits Explain the Rise and Fall of Cultural Groups in America*. New York: Penguin Books.

Church of Jesus Christ of Latter-day Saints. 1998. *Church Handbook of Instructions*. Book 1. Salt Lake City, UT: Intellectual Reserve.

Cizre, Ümit. 2007. *Democratic Oversight and Reform of the Security Sector in Turkey. 2005/2006 Status Report*. Piscataway, NJ: Transaction.

Clark, James. 1965. *Messages of the First Presidency*. Vol. 3. Salt Lake City, UT: Deseret Book.

Coleman, James. 1988. "Social Capital in the Creation of Human Capital." *American Journal of Sociology* 94:S95–S120.

———. 1990. *Foundations of Social Theory.* Cambridge, MA: Belknap Press of Harvard Univ. Press.

Cranny, Garr. 1992. "Schools." In *Encyclopedia of Mormonism,* edited by Daniel Ludlow, 1267–69. New York: Macmillan.

Croft, Q. Michael. 1985. "Influence of LDS Church on Utah Politics, 1945–1985." PhD diss., Univ. of Utah.

Çaha, Ömer. 1998. "İdeolojik Kamusalın Sivil Kamusala Dönüşümü" (Transformation of the Ideological Public into Civil Public). *Doğu Batı* 2, no. 5:76–79.

Çaha, Ömer, Ferhat Kentel, Yasin Aktay, and Ramazan Yelken. 2011. *Türk Toplumunda Cemaat Algısı* (Perception of Religious Communities in the Turkish Public). Istanbul: ANDY-AR Center for Social Research.

Çınar, Alev. 1998. "Bodies, Places, and Time: Islamic Visibilities in the Public Sphere and the Contestations of Secular Modernity in Turkey." PhD diss., Univ. of Pennsylvania.

———. 2005. *Modernity, Islam, and Secularism in Turkey: Bodies, Places, and Time.* Minneapolis: Univ. of Minnesota Press.

Dağı, İhsan. 2004. "Rethinking Human Rights, Democracy, and the West: Post-Islamist Intellectuals in Turkey." *Critique: Critical Middle Eastern Studies* 13, no. 2:135–51.

Ebaugh, Helen Rose. 2009. *The Gülen Movement: A Sociological Analysis of a Civic Movement Rooted in Moderate Islam.* New York: Springer.

Eckstein, Harry. 1975. "Case Study and Theory in Political Science." In *Handbook of Political Science,* edited by F. I. Greenstein and N. W. Polsby, 79–138. Reading, MA: Addison-Wesley.

Erdoğan, Latif. 1995. *Fethullah Gülen Hocaefendi: Küçük Dünyam.* Istanbul: AD Yayıncılık.

Erdoğan, Mustafa. 1999. "Kamu Alanı ve Liberalizm: Birkaç Not" (Public Sphere and Liberalism: A Few Points). *Yeni Türkiye* 25:7–15.

Ergil, Doğu. 2010. *100 Soruda Fethullah Gülen ve Hareketi.* Istanbul: Timaş Yayınları.

Feldman, Noah. 2006. *Divided by God: America's Church-State Problem—and What We Should Do About It.* New York: Farrar, Straus & Giroux.

———. 2008. "Why Sharia?" *New York Times Magazine,* March 16, 2008.

Flake, Kathleen. 2004. *The Politics of American Religious Identity: The Seating of Senator Reed Smoot, Mormon Apostle.* Chapel Hill: Univ. of North Carolina Press.

Fowler, Robert B., Allen D. Hertzke, Laura R. Olson, and Kevin R. Den Dulk. 2010. *Religion and Politics in America: Faith, Culture, and Strategic Choices*. Boulder, CO: Westview.

Fowles, John Lessing. 1990. "A Study Concerning the Mission of the Weekday Religious Educational Program of the Church of Jesus Christ of Latter Day Saints from 1890–1990: A Response to Secular Education." PhD diss., Univ. of Missouri-Columbia.

Fox, Jeffrey Carl. 2006. *Latter-Day Political Views*. Lanham, MD: Lexington Books.

Fraser, Nancy. 1992. "Rethinking The Public Sphere: A Contribution to the Critique of Actually Existing Democracy." In *Habermas and the Public Sphere*, edited by Craig Calhoun, 109–42. Cambridge: MIT Press.

Gage, Tom. 2013. *Gülen's Dialogue on Education*. Seattle: Cune.

Ganser, Daniele. 2005. *NATO's Secret Armies: Operation Gladio and Terrorism in Western Europe*. London: Frank Cass.

Gardner, David. 1992. "Education." In *Encyclopedia of Mormonism*, edited by Daniel Ludlow, 441–46. New York: Macmillan.

Garr, Arnold K. 2009. "Joseph Smith: Campaign for President of the United States." *Ensign*, February 2009, 48–52.

Givens, Terryl. 2004. *The Latter-day Saint Experience in America*. Westport, CT: Greenwood.

Göle, Nilüfer. 1994. "Towards an Autonomization of Politics and Civil Society in Turkey." In *Politics in the Third Turkish Republic*, edited by Metin Heper, 213–22. Boulder, CO: Westview.

———. 2000. *İslam'ın Yeni Kamusal Yüzleri: İslam ve Kamusal Alan Üzerine Bir Atölye Çalışması*. Istanbul: Metis Yayınları.

Gordon, Sarah Barringer. 2002. *The Mormon Question: Polygamy and Conflict in Nineteenth-Century America*. Chapel Hill: Univ. of North Carolina Press.

———. 2010. *The Spirit of the Law: Religious Voices and the Constitution in America*. Cambridge, MA: Harvard Univ. Press.

Gulalp, Haldun. 2001. "Globalization and Political Islam: The Social Base of Turkey's Welfare Party." *IJMES* 89, no. 1:22–41.

———. 2003. "Whatever Happened to Secularization? The Multiple Islams in Turkey." *South Atlantic Quarterly* 102, no. 2:381–95.

Gülen, Fethullah. 1997. *İ'la-yı Kelimetullah veya Cihad*. Izmir: Nil Yayinevi.

———. 1998. *Ruhumuzun Heykelini Dikerken*. Istanbul: Nil Yayinevi.

———. 2001. "A Comparative Approach to Islam and Democracy." *SAIS Review* 21, no. 2:133–38.

———. 2006. *Pearls of Wisdom*. Translated by Ali Ünal. Somerset, NJ: Light.

———. 2007. *Prizma*. Izmir: Nil Yayınları.

———. 2008. "Dinin Özündeki Kolaylık ve Zor Şartlarda Namaz" [The Ease at the Core of Religion and Prayer under Difficult Conditions). Audio lecture, December 15, 2008, http://www.herkul.org/bamteli/index.php?article_id=6412.

———. 2009. "Almanya Konferansı ve Bal İnsanlar." Audio lecture, June 8, 2009, http://www.herkul.org/bamteli/index.php?article_id=7135.

Gündem, Mehmet. 2005. *Fethullah Gülen'le 11 Gün: Sorularla Bir Hareketin Analizi*. Istanbul: Alfa.

Gürbüz, Mustafa. 2007. "Performing Moral Opposition: Musings on the Strategy and Identity in the Gülen movement." Presented at "Muslim World in Transition: Contributions of the Gülen Movement" Conference, London.

Gürcan, Ayşe Ezgi. 2015. "The Problems of Religious Education in Turkey: Alevi Citizen Action and the Limits of ECTHR." Istanbul Policy Center Policy Brief, http://ipc.sabanciuniv.edu/wp-content/uploads/2015/10/The-Problems-Of-Religious-Education-In-Turkey-Alevi-Citizen-Action-And-The-Limits-Of-Ecthr.pdf.

Gürüz, Kemal. 2004. "European Turkey: Modernization, Secularism and Islam." Presented at the Cornell Univ. Turkish Forum "European Turkey: Modernization, Secularism, and Islam," Ithaca, NY.

Guth, James L. 2012. "The Religious Roots of Foreign Policy Exceptionalism." *Review of Faith & International Affairs* 10, no. 2:77–85.

Habermas, Jürgen. 1989a. *The Structural Transformation of the Public Sphere: An Inquiry into a Category of Bourgeois Society*. Cambridge, MA: MIT Press.

———. 1989b. "The Public Sphere: An Encyclopedia Article." In *Critical Theory and Society: A Reader*, edited by Stephen Bronner and Douglas Kellner, 136–42. New York: Routledge.

Hardy, B. Camon. 2012. *Solemn Covenant: The Mormon Polygamous Passage*. Urbana: Univ. of Illinois Press.

Hafen, Bruce. 1992. "Disciplinary Procedures." In *Encyclopedia of Mormonism*, edited by Daniel Ludlow, 385–87. New York: Macmillan.

Hammond, Philip. 1999. "Can Religion be Religious in Public." In *The Power of Religious Publics: Staking Claims in American Society*, edited by William H. Swatos Jr., and James K. Wellman Jr., 19–31. Westport, CT: Praeger.

Hampshire, Annette P. 1985. *Mormonism in Conflict: The Nauvoo Years.* New York: E. Mellen.

Hanioğlu, M. Şükrü. 1995. *The Young Turks in Opposition.* New York: Oxford Univ. Press.

———. 2008. *A Brief History of the Late Ottoman Empire.* Princeton, NJ: Princeton Univ. Press.

Hansen, Suzy. 2010. "The Global Imam." *New Republic*, December 2, 2010.

Harris, Frederick. 2003. "Ties that Bind and Flourish: Religion as Social Capital in African American Politics and Society." In *Religion as Social Capital: Producing the Common Good*, edited by Corwin E. Smidt, 121–38. Waco, TX: Baylor Univ. Press.

Haynes, Jeffrey. 1998. *Religion in Global Politics.* London: Longman.

Heinerman, John, and Anson D. Shupe. 1985. *The Mormon Corporate Empire.* Boston: Beacon.

Hendrick, Joshua. 2014. *Gülen: The Ambiguous Politics of Market Islam in Turkey and the World.* New York: New York Univ. Press.

Henetz, Patty. 1991. "Church Evaluating Reports of Satanic Cults in Utah." *Deseret News*, October 25, 1991.

Hobbes, Thomas. 2008. *Leviathan.* Translated by Marshall Missner. New York: Pearson Longman.

Hough, C. Merrill. 1960. " Two School Systems in Conflict: 1867–1890." *Utah Historical Quarterly* 28, no. 2:112–28.

Howe, Daniel Walker. 2015. "Emergent Mormonism in Context." In *The Oxford Handbook of Mormonism*, edited by Terry L. Givens and Philip L. Barlow, 24–37. New York: Oxford Univ. Press.

Jenkins, Gareth H. 2009. "Between Fact and Fantasy: Turkey's Ergenekon Investigation." Central Asia—Caucasus Institute, Silk Road Paper, July 2009, http://www.silkroadstudies.org/resources/pdf/SilkRoadPapers/2009_08_SRP_Jenkins_Turkey-Ergenekon.pdf.

Kadıoğlu, Ayşe. 2005. "Civil Society, Islam, and Democracy in Turkey: A Study of Three Islamic Non-Governmental Organizations." *Muslim World* 95, no. 1:23–41.

Kardam, Filiz, and Cengiz, Kurtuluş. 2011. "Republican Citizenship in Turkey: Historical Development, Perceptions and Practices." *Middle Eastern Studies* 47, no. 1:151–65.

Karpat, Kemal H. 1973. *An Inquiry into the Social Foundations of Nationalism in the Ottoman State: From Social Estates to Classes, from Millets to Nations.* Princeton, NJ: Center of International Studies, Princeton Univ.

Kasaba, Reşat. 1993. "Populism and Democracy in Turkey: 1946–1961." In *Rules and Rights in the Middle East: Democracy, Law, and Society,* edited by E. Goldberg, R. Kasaba, and J. S. Migdal, 43–68. Seattle: Univ. of Washington Press.

Keyman, E. Fuat. 1998. "Kamusal Alan ve Cumhuriyetçi Liberalizm: Türkiye'de Demokrasi Sorunu." *Doğu Batı* 2, no. 5:57–72.

Kılınç, Ramazan. 2007. "The Patterns of Interaction Between Islam and Liberalism: The Case of the Gülen Movement." In *Muslim World in Transition: The Contributions of the Gülen Movement,* edited by Ihsan Yilmaz, 118–39. London: Leeds Metropolitan Univ. Press.

King, Gary, Robert O. Keohane, and Sidney Verba. 1994. *Designing Social Inquiry: Scientific Inference in Qualitative Research.* Princeton, NJ: Princeton Univ. Press.

Klandermans, Bert. 1997. *The Social Psychology of Protest.* Oxford: Blackwell.

Knowlton, Brian. 2010. "Turk Who Leads a Movement Has Advocates and Critics." *New York Times,* June 11, 2010.

Köse, Talha. 2010. "The AKP and the Alevi Opening: Understanding the Dynamics of the Rapprochement." *Insight Turkey* 12, no. 2:143–65.

Kruse, Kevin M. 2015. *One Nation Under God: How Corporate America Invented Christian America.* New York: Basic Books.

Kuru, Ahmet T. 2003. "Fethullah Gülen's Search for a Middle Way between Modernity and Muslim Tradition." In *Turkish Islam and the Secular State: The Gülen Movement,* edited by Hakan Yavuz and John Esposito, 115–30. Syracuse, NY: Syracuse Univ. Press.

———. 2007. "Changing Perspectives on Islamism and Secularism in Turkey: The Gülen Movement and the AK Party." Presented at "Muslim World in Transition: Contributions of the Gülen movement Conference," London.

———. 2009. *Secularism and State Policies toward Religion: The United States, France, and Turkey.* Cambridge: Cambridge Univ. Press.

Kurucan, Ahmet. 2010. "Hizmet Hareketi mi Yoksa Gülen Hareketi mi?" (Gülen Movement or Gülen Movement?) *Zaman*, November 27, 2010.

Lacy, Helen, Dean L. May, Linda Seeger, and Kirk Strickland. 1988. *The Americanization of Utah.* Department of History, Univ. of Utah, video recording. Salt Lake City, UT: Instructional Media Services.

Lapidus, Ira M. 2002. *A History of Islamic Societies.* Cambridge: Cambridge Univ. Press.

Levine, Carrie. 2009. "For Italian Job, Mormons Ask a DC Insider for Help: Church's Rare Lobbying Foray Aims to Gain Legal Rights in Italy." *National Law Journal*, October 6, 2009.

Linz, Juan J., and Alfred Stepan. 1996. "Toward Consolidated Democracies." *Journal of Democracy* 7, no. 2:14–33.

Locke, John. 2004. *Second Treatise of Government.* New York: Barnes & Noble Books.

Lythgoe, Dennis L. 1968. "The Changing Image of Mormonism." *Dialogue: A Journal of Mormon Thought* 3, no. 4:45–58.

Macedo, Stephen. 1991. *Liberal Virtues. Citizenship, Virtue, and Community in Liberal Constitutionalism.* Oxford: Clarendon.

Magleby, David B. 2006. "Religious Interest Group Activity in Utah." In *Representing God at the Statehouse*, edited by Edward L. Cleary and Allen D. Hertzke, 177–200. New York: Rowman & Littlefield.

Mahçupyan, Etyen. 1998. "Osmanlıdan Günümüze Parçalı Kamusal Alan ve Siyaset." *Doğu Batı* 2, no. 5:22–48.

Mardin, Şerif. 1962. *The Genesis of Young Ottoman Thought: A Study in the Modernization of Turkish Political Ideas.* Princeton, NJ: Princeton Univ. Press.

———. 1969. "Power, Civil Society, and Culture in the Ottoman Empire." *Comparative Studies in Society and History* 11, no. 3:258–81.

McAdam, Doug, John D. McCarthy, and Mayer N. Zald. 1996. *Comparative Perspectives on Social Movements: Political Opportunities, Mobilizing Structures, and Cultural Framings.* Cambridge: Cambridge Univ. Press.

McAdam, Doug, Sidney Tarrow, and Charles Tilly. 2002. "Toward an Integrated Perspective on Social Movements and Revolution." In *Comparative Politics: Rationality, Culture and Structure*, edited by Mark Lichbach and Alan Zuckerman, 142–73. Cambridge: Cambridge Univ. Press.

McGreevy, John T. 2004. *Catholicism and American Freedom: A History.* New York: W. W. Norton.

Mercan, Faruk. 2016. *Demokrasiden Geriye Donus Yok: Dünden Bugüne Fethullah Gülen'in Düşünce İstikameti.* Clifton, NJ: Blue Dome, iBooks edition.

Michel, Thomas. 2014. *Peace and Dialogue in a Plural Society: Contributions of the Hizmet Movement at a time of Global Tensions.* Clifton, NJ: Blue Dome.

Migdal, Joel S., Atul Kohli, and Vivienne Shue. 1994. *State Power and Social Forces: Domination and Transformation in the Third World.* Cambridge: Cambridge Univ. Press.

Mill, John Stuart. 2006. *The Collected Works of John Stuart Mill.* Indianapolis: Liberty Fund.

Monson, Quin J., and Kara L. Norman. 2007. "Salt Lake City's Main Street Plaza Controversy." In *Religious Interests in Community Conflict: Beyond the Culture Wars,* edited by Paul A. Djupe and Laura R. Olson, 173–94. Waco: Baylor Univ. Press.

The Mormons. 2008. PBS Home Video.

Nasr, Vali. 2003. "Lessons from the Muslim World." *Daedalus* 132, no. 3:67–72.

Navaro-Yashin, Yael. 2002. *Faces of the State: Secularism and Public Life in Turkey.* Princeton, NJ: Princeton Univ. Press.

Nursi, Bediuzzaman Said Nursi, 2013. *Mesnevi-i Nuriye.* Risale Press, e-book.

Ocak, Ahmet Yaşar. 2000. *Türkler, Türkiye ve İslâm.* Istanbul: İletişim Yayınları.

O'Donnell, Guillermo. 1998. "Horizontal Accountability in New Democracies." *Journal of Democracy* 9, no. 3:112–26.

Öniş, Ziya. 2004. "Turgut Özal and his Economic Legacy: Turkish Neo-Liberalism in Critical Perspective." *Middle Eastern Studies* 40, no. 4:113–34.

Öniş, Ziya, and Barry M. Rubin. 2003. *The Turkish Economy in Crisis.* London: Frank Cass.

Öniş, Ziya, and Fikret Şenses. 2009. *Turkey and the Global Economy: Neoliberal Restructuring and Integration in the Post-Crisis Era.* London: Routledge.

Ostling, Richard N., and Joan K. Ostling. 2007. *Mormon America: The Power and the Promise.* New York: Harper One.

Özbudun, Ergun. 1976. *Social Change and Political Participation in Turkey.* Princeton, NJ: Princeton Univ. Press.

Özbudun, Ergun, and Ömer Faruk Gençkaya. 2009. *Democratization and the Politics of Constitution-Making in Turkey.* Budapest: Central European Univ. Press.

Özdalga, Elisabeth. 2003a. "Secularizing Trends in Fethullah Gülen's Movement: Impasse or Opportunity for Further Renewal." *Critique: Critical Middle Eastern Studies* 12, no. 1:61–73.

———. 2003b. "Worldly Asceticism in Islamic Casting: Fethullah Gülen's Inspired Piety and Activism." *Critique: Critical Middle Eastern Studies* 17 (Fall): 83–104.

———. 2005. "Redeemer or Outsider? The Gülen Community in the Civilizing Process." *Muslim World* 95, no. 3:429–46.

Pamuk, Sevket. 2008. "Economic Change in Twentieth-Century Turkey: Is the Glass More than Half Full." In The *Cambridge History of Turkey: Turkey in the Modern World*, edited by Resat Kasaba, 266–300. Cambridge: Cambridge Univ. Press.

Pandya, Sophia and Nancy Gallagher. 2012. *The Gulen Hizmet Movement and its Transnational Activities.* Boca Raton, FL: Brown Walker.

Paulos, Michael H. 2008. *The Mormon Church on Trial: Transcripts of the Reed Smoot Hearings.* Salt Lake City, UT: Signature Books.

Pettit, Philip. 1997. *Republicanism: A Theory of Freedom and Government.* New York: Oxford Univ. Press.

Prince, Gregory A., and Robert Wright. 2005. *David O. McKay and the Rise of Modern Mormonism.* Salt Lake City, UT: Univ. of Utah Press.

Przeworski, Adam, and Henry Tune. 1970. *Logic of Comparative Social Inquiry.* New York: Wiley-Interscience.

Putnam, Robert. 1993. "The Prosperous Community: Social Capital and Public Life." *American Prospect* 13:35–42.

———. 1994. *Making Democracy Work: Civic Traditions in Modern Italy.* Princeton, NJ: Princeton Univ. Press.

———. 1995. "Bowling Alone: America's Declining Social Capital." *Journal of Democracy* 6, no. 1:65–78.

———. 2000. *Bowling Alone: The Collapse and Revival of American Community.* New York: Simon & Schuster.

Quinn, D. Michael. 1993. "Ezra Taft Benson and Mormon Political Conflicts." *Dialogue: A Journal of Mormon Thought* 26, no. 2:1–87.

———. 1994. *The Mormon Hierarchy: Origins of Power.* Salt Lake City, UT: Signature Books in association with Smith Research Associates.

———. 1997. *The Mormon Hierarchy: Extensions of Power.* Salt Lake City, UT: Signature Books in association with Smith Research Associates.

Rawls, John. 1999. *A Theory of Justice.* Cambridge, MA: Belknap Press of Harvard University Press.

———. 2005. *Political Liberalism.* New York: Columbia Univ. Press.

Rousseau, Jean-Jacques. 1986. *The Social Contract and Discourses.* Translated by G. D. H. Cole, J. H. Brumfitt, and John C. Hall. London: J. M. Dent/C. E. Tuttle.

Sahin, Mustafa G. 2011. "Said Nursi and the Nur Movement in Turkey: An Atomistic Approach." *Digest of Middle East Studies* 20:226–27.

Şahin, M. Abdülfettah. 1990. *Ölçü ve Yoldaki Işıklar-3* (Criteria or Lights of the Way). Izmir: TOV.

Saritoprak, Zeki. 2003. "Fethullah Gülen: A Sufi in His Own Way." In *Turkish Islam and the Secular State: The Gülen Movement*, edited by Hakan Yavuz and John Esposito, 156–69. Syracuse, NY: Syracuse Univ. Press.

Sehat, David. 2007. "The American Moral Establishment: Religion and Liberalism in the Nineteenth Century." PhD diss., Univ. of North Carolina.

———. 2014. *The Myth of American Religious Freedom.* Oxford: Oxford Univ. Press.

Sevindi, Nevval. 1997. *Fethullah Gülen ile New York Sohbeti.* Istanbul: Sabah Kitapları.

Sharkansky, Ira. 1997. "Religion and Politics in Israel and Utah." *Journal of Church & State* 39, no.3:523–41.

Shipps, Jan. 1985. *Mormonism: The Story of a New Religious Tradition.* Urbana: Univ. of Illinois Press.

———. 2004. "Spinning Gold: Mormonism and the Olympic Games." *Dialogue: A Journal of Mormon Thought* 36, no. 1:113–49.

———.2016. "Ezra Taft Benson and the Conservative Turn of 'Those Amazing Mormons.'" In *Mormonism and American Politics*, edited by Randall Balmer and Jana Riess, 73–84. New York: Columbia Univ. Press.

Sikkink, David. 2003. "From Christian Civilization to Individual Civil Liberties: Framing Religion in the Legal Field, 1880–1949." In *The Secular Revolution*, edited by C. Smith, 310–54. Berkeley: Univ. of California.

Sikkink, Kathryn, and Martha Finnemore. 2001. "Taking Stock: The Constructivist Research Program in International Relations and Comparative Politics." *Annual Review of Political Science* 4, no. 1:391–416.

Smidt, Corwin E. 2003. *Religion as Social Capital: Producing the Common Good.* Waco, TX: Baylor Univ. Press.

Smith, Joseph. 1842. "The Articles of Faith of the Church of Jesus Christ of Latter-day Saints: A Statement by Joseph Smith." *Times and Seasons*, March 1, 1842.

Smith, Joseph, and Church of Jesus Christ of Latter-day Saints. 1981. *The Book of Mormon: An Account Written by the Hand of Mormon upon Plates Taken from the Plates of Nephi.* Salt Lake City, UT: Church of Jesus Christ of Latter-day Saints.

Stack, Peggy Fletcher. 2007. "Romney Once Tilted Left, Now Right, of Official Mormon Teaching." *Salt Lake Tribune*, February 21, 2007.

———. 2008. "Mitt's Bid for White House Took the Pulse of Nation on Mormonism." *Salt Lake Tribune*, February 8, 2008.

Stepan, Alfred C. 1988. *Rethinking Military Politics: Brazil and the Southern Cone.* Princeton, NJ: Princeton Univ. Press.

———. 2001. *Arguing Comparative Politics.* Oxford: Oxford Univ. Press.

Tarrow, Sidney. 2001. "Transnational Politics: Contention and Institutions in International Politics." *Annual Review of Political Science* 4, no. 1:1–20.

Tas, Hakki. 2014. "Turkey's Ergenekon Imbroglio and Academia's Apathy." *Insight Turkey* 16, no. 1:163–79.

Tekeli, İlhan. 1998. *Katılımcı Demokrasi, Kamusal Alan ve Yerel Yönetim.* Istanbul: WALD.

Tittensor, David. 2014. *The House of Service: The Gulen Movement and Islam's Third Way.* New York: Oxford Univ. Press.

Turam, Berna. 2007. *Between Islam and the State: The Politics of Engagement.* Stanford, CA: Stanford Univ. Press.

Turgut, Pelin. 2010. "The Turkish Imam and His Global Education Mission." *Time*, April 26, 2010.

Turley, Richard E., and Ronald W. Walker. 2009. *Mountain Meadows Massacre: The Andrew Jenson and David H. Morris Collections.* Provo, UT: Brigham Young Univ. Press.

Ugur, Etga. 2004. "Intellectual Roots of 'Turkish Islam' and Approaches to the 'Turkish Model.'" *Journal of Muslim Minority Affairs* 24, no. 2:327–45.

Ünver, H. Akin. 2009. "Turkey's 'Deep-State' and the Ergenekon Conundrum." *Middle East Institute Policy Brief* no. 23:137–44.

Vahide, Sukran, and Ibrahim M. Abu-Rabi, ed. 2005. *Islam in Modern Turkey: An Intellectual Biography of Bediuzzaman Said Nursi*. Albany: State Univ. of New York Press.

Van Zile, P. T. 1882. "The Twin Relic." In *The Women of Mormonism: As Told by the Victims*, edited by J. A. Froiseth, 312–36. Detroit, MI: C. G. Paine.

Verdoia, Ken, dir. 1996. *Utah: The Struggle for Statehood*. DVD. Salt Lake City, UT: KUED Productions.

Wald, Kenneth D., Adam L. Silverman, and Kevin S. Fridy. 2005. "Making Sense of Religion in Political Life." *Annual Review of Political Science* 8, no. 1:121–43.

Walton, Jeremy. 2009. "Horizon and Histories of Liberal Piety: Civil Islam and Secularism in Contemporary Turkey." PhD diss., Univ. of Chicago.

Welch, John W., and Jeannie Welch. 1985. *The Doctrine and Covenants by Themes: The Text of the Doctrine and Covenants Arranged Topically*. Salt Lake City, UT: Bookcraft.

White, Jean Bickmore. 1996. *Charter for Statehood: The Story of Utah's State Constitution*. Salt Lake City, UT: Univ. of Utah Press.

Wildavsky, Aaron. 1987. "Choosing Preferences by Constructing Institutions: A Cultural Theory of Preference Formation." *American Political Science Review* 81, no. 1:3–22.

Willan, Philip. 2002. *Puppetmasters: The Political Use of Terrorism in Italy*. London: Constable.

Williams, J. D. 1967. "Separation of Church and State in Mormon Theory and Practice." *Journal of Church and State* 9, no. 2 (Spring): 238–62.

Williams, Rhys. 2003. "The Language of God in the City of Man: Religious Discourse and Public Politics in America." In *Religion as Social Capital: Producing the Common Good*, edited by Corwin E. Smidt, 171–90. Waco, TX: Baylor Univ. Press.

Wolfe, Alan. 1997. "Public and Private in Theory and Practice: Some Implications of an Uncertain Boundary." In *Public and Private in Thought and Practice: Perspectives on a Grand Dichotomy*, edited by J. A. Weintraub and K. Kumar, 182–203. Chicago: Univ. of Chicago Press.

Woolcock, Michael. 1998. "Social Capital and Economic Development: Toward a Theoretical Synthesis and Policy Framework." *Theory and Society* 27, no. 2:151–208.

Yavuz, M. Hakan. 2003a. *Islamic Political Identity in Turkey.* Oxford: Oxford Univ. Press.

———. 2003b. "Nur Study Circles (Dersanes) and the Formation of New Religious Consciousness in Turkey." In *Islam at Crossroads: On the Life and Thought of Bediuzzaman Said Nursi*, edited by I. M. Abu-Rabi, 297–316. Albany: State Univ. of New York Press.

———. 2003c. "The Gülen Movement: The Turkish Puritans." In *Turkish Islam and the Secular State: The Gülen Movement*, edited by M. Hakan Yavuz and John L. Esposito, 19–47. Syracuse, NY: Syracuse Univ. Press.

———. 2009. *Secularism and Muslim Democracy in Turkey.* Cambridge: Cambridge Univ. Press.

———. 2013. *Toward an Islamic Enlightenment: The Gülen Movement.* New York: Oxford Univ. Press.

Yılmaz, Hakan. 1998. "Kamu, Kamu Otoritesi ve Devlet: Habermas'ın Işığında Türkiye'yi Düşünmek." *Cogito* 15:159–69.

Yorgason, Ethan. 2003. *Transformation of the Mormon Culture Region.* Urbana. Univ. of Illinois Press.

———. 2016. "Contests over Latter-day Space: Mormonism's Role within Evangelical Geopolitics as seen through Last-days Novels." In *Mapping the End Times: American Evangelical Geopolitics and Apocalyptic Visions*, edited by Jason Dittmer and Tristan Sturm, 49–72. New York: Routledge.

Index

Etga Ugur is an Assistant Professor at the University of Washington, Tacoma. He teaches classes on comparative politics, American foreign policy, and Middle East politics. He received his PhD in Political Science from the University of Utah in 2011. He subsequently worked as a Postdoctoral Fellow in the Muslim Studies Program at Michigan State University and a Visiting Assistant Professor at James Madison College.